Praise for *Up and Out of Poverty*

"Philip Kotler, pioneer in social marketing, and Nancy Lee bring their incisive thinking and pragmatic approach to the problems of behavior change at the bottom of the pyramid. Creative solutions to persistent problems that affect the poor require the tools of social marketing and multi-stakeholder management. In this book, the poor around the world have found new and powerful allies. A must read for those who work to alleviate poverty and restore human dignity."

—**CK Prahalad**, Paul and Ruth McCracken Distinguished University Professor, Ross School of Business, The University of Michigan, Ann Arbor; and author of *The Fortune at the Bottom of the Pyramid,* 5th Anniversary Edition

"*Up and Out of Poverty* will prove very helpful to antipoverty planners and workers to help the poor deal better with their problems of daily living. Philip Kotler and Nancy Lee illustrate vivid cases of how the poor can be helped by social marketing solutions."

—**Mechai Viravaidya**, founder and Chairman, Population and Community Development Association, Thailand

"Helping others out of poverty is a simple task; yet it remains incomplete. Putting poverty in a museum is achievable within a short span of time—if we all work together, we can do it!"

—**Muhammad Yunus**, winner of the Nobel Prize for Peace; and Managing Director, Grameen Bank

"In *Up and Out of Poverty*, Kotler and Lee remind us that 'markets' are people. A series of remarkable case studies demonstrate conclusively the power of social marketing to release the creative energy of people to solve their own problems. Here's a blueprint for government, corporations, and communities who want to change the world by arming the poor with the savvy of modern marketing."

—**Bill Smith**, Executive Vice President, Academy for Educational Development

"As an MBA student at Wharton in the 1970s, Philip Kotler's textbook was the marketer's Bible. Now, decades later, Philip Kotler and Nancy Lee have made a profound contribution to understanding and addressing the blight of global poverty. Marketing seems an unlikely weapon in the fight against poverty. But poverty is affected by behavioral choices, and behavior is influenced by information. Social marketing views the poor as rational consumers of information who change their behaviors when presented with information in a compelling way…the very thing marketers do so well, whether selling the benefits of a toothpaste which prevents cavities or those of bednets which can prevent malaria."

—**Rich Stearns**, President, World Vision US

"This is a much needed contribution on how social marketing can help people escape from poverty. Throughout the book, Kotler and Lee lay out the methodology and tools for achieving large scale behavior change for social good and demonstrate the principles in action from over 30 years of work in addressing public health and social problems. The book consistently underscores the authors' belief that much of the work of helping the poor lies in using marketing tools to understand, influence, and empower the poor to participate in developing their own solution. This work positions social marketing as a policy instrument that deserves wide appreciation and use among policymakers, program planners, and local leaders to address the problems of poverty in a deliberate and systematic fashion."

—**Craig Lefebvre**, research professor, Public Health Communication and Marketing Program, The George Washington School of Public Health and Health Services; and former Chief Technical Officer, Population Services International

"Kotler and Lee set the record straight in this important book: Social marketing uses a range of tools to influence behavior and reduce poverty, beyond simply the sale of subsidized commodities like condoms and mosquito nets. Kotler's pioneering work in this field continues to inspire practitioners."

—**Karl Hofmann**, President and Chief Executive Officer of PSI (Population Services International)

Up and Out of Poverty
The Social Marketing Solution

Philip Kotler and Nancy R. Lee

Vice President, Publisher: Tim Moore
Associate Publisher and Director of Marketing: Amy Neidlinger
Wharton Editor: Steve Kobrin
Editorial Assistant: Pamela Boland
Development Editor: Russ Hall
Operations Manager: Gina Kanouse
Digital Marketing Manager: Julie Phifer
Publicity Manager: Laura Czaja
Assistant Marketing Manager: Megan Colvin
Cover Designer: Chuti Prasertsith
Managing Editor: Kristy Hart
Project Editor: Anne Goebel
Copy Editor: Gayle Johnson
Proofreader: Kathy Ruiz
Indexer: Erika Millen
Compositor: Nonie Ratcliff
Manufacturing Buyer: Dan Uhrig

© 2009 by Pearson Education, Inc.
Publishing as Wharton School Publishing
Upper Saddle River, New Jersey 07458

Wharton School Publishing offers excellent discounts on this book when ordered in quantity for bulk purchases or special sales. For more information, please contact U.S. Corporate and Government Sales, 1-800-382-3419, corpsales@pearsontechgroup.com. For sales outside the U.S., please contact International Sales at international@pearson.com.

Company and product names mentioned herein are the trademarks or registered trademarks of their respective owners.

Printed in the United States of America

First Printing June 2009

ISBN-10: 0-13-714100-9
ISBN-13: 978-0-13-714100-5

Pearson Education LTD.
Pearson Education Australia PTY, Limited.
Pearson Education Singapore, Pte. Ltd.
Pearson Education North Asia, Ltd.
Pearson Education Canada, Ltd.
Pearson Educación de Mexico, S.A. de C.V.
Pearson Education—Japan
Pearson Education Malaysia, Pte. Ltd.

Library of Congress Cataloging-in-Publication Data

Kotler, Philip.

  Up and Out of Poverty: The Social Marketing Solution / Philip Kotler, Nancy R. Lee.
    p. cm.

  ISBN 978-0-13-714100-5 (hardback : alk. paper) 1. Poverty. 2. Poor. 3. Poverty—Government policy. 4. Poverty—Case studies. 5. Poor—Case studies. 6. Poverty—Government policy—Case studies. I. Lee, Nancy, 1932- II. Title.

  HC79.P6K68 2009

  362.5'561—dc22

                              2008046582

To the four billion poor in our world, and to those working to help them achieve a better life

Contents

Case Stories

Acknowledgments

We have benefitted greatly from those who have written about poverty and proposed several lines of action, among them Jeffrey Sachs, Muhammad Yunus, Amartya Sen, CK Prahalad, Paul Collier, and many others. We admire those who are working in the field and/or financing efforts to help the poor, including CARE, The Bill & Melinda Gates Foundation, Population Services International, Plan International, World Vision, The World Bank, USAID, Doctors Without Borders, Habitat for Humanity International, Save the Children, William J. Clinton Foundation, Academy for Educational Development, and Mercy Corps.

We are indebted to Ned Roberto, one of the most thorough researchers into the needs and lives of the poor, for early help, and to Tony Leisner for his assistance in researching the poverty literature and solutions.

We are grateful to the staff at Wharton School Publishing, including Tim Moore, Russ Hall, Anne Goebel, Gayle Johnson, Pamela Boland, and Steve Kobrin, who helped us shape our book into its present form.

About the Authors

Philip Kotler (M.A., University of Chicago; Ph.D., MIT) is the S. C. Johnson Distinguished Professor of International Marketing at the Kellogg School of Management, Northwestern University. He has published the 13th edition of *Marketing Management*, the world's leading textbook on teaching marketing to MBAs. He has also published *Strategic Marketing for Nonprofit Organizations*, *Social Marketing*, *Corporate Social Responsibility*, *Marketing in the Public Sector*, and 30 other books. His research covers social marketing, strategic marketing, innovation, services marketing, and Internet marketing. He has received 12 honorary doctorate degrees from major universities in the U.S. and abroad.

Nancy R. Lee (MBA, University of Puget Sound) has more than 25 years of practical marketing experience in the private, nonprofit, and public sectors. As an adjunct faculty member at the University of Washington and Seattle University, she teaches Social Marketing, Marketing in the Public Sector, and Marketing for Nonprofit Organizations. As president of Social Marketing Services, Inc., Lee is a frequent speaker at conferences, seminars, and workshops and serves as a strategic adviser on a variety of local and national social marketing campaigns. This is the fifth book she has coauthored with Philip Kotler.

For more information about this book, visit Kotler and Lee's Web site dedicated to this topic at www.upandoutofpoverty.com.

Foreword

Philip Kotler and Nancy Lee lay out a compelling case for the power of social marketing to promote social change and to address itself to the problems of the poor. This is no surprise to those who have followed Dr. Kotler's work since his founding of the field some 40 years ago. But if you think that marketing is about branding, slogans, and advertising campaigns, this book provides ample evidence of the importance of "total" marketing—the creation, distribution, and promotion of products, services, and experiences that meet human needs. Over the years Kotler has tackled the role of social marketing in healthcare and nonprofit management and has described multiple applications of social marketing to social change. But here, in *Up and Out of Poverty*, Kotler and Lee tackle one of the world's most intransigent and disgraceful realities: poverty and its devastating human, social, and political consequences.

Poverty has many fathers: war, natural disaster, racism, discrimination, ignorance, and avarice. The masses who labored to build the pyramids; the peasants who fed the czars' empire; and the unemployed youth who roam the streets of Palestine, Johannesburg, and Bangkok today share a common anonymity. No monuments are raised in their names; no record of their individuality exists. They are simply "the poor."

The world continues to treat poverty like an epidemic of polio—a single disease with a common cause. Experts proclaim the discovery of a never-ending array of "poverty vaccines"—microfinance, healthcare, basic education, girls' education, democracy-building, foreign investment, foreign aid, political and social stability, peace education, and many more. Economists search for answers in the success of Asian tigers. Anthropologists look at primitive societies for root causes. Educators decry the lack of classrooms and quality education for the poor. Rock stars and celebrities both stir and calm our conscience with fund-raisers. Public health experts promise that the eradication of malaria, HIV/AIDS, and TB will lead to the eradication of poverty.

These approaches to poverty reduction make sense if you assume that poverty is a "vaccine-preventable disease." The metaphor of disease vaccines is attractive. A vaccine for polio works reliably for people of all ages and both genders. It does not matter to a polio vaccine whether people are angry or dispirited, whether they love their children, or whether they believe in their ancestors or trust their church. A polio vaccine is indifferent to their desire to escape the boredom of poverty in drink or the oppression of poverty in wife beating. A polio vaccine is stable over time. After it is administered, it is resistant to war, natural disaster, racism, divorce, and economic downturn.

These views of poverty are credible because the poor remain anonymous and silent. And this is precisely where Kotler and Lee make their most convincing argument for social marketing's role in the intelligent fight against poverty. Their ambitious title, *Up and Out of Poverty*, reflects more their determination to end poverty than their conviction that social marketing is another magic vaccine against poverty. No, the importance of this work is the focus on reframing poverty. It isn't a communicable disease susceptible to vaccine development. Poverty is a chronic human condition, more like diabetes than polio, susceptible to external events and influenced by individual and community differences.

Up and Out of Poverty illustrates the power of social marketing to contribute to poverty reduction in three uniquely marketing ways: exchange theory, market segmentation, and competitiveness. *Exchange theory* suggests the disquieting thought that the poor have the right to want what the rich want. The notion of paternalism, in which development is guided by the "needs" of the poor (needs conveniently defined by the rich), is discarded. Kotler and Lee emphasize the ability of market research to identify what the poor want—companionship, the chance to lead or help others. They illustrate how social marketing translates those desires into products and services such as condoms, oral rehydration, and malaria bed nets. In exchange, the poor are willing to use these products and services to alleviate their poverty.

Market segmentation offers the seemingly novel thought that the poor might not all be alike. Some of them might be more efficient targets of change than others. The notion of *competitiveness* emerges from commercial marketing, where it is assumed that every new product or service competes in the minds of consumers with existing consumer choices. For years development experts have assumed that the poor are sitting around waiting for help. The idea that development programs had to compete for the poor's attention seemed ludicrous. In fact, the poor make choices every day on how to survive. And some of those choices are resistant to change. A development program must not only be good, it also must be better than what the poor already value.

Perhaps most importantly, Kotler and Lee stress the importance of integrating public- and private-sector resources to create programs large enough, focused enough, and continuous enough to make a difference in the immense weight of the poverty problem. The whole concept of continuity to development programs brings into question one of the development community's most cherished, if least accomplished, goals—sustainability. Sustainability has come to mean that after two to five years of a program, its effects should last long after the program has ended. The logic is attractive. There are so few resources, and the problem is so immense. But as Kotler and Lee suggest, marketing emerges from a paradigm in the commercial world in which marketing is a continuous business function, not a start-up cost.

Perhaps most appealing is the work that the authors have done to track down relevant case studies and use them to illustrate their points. This new book is not only an eye-opener for the development professional, but also a darn good read.

—Bill Smith, EdD
Innovations Management/Academy for Educational Development
Associate Editor, *Social Marketing Quarterly*

Preface

Many books have been written about the scourge of poverty. They offer different theories on poverty and different solutions. Some outline macro solutions, and others deal with micro solutions. Our book takes a very different look at the problem and offers a different model for helping the poor escape from poverty. We examine the power of "social marketing methodology" to abate the suffering of the poor. This preface describes the major approaches to fighting poverty and how our approach adds to the set of tools for helping the poor achieve a better life.

Of all the problems facing mankind—disease, hard drugs, crime, corruption, armed conflict, global warming, nuclear risks, environmental sustainability—poverty is among the most persistent and shameful. Furthermore, poverty contributes greatly to the other problems. The poor suffer more from disease, and their hopeless condition leads some of the poor into lives of crime, hard drugs, and armed conflict. This means that the cost of poverty far exceeds the cost that the poor themselves bear. Poverty pours its poison on the rest of mankind.

Until the nineteenth century, the poor received little attention. Poverty was seen as inevitable. Governments and do-gooders could do little about it. The Industrial Revolution exacerbated the problem by attracting poor rural peasants to the cities in search of work. This led to the establishment of shantytowns and poorhouses. The plight of the poor became more visible. Caring researchers such as Beatrice and Sidney Webb in the U.K. started to count the poor and write about their plight. Charles Dickens, in *Oliver Twist*, vividly dramatized the conditions and exploitation of the poor.

The concept of creating antipoverty programs began in the nineteenth century and continues today. One sixth of the world's population earns less than $1 a day. Another 2 billion of the world's 6 billion people earn less than $2 a day. In the year 2000, the United Nations outlined its multilateral plan for reducing world poverty. The United

Nations formulated the Millennium Development Goals (MDG)—eight goals with 18 accompanying targets, designed to significantly reduce poverty levels by 2015. Target 1 was to cut in half between 1990 and 2015 the proportion of people whose income is less than $1 a day. The goal is ambitious and is not likely to be achieved, given the tumultuous new circumstances of rising food and energy costs and continued armed conflict in the world.

Experts have put forth different theories of the causes of the problem and therefore have advocated different measures to cure the problem. We can distinguish between experts who see poverty as having a major basic cause and those who see many causal factors at work.

The simplest theory is that the poor have brought the condition on themselves. The assertion is that many are shiftless, lazy, and uneducated and prefer to live on handouts rather than exerting effort to lift themselves out of poverty. The implied solution from this view is to either find a way to change their attitude and behavior or leave them in their penurious state. Granted, some of the poor are responsible for their condition. However, there is evidence that most of the poor would be ready and willing to escape their penurious conditions if they could find employment and have a decent place to live.

Another simplistic theory is that poverty is the result of the poor having too many children. Each new child makes a poor family poorer. The argument goes further to say that the Earth has a limited population "carrying capacity" for resources and food to permit a decent standard of living for 6 billion people (let alone the 9 billion people projected by 2020). Therefore, poverty continues to be a problem because of overpopulation. This is a variation on Thomas Malthus' proposition that the rate of population growth will exceed the rate of growth of food supply, resulting in starvation, war, and the continuation of poverty.[1] The major modern version of this view is found in the book *The Limits to Growth*.[2] Here the solution follows that much poverty would abate if poor families would limit the number of their offspring voluntarily or by edict. China represents the latter in restricting families to only one child. Certainly this has been one of the major contributors to China's impressive reduction in the number of families living in poverty.

Another singular theory is that poverty persists because the poor don't own any fungible property on which they could borrow money. They lack tradeable assets. This theory has been propounded by the highly respected though controversial Peruvian economist Hernando de Soto in his book *The Mystery of Capital: Why Capitalism Triumphs in the West and Fails Everywhere Else.*[3] De Soto argues that the real source of wealth is real property—that is, well-defined and socially accepted property rights. Property is an asset that can be used to get or make a loan or mortgage, or obtain insurance or own stock, and other things that make capitalism so effective in producing economic growth and prosperity. But de Soto says this doesn't work in poor communities and countries because the institutions don't recognize the assets of the poor. The poor have plenty of assets (land, homes, businesses), but they typically lie in the extralegal, informal realm. The legal system has not adapted to this reality. The costs of making these assets legal (obtaining proper title to a house, registering a business) are so prohibitive in terms of time and money that the assets end up being "dead capital." The poor cannot use their assets to achieve any of the normal capitalist tools to achieve upward mobility. Because these assets are not recognized, they create an extralegal style of living within their informal social circles. For de Soto, the singular solution is to push the legal system to allow the monetization of these assets so that the dead capital becomes alive.

Besides these grand singular theories, the majority of experts recognize poverty as resulting from many interrelated causes, all of which must be addressed in an integrated fashion. Consider Paul Collier's views in his book *The Bottom Billion: Why the Poorest Countries Are Failing and What Can Be Done About It.*[4] According to Collier, the billion people at the bottom live in "trapped countries." He identifies four elements that cause countries to become trapped:

- *Civil war.* Nearly three-quarters of the bottom billion have been through or are currently experiencing civil war. Civil wars usually occur where there are large numbers of unemployed and uneducated young men and ethnic imbalances.
- *Natural resources curse.* Almost 30% of these countries rely on exporting some raw materials, such as oil or minerals. Countries with large amounts of natural resources tend not to

develop the skill sets of their people, and they tend not to hold democratic elections. Corrupt governments and impoverished and violent masses often result.

- *Landlocked countries.* About 30% of the countries with desperate poor are landlocked or surrounded by bad neighbors. This leaves them economically disadvantaged.

- *Bad governance.* About 75% of the countries suffer from bad governance or autocratic leaders who exploit their people.

Each condition requires a different type of solution. Collier favors legitimate military interventions in areas being torn apart by civil war. Countries with large amounts of natural resources should develop skills that raise the value of their exports and should not simply export raw materials at world market prices. Landlocked countries must learn to work with neighboring port-based countries to build roads that will give them access to ports. Bad governance is the hardest problem to solve. Robert Mugabe ran Zimbabwe into the ground, and the rest of the world stood helplessly by.

Collier's chief recommendation to fight poverty is to "narrow the target and broaden the instruments." Narrowing the target means focusing on the one billion of the world's people (70% of whom are in Africa) who are in countries that are failing. Broadening the instruments means shifting focus from aid to an array of policy instruments: better delivery of aid, occasional military intervention, international charters, and smarter trade policy.

What about foreign aid as a partial solution to the problems of the poor? Two experts have sharply different views of the value of foreign aid. Jeffrey Sachs, author of *The End of Poverty*, wants the West to be more generous and to give substantially more foreign aid to poor countries.[5] On the other hand, William Easterly, in *The White Man's Burden*, advances strong arguments against foreign aid.[6] He describes Jeffrey Sachs as one of those big "top-down planners" who is never embarrassed about the many failures of foreign aid. Some estimate that as little as 15% of foreign aid reaches the deserving poor as a result of high administrative expenses and corruption. Foreign-aid relief agencies' tendency to do "top-down planning" fails to provide information on variations in local needs for medicines and foods.

Foreign aid also creates a dependency that keeps countries from reaching for their own solutions. Foreign aid hurts a country's private businesses that produce or sell the same foreign-aid items. Easterly sees the work of large foreign-aid bureaucracies and their vast past expenditures and interventions as largely a failure. At the same time, Easterly acknowledges some good deeds of these large aid agencies, especially when they concentrate on particular needs. These include drilling and maintaining local wells, building and maintaining local roads or sewage systems, or distributing medicine or food in particular places where they are needed.

The major problem of top-down planning is that huge agencies at the international and national levels have to decide how to allocate money to the different poverty-alleviation tools. They do this by setting priorities that reflect the country's modal conditions. But the priorities may vary from village to village and city to city. This means that some communities receive more to spend on causes that are not important, and other communities receive less than they need.

This makes it desirable to add a "bottom-up planning approach" that engages all the communities to develop their own proposals and programs of need, which are then passed upward. These programs must meet certain criteria, such as taking a long view of what would develop the community, and explaining the program's logic. The need is to "Take the mountain into the valley." C. K. Prahalad, in his book *The Fortune at the Bottom of the Pyramid: Eradicating Poverty Through Profits*, eloquently describes how local innovation and financial assistance to the poor can give the poor an incentive to help themselves escape from poverty.

Given these different approaches to understanding and reducing poverty, we are ready to state the main features of this book:

- This book doesn't believe that one major solution (such as foreign aid or population control) provides a full answer to the poverty-alleviation problem.
- We believe that the best solutions will involve more than government solutions and nongovernment organization (NGO) solutions. The solutions will involve the private sector as well, working closely with government agencies and civil organizations.

- We believe that much of the work of helping the poor lies in using tools to understand, influence, and assist the poor in participating in developing their own solutions.
- We link the big national picture of the problem with the specific conditions found in each local situation.
- We describe and illustrate with actual cases the major steps in the social marketing planning, implementation, monitoring, and control program. We believe that this level of analysis has been missing in all the previous work on helping the poor.

In essence, our book aims to describe what to do and how to do it in helping the poor escape poverty.

We have written this book so that those working to help reduce poverty will understand and use the powerful tool of social marketing. We believe that social marketing can help people move up and out of poverty, ensure that they don't slip backward, and even keep them from entering this situation in the first place. We think it has been missing as a major player in the poverty solution mix.

Part I, "Understanding the Poverty Problem and Its Broad Solutions," summarizes the various definitions used to measure the number of people living in poverty, major factors that cause or reflect poverty, and ways in which the nonpoor are also impacted by poverty. We then examine the barrel of current poverty solutions and describe how the social marketing solution differs.

Part II, "Applying Marketing Perspectives and Solutions," is more practical, outlining various theories, principles, and techniques that have been used to create behavior-change campaigns. These are illustrated with successful poverty-reducing cases from around the world.

Part III, "Ensuring an Integrated Approach," focuses on the unique role that the three major sectors (public, nonprofit, and private) play in poverty reduction. The final chapter stresses the critical need for these three sectors to work together, ensuring an integrated approach.

We believe you'll find the marketing concept easy to grasp. We adopt a customer-oriented mind-set. We define who our customers are and what they need and want in order to adopt the desired behaviors we have in mind—ones that will help them move up and out of poverty.

Endnotes

[1] Thomas Malthus, *Principles of Political Economy* (London: William Pickering, 1836).

[2] Donella H. Meadows (and others), *The Limits to Growth: A Report for the Club of Rome's Project on the Predicament of Mankind* (New York: Universe Books, 1972).

[3] Hernando de Soto, *The Mystery of Capital: Why Capitalism Triumphs in the West and Fails Everywhere Else* (New York: Basic Books, 2000).

[4] Paul Collier, *The Bottom Billion: Why the Poorest Countries Are Failing and What Can Be Done About It* (Oxford, U.K.: Oxford University Press, 2007).

[5] Jeffrey Sachs, *The End of Poverty: Economic Possibilities for Our Time* (New York: Penguin Press, 2005).

[6] William Easterly, *The White Man's Burden: Why the West's Efforts to Aid the Rest Have Done So Much Ill and So Little Good* (New York: Penguin Press, 2006). The same skepticism about foreign aid is articulated in Clark C. Gibson, Krister Andersson, Elinor Ostrom, and Sujai Shivakumar, *The Samaritan's Dilemma: The Political Economy of Development Aid* (Oxford, U.K.: Oxford University Press, 2005).

Part I

Understanding the Poverty Problem
and Its Broad Solutions

1

Why Poverty Hurts Everyone

"Poverty is a call to action—for the poor and the wealthy alike—a call to change the world so that many more may have enough to eat, adequate shelter, access to education and health, protection from violence, and a voice in what happens in their communities."

—The World Bank[1]

At 5 a.m. in Zimbabwe, 13-year-old Chipo walks two miles to draw water to bring back to quench the thirst of her four younger siblings, ages 5 to 11. She prepares a slim pot of porridge, wondering where she will get something to feed them that night. She will have to carry her youngest sibling, who has had diarrhea for a week, to a medical clinic four miles away, where she expects a long wait. Her parents died from AIDS earlier in the year. Her neighbors are poor too, but they have provided a little help. She has no thought of schooling; her siblings and their survival are her only concern.

Meanwhile, near a vending machine at a gas station in Newark, New Jersey, Jim spots Suzanne after not seeing her for a long time. He is taken aback by her gaunt frame and worn-looking clothing. She breaks down and explains that she hasn't been eating much because she doesn't have money for food. Three years ago, she was hit by a drunk driver, and the accident shattered many bones in her body. She spent months in the hospital, and when she returned home, her husband divorced her. She has been living on $700 per month in alimony and $60 in food stamps. She applied for disability assistance but was told she was ineligible. She also has applied for part-time jobs, but she feels that when employers see her cane for walking, they immediately dismiss the idea of hiring her. Her rent is $430, her utility bill is $90, and her phone bill is $60. She spends over $70 a month on co-payments for doctor visits and prescription medication, and $40 a month for gas. That leaves $10 for food, since she usually runs out of food stamps toward the middle of the month. Suzanne fights back tears as she explains how awful she feels about not bathing, but soap and shampoo are not covered by food stamps.

Most of the terrible fates experienced by the poor like Chipo and Suzanne are familiar to many of us. We see the faces of the hungry, unemployed, and homeless. We read about gender inequalities, those who are illiterate, and villagers who have to travel an hour for health care or to get clean water—on foot. We know about mothers who experience their children dying young from diarrhea, who die in childbirth, and who age prematurely. We are frequently reminded of the vast numbers who have tuberculosis, malaria, or HIV/AIDS. And we hear about those whose farmland is producing less each year, whose livestock are not healthy, and whose water is contaminated.

But what is the impact on the rest of us—the nonpoor? We suggest it is enormous, and we make the case in this chapter. Over the years, many books have been written about poverty and its causes and cures. Some take a 360 degree view and offer broad policy and solution ideas often involving economic measures. Others get very close to the victims of poverty and describe their hardships and sufferings. Our book differs as it focuses on the fieldwork aspects of trying to solve specific problems of hunger, disease, inadequate schooling, family planning, inadequate or foul water, and other problems contributing to poverty. We believe that the developing field of *social marketing*, with its apparatus of concepts, tools, and principles can make a deep dent in these problems and has been missing in the poverty solution mix.

Our relentless focus and attention is on those poor who want to help themselves. What do they want and need that will address the barriers and support the behaviors that will move them out of poverty, even keep them out in the first place? They are the homeless people who don't know what resources are available or how to access them; the millions of women who want to use family planning, but can't convince their husbands; poor farmers who are afraid to try chemical fertilizers because they heard they might be bad for their livestock; sexworkers who fear they will lose business, even be jailed, if they suggest that their clients use condoms; fishermen who thought the mosquito net delivered to their door was for catching more fish; young adults wanting a job requiring computer skills they don't have; tuberculosis patients who think because they feel better they can discontinue their medications; poor families wanting to save money but not trusting financial institutions; children dropping out of school because their itching from riverblindness makes them the brunt of teasing; and the high school students who end up not graduating because their attendance is so poor they get behind.

We will describe many cases in this book where social marketing theory and practice has been successfully applied to influence behaviors that reduced poverty and improved the quality of lives. We believe that the need to accelerate our progress in fighting poverty is growing more urgent than ever as a result of the financial meltdown starting in 2008 that has caused more people to lose their jobs and many to lose their homes and increase the numbers of poor. Hopefully help will be forthcoming along with these new tools and concepts for addressing the issues.

We begin with a brief picture of the poverty landscape, answering the questions: Who are the poor? How many are there? Where do they live? Why are they poor?

Who and How Many Are the Poor?

Governments are interested in measuring poverty for several reasons: to know its percentage in the population, to track whether it is rising or falling, to know its percentage among different groups, and, perhaps most importantly, to provide direction for developing poverty-reduction strategies. Several commonly used definitions of "poor" appear in the sidebar titled "Definitions of Poverty."

The World Bank reports that a person is considered poor if his or her consumption or income level falls below some minimum level necessary to meet basic needs. This minimum level is called the *poverty line*. Because basic needs vary across time and societies, poverty lines vary in time and place. Each country uses a line that is appropriate to its level of development, societal norms, and values. Information on consumption and income is obtained through sample surveys of households, conducted fairly regularly in most countries. When estimating poverty worldwide, the same poverty reference needs to be used, providing a common unit across countries. Since 2005, the World Bank has used reference lines set at $1.25 and $2 per day of income, per person.[2]

Jeffrey Sachs, in his book *The End of Poverty*, distinguishes and describes three degrees of poverty. For each, we have applied the World Bank's reference lines to estimate the size of each group:

- Those in *extreme poverty* are households that "cannot meet basic needs for survival. They are chronically hungry, unable to access health care, lack the amenities of safe drinking water and sanitation, cannot afford education for some or all of the children, and perhaps lack rudimentary shelter—a roof to keep the rain out of the hut, a chimney to remove the smoke from the cookstove—and basic articles of clothing, such as shoes."[3] Using the World Bank's most recent data (2005), economists estimated that 1.4 billion people were living in extreme poverty, less than US$1.25 a day.[4]

- For those in *moderate poverty*, "[the] basic needs are met, but just barely."[5] These people still must forgo many of the things that many of us take for granted, such as education and health care. The smallest misfortune (poor health, job loss, natural disasters, drought, inflation) threatens their survival or might cause them to spiral down to extreme poverty levels. By defining the moderate poor as people earning between $1.25 and $2 per day, the number is estimated at 1.6 billion.[6]

- A household in *relative poverty* has an "income level below a given proportion of average national income."[7] It is a reflection of the distribution of income in a given country. "The relative poor, in high-income countries, lack access to cultural goods, entertainment, recreation, and to quality health care, education, and other prerequisites for upward social mobility."[8] They may also have received less attention with the focus on solving the problem of the extreme and moderate poor, where suffering is more obvious. Although no formal estimate of the global relative poor exists, it would not be surprising if more than another billion may be in this class, making the world's total number of poor people about 4 billion—a majority of us.

Definitions of Poverty

- *Absolute definition.* As of 2005, the World Bank defines the number of people living in extreme poverty as those earning less than $1.25 a day, and those living in moderate poverty as those earning between $1.25 and $2 a day.

- *Food-defined definition.* Defining a threshold that says that the cost of obtaining a sufficient amount of food for a given family's size should not exceed 33% of the family's disposable income. Thus, a family of four should earn at least $19,991 because they need to spend $6,663 to obtain an adequate amount of food to feed the family. This family of four is defined as poor if it earns less than $19,991 a year. This measure has historically been used in the United States but is not used by most other nations.

- *Human poverty index definition.* The United Nations Development Programme defines an index composed of four factors: the likelihood of a child not surviving to age 60, the functional illiteracy rate, long-term unemployment, and the population living on less than 50% of the median national income.

- *By situation.* The United Nations (UN) defines poverty as "a human condition characterized by the sustained or chronic deprivation of the resources, capabilities, choices, security, and power necessary for the enjoyment of an adequate standard of living and other civil, cultural, economic, political, and social rights."[9]

- *Definitions by where the poor live.* The *village poor* are found in thousands of villages in Africa, Asia, and elsewhere where little is grown and little industry exists. The *rural poor* live in small communities that have become depressed as a result of drought or industry abandonment and where few job opportunities exist. And the *urban poor* are where people live in relative poverty, in the worst cases in crowded and dirty slums.

Where Do the Poor Live?

Over 90% of the extreme poor live in three regions of the world: Sub-Saharan Africa, East Asia, and South Asia. Looking at extreme poverty by country, Table 1.1 shows the percentage of the world's poor who live in each of these countries, with "poor" defined as living below the global poverty line of US$1 per day.[10] As indicated, ten countries represent 84.24% of the world's poor and almost two thirds (63%) live in India or China.

TABLE 1.1   The Top Ten Countries Representing 84.24% of the World's Poor (Below US$1 Per Day)

Rank	Country	Percentage of the World's Poor
1	India	41.01%
2	China	22.12%
3	Nigeria	8.03%

Rank	Country	Percentage of the World's Poor
4	Pakistan	3.86%
5	Bangladesh	3.49%
6	Brazil	1.82%
7	Ethiopia	1.82%
8	Indonesia	1.49%
9	Mexico	1.43%
10	Russia	.99%

Source: NationMaster, 2008

To understand how "poor" a country is, however, it is more relevant to consider what proportion of its population lives in extreme poverty. Table 1.2 shows this statistic for all countries with 50% or more people living below the poverty line. As you can see, the vast majority (70%) of these countries are on the continent of Africa.

TABLE 1.2 Countries with 50% or More of Their People Living Below the Poverty Line[11]

Rank	Country	Percentage of the Population Living Below the Poverty Line
#1	Liberia: (Africa)	80%
#2	Gaza Strip: (Middle East)	80%
#3	Haiti: (Central America)	80%
#4	Zimbabwe: (Africa)	80%
#5	Chad: (Africa)	80%
#6	Sierra Leone: (Africa)	70.2%
#7	Suriname: (South America)	70%
#8	Mozambique: (Africa)	70%
#9	Angola: (Africa)	70%
#10	Nigeria: (Africa)	70%
#11	Swaziland: (Africa)	69%
#12	Burundi: (Africa)	68%
#13	Tajikistan: (Asia)	60%
#14	Bolivia: (South America)	60%
#15	Rwanda: (Africa)	60%

(continued)

TABLE 1.2 Continued

Rank	Country	Percentage of the Population Living Below the Poverty Line
#16	Comoros: (Africa)	60%
#17	Guatemala: (Central America)	56.2%
#18	Malawi: (Africa)	55%
#19	Senegal: (Africa)	54%
#20	São Tomé and Príncipe: (Africa)	54%
#21	Afghanistan: (Asia)	53%
#22	Honduras: (Central America)	50.7%
#23	Kenya: (Africa)	50%
#24	Namibia: (Africa)	50%
#25	Ethiopia: (Africa)	50%
#26	Madagascar: (Africa)	50%
#27	Eritrea: (Africa)	50%
#28	South Africa:	50%

Source: NationMaster, 2009

Some are surprised to learn that India has (only) 25% living below the poverty line, China has 10%, and the United States has 12%. More detail on the United States is provided in the following sidebar.

Poverty in the United States

In the United States, an estimated 37 million Americans (12%) live below the official poverty line. Many are surprised by the following additional facts, published in 2007 prior to the collapse of the mortgage industry and the rise of gasoline prices:[12]

- One in eight Americans lives in poverty. A family of four is considered poor if the family's income is below $19,991.

- One third of all Americans will experience poverty within a 13-year period. In that period, one in 10 Americans are poor for most of the time, and one in 20 is poor for 10 or more years.

- Poverty in the United States is far higher than in many other developed nations. At the turn of the 21st century, the United States ranked 24th among 25 countries when measuring the share of the population below 50% of the median income.

U.S. poverty rates vary significantly by race, age, education level, and other economic, social, and demographic characteristics. The overall poverty rate for minors (those younger than 18) is 22%, the highest in the developed world. The rate is highest for African-American minors (30%). And U.S. poverty has increased in recent years because of the rise in oil prices, the collapse of housing prices, the high debt burden, and deindustrialization resulting from the foreign outsourcing of more goods that normally would have supported blue-collar jobs in America.

A lot of controversy surrounds poverty measurements and solutions in the United States. Liberals tend to state that poverty levels are underestimated because these measurements ignore the medical costs of the poor, child support payments, and other costs. Liberals typically want government to spend more on antipoverty programs. Conservatives tend to believe that poverty levels are overestimated by failing to take into account the noncash benefits the poor receive, such as food stamps, public housing, church charity, and odd jobs. Conservatives also argue that living in poverty today is not as bad as it was in the past, with many poor people having TV sets, kitchen appliances, and even cars. They cite the 91% of households in the bottom 10% who own a color television, 55% who own a VCR, and 42% who own a stereo. They point to economic growth as the solution, not handouts.

Why Are They Poor?

There are ongoing debates over the causes of poverty, directly influencing the design and implementation of poverty-reduction programs that will be highlighted in Chapter 2, "Examining a Barrel of Current Solutions." Most factors cited as contributing to poverty, however, are related to a few major categories: health, the environment, the economy, infrastructures, education, social factors, and family planning. Examples include the following:

- *Poor health* that may be caused by lack of access to affordable health care, inadequate nutrition, low levels of physical activity, chronic diseases, clinical depression, substance abuse, lack of immunizations, and/or the spread of diseases such as AIDS, malaria, and tuberculosis.

- *Adverse environmental factors*, including erosion leading to soil infertility, overgrazing, overplanting, deforestation, natural disasters, drought, water contamination, and climate change.

- *Hard economic conditions* such as widespread unemployment, low wages, overspending, or economic failures of governments.

- *Lack of basic infrastructures and services* such as roads, sewage treatment, water supply, and electricity.

- *Poor access to education* or families keeping children from attending school because the children are needed to work on the farm or in other family businesses.

- *Strong social factors*, including crime, domestic violence, wealth distribution, war, discrimination, gender inequities, and individual beliefs, actions, and choices.

- *Lack of family planning*, sometimes reflecting lack of access to counseling and related services, and sometimes a result of religious or long-held cultural beliefs.

New forces operating in today's world are further threatening food supplies, raising food costs, and deepening the suffering of poor people. Major negative forces include the following:

- *High energy prices.* The world's economies in the past ran on cheap oil. The price of a barrel of oil shot up to $140 in mid-2008, causing the transportation, food, and other costs to rise significantly. Oil prices subsequently fell to $45 a barrel, which reduced energy costs but hurt oil-rich countries such as Venezuela and others that depended on higher oil revenues, causing an increase in unemployment in those countries.

- *The rise of China.* China's spectacular economic growth has required huge purchases of the world's steel, construction materials, food, and other items, causing their prices to rise significantly.

- *Biofuels.* The conversion of much farmland to growing corn to be made into biofuels has raised the price of farmland and many food products.

- *Droughts.* Long-lasting droughts in Australia, China, and other countries have significantly reduced the output of rice, causing rice prices to escalate, resulting in food shortages and riots in heavy rice-importing countries such as Haiti and Egypt.

- *Dietary changes.* People in emerging countries that are experiencing high economic growth are increasing their meat consumption, which has increased the need for grain to feed cattle and pigs, thus moving food prices higher.

- *Global warming.* Global warming tends to hurt food production in countries nearer to the equator by contributing to drought conditions.

- *Financial meltdown of 2008.* The U.S. economy suddenly turned from strong to weak as a result of loose credit standards leading to overbuilt housing and falling prices where many mortgage holders could not make their monthly payments. Home prices plummeted, banks stopped lending, and major "iconic" companies—Lehman Brothers, AIG Insurance, Citicorp—dove into bankruptcy or bailouts. The U.S. problem spread to all other countries that held "junk" mortgages, and a new mood of cost-cutting rather than spending on the part of consumers and businesses led to a worldwide recession filled with factory closings, lost jobs, and increases in the number of the poor.

The impact of these forces on living costs, credit availability, and joblessness has deepened the level of poverty. In 2008, for example, food riots broke out in Bangladesh and Egypt and required military interventions in Asia. Even in the United States, food banks and soup kitchens reported a 20% increase in visitors, and the number of citizens enrolled in food stamp programs grew by 1.3 million.[13]

And then there is the vicious cycle of poverty. Unfortunately, poverty has a built-in tendency to persist for generations within the poor and their offspring. Every baby born into a poor family faces a higher-than-average chance of dying at birth or shortly thereafter due to inadequate health facilities and abominable living conditions. If the baby survives, he or she will be exposed to hunger, polluted water, diseases such as malaria and dysentery, and other serious risks. The child, if he survives, is likely to grow up with little adult supervision because of parents who work in the fields or who are too weak to work. The urban poor child will grow up in slum conditions. He will receive either minimal or no schooling. The child will more likely bond with peers as he grows into his teens, many of whom will form gangs for mutual protection. Some children will end up in beggary or burglary or drug pushing. Early sexual intercourse is likely, resulting in young girls getting pregnant because of little parental supervision or ignorance about birth control methods. These young girls then bring into the world their newborns, who have no better chance than their parents of escaping poverty.

Why Should We Care About the Poor?

Poverty is a disgraceful and unjust condition that has always haunted mankind. Most people see the problem as insoluble. They see previous solutions that have failed. Some even think that previous remedies have worsened the condition of the poor. They claim that assisting the poor increases dependency and produces a "culture of poverty" that persists from generation to generation. Some go further and blame the poor for their problems. They think many of the poor are shiftless, lazy, unintelligent, or even parasitic. All that said, there is widespread pessimism about mankind's ability to reduce the world's level of poverty and wasted lives.

Why is it important to be optimistic about mankind's ability to reduce the number of people who waste their lives living in penurious conditions? What will the nonpoor gain if the lives of the poor are improved? The answer is that the nonpoor, as well as the poor, can benefit for seven reasons.

First, poverty means *wasted lives*—lives of people who could have grown to their full potential, prospered, and contributed. How many could have become doctors, scientists, professionals, and contributors to the well-being of their families, friends, and society at large? Chapter 7, "Understanding Barriers, Benefits, and the Competition for Change," tells the story of Cheong Chuon, a Cambodian farmer who, because of the Farmer Field School program he attended, learned to feed his chickens well and for less money by giving them earthworms, and to feed his tadpoles termites from a termite mound. He was also helped to apply for a microloan that he used to buy more chickens and build a chicken house. He was able to repay the loan with his increased productivity.

Second, poverty breeds desperation and leads some desperate poor people into wasted lives, in some extremes even to *crime*. Beggars abound in poor countries; in some cases they are even organized as a business. Some who are deprived of good things turn to criminal activities—burglary, holdups, prostitution, or drug running. The victims of crime include the poor themselves as well as many members of society at large. How many could be organized and supported to become productive instead of destructive? In Chapter 5, "Evaluating and Choosing Target Market Priorities," you'll read about scavengers who live in the slums outside Manila in the Philippines. They gather, on a daily basis, to dig through the 130-foot mountain of garbage at the city's biggest dump. Their cottage industries thrive as thousands sort through the baskets that are then brought back to the slums. Consider what would have happened to these 150,000 residents if their activities weren't supported by the city.

Third, the poor are more prone to illnesses and *health problems*. Consider that in today's fast-moving world, diseases travel at break-neck speeds. Although it took decades for AIDS to spread, the bird flu showed signs of doing that in months. Those with only a few fowl to provide eggs and a few underfed chickens to eat will not destroy their only food source to save someone from the bird flu living in a land they have never seen. And, as described in Chapter 4, "Segment-ing the Poverty Marketplace," consider the fate of New York City if an aggressive condom distribution campaign had not been launched on Valentine's Day in 2007. The city, with only 3% of the country's population, had 18% of the HIV/AIDS cases.

Fourth, the hopelessness felt by the poor makes them apt to *follow any demagogue* who promises salvation, whether it is through communism, fascism, or religious extremism. Osama bin Laden operated in the Sudan for years and found an eager following. Poverty, and its accompanying hopelessness, is a primary source of suicide bombers willing to trade their life for the small rewards given to their surviving families. In Chapter 6, "Determining Desired Behavior Changes," you'll read about Gulbibi, living in Pakistan, who was married at the age of 16. By the time she was 26, she had been pregnant five times, suffered one miscarriage, and given birth to four children. Eventually, with the help of a family clinic, she was able to convince her husband they could not afford to have any more chil-dren for a while. But what would her future and potentially that of many others have been if she hadn't taken action?

Fifth, the poor represent far more than a group that deserves our sympathy and charity. Helping the poor escape from poverty will also help *raise the incomes of the rest of the world*. The poor constitute a major untapped market opportunity for businesses that can imagine new ways to bring down the cost of products and services to the poor. Up to now, companies have largely failed to recognize "the fortune that lies at the bottom of the pyramid."[14] Through microfinance loans, smaller package sizes, and less expensive equipment (computers, cell phones, and so on), most of the poor would have access to the material fruits of modern society. Business and commerce need to pay attention to the poor if they want to know where they will sell or rent the next billion cell phones or computers.

Today millions of Chinese and Indians are employed making low-cost products to sell to other less-developed countries. Stripped-down models of electric generators that meet basic needs are sold for less than $200 in Africa to the working poor. Comparable output units but with more gadgets sell for three to four times as much in developed countries. Cell phone prices are dropping below $30, in part because they aren't loaded with features that many customers don't need. An inexpensive cell phone in a country such as Mali, where there is only one landline phone per 1,000 people, is a business opportunity, not just a convenience. The owner of that phone charges other people for calls by the minute and creates a livelihood.

C. K. Prahalad,[15] in his book *The Fortune at the Bottom of the Pyramid*, makes a compelling case for adapting products for the poor to make them affordable. Using Prahalad's math, the extreme and moderate poor have buying power equal to $8 billion per day. This makes the poor a multitrillion-dollar annual market for the world's products. Prahalad believes that the poor are an opportunity, not a burden. Western companies can resurrect earlier and simpler models of successful products and provide them at lower costs to this vast marketplace.

A sixth reason that more advanced nations should worry about nations filled with poor people. These nations often collapse into "failed states" that fall into conflicts and violence that necessitate *military intervention* by U.S. or NATO or UN forces. This happened with Honduras, Lebanon, Somalia, and Bosnia-Herzegovina—each violent outbreak within or between countries posing a threat to U.S. and European national security. As described in Chapter 11, "The

Nonprofit Sector's Role in Poverty Reduction," lack of preparation for natural disasters can also lead to failed states and increased need for international support. The massive disaster in Central America from Hurricane Mitch in 1998 served as a wake-up call, inspiring the government to take several actions to minimize the impact of inevitable future emergencies.

Seventh, the poor are desperate to leave their surroundings and enter other countries legally, or more often illegally, to better their lives. The United States itself estimates that 12 million Mexicans and other Latin Americans have entered the United States illegally in spite of billions spent on U.S. border control. Europe is beginning to feel the enormous pressures of illegal immigration from desperate people fleeing appalling circumstances in Africa and Asia. Not only is there the fear that they will take jobs away from workers in the developed countries, but that they will end up living in burgeoning slums along with some imports of criminality. Clearly the working class (middle and upper classes) in developed nations cannot claim they are safe and unaffected by poverty. The poor are no longer only a problem for the poor but a problem for all of us.

Summary

This chapter has presented the various definitions used to measure the number of people living in poverty. The "absolute definition" of people who live in extreme poverty is those who earn less than $1.25 a day (an estimated 1.4 billion). Those who live in moderate poverty earn between $1.25 and $2 a day (an estimated 1.6 billion). Adding to this the additional 1 billion estimated to be living in relative poverty, 4 billion could be considered poor. Although the majority (63%) of the extreme poor live in India and China, Africa has the greatest percentage of its population living in poverty.

Several major factors related to causing or reflecting poverty include those related to health, the environment, the economy, infrastructures, education, social factors, and family planning. Existing ideas (a barrel of solutions) for addressing these are presented in Chapter 2.

We concluded with ways that the nonpoor are also impacted by poverty, citing seven reasons we should all do all we can:

- Wasted lives that may have contributed to family, friends, communities, and society
- Crime
- Spread of illnesses and health problems
- Potential to follow demagogues
- Untapped market potential
- The collapse of failed states that then require our resources
- Illegal immigration into the developed world

Endnotes

[1] The World Bank. "Poverty Analysis—Overview." Retrieved August 30, 2008 from http://web.worldbank.org/WBSITE/EXTERNAL/TOPICS/ EXTPOVERTY/EXTPA/0,,contentMDK:20153855~menuPK:435040~pagePK: 148956~piPK:216618~theSitePK:430367,00.html.

[2] The World Bank. "World Bank Updates Poverty Estimates for the Developing World." August 26, 2008. Retrieved August 31, 2008 from http://econ. worldbank.org/WBSITE/EXTERNAL/EXTDEC/EXTRESEARCH/0,,print: Y~isCURL:Y~contentMDK:21882162~pagePK:64165401~piPK:64165026~ theSitePK:469382,00.html.

[3] Jeffrey Sachs, *The End of Poverty: Economic Possibilities for Our Time* (New York: Penguin Press, 2005), p. 20.

[4] The World Bank, op. cit.

[5] Sachs, op. cit. p. 20.

[6] The World Bank, op. cit.

[7] Sachs, op. cit. p. 20.

[8] Sachs, op. cit. p. 20.

9   United Nations. Human Rights in Development. "Poverty: What is poverty?"
    Retrieved September 1, 2008 from http://www.unhchr.ch/development/poverty-
    02.html.

10 NationMaster. Poverty: Share of all poor people (most recent) by country.
    Retrieved August 31, 2008 from http://www.nationmaster.com/red/graph/
    eco_pov_sha_of_all_poo_peo-poverty-share-all-poor-people&b_printable=1.
    Data source reported as World Bank 2002 for population numbers and propor-
    tion of population living on less than a dollar a day is from the Millennium
    Indicators (millenniumindicators.un.org).

11 NationMaster. Population below poverty line (most recent) by country.
    Retrieved February 27, 2009 from http://www.nationmaster.com/graph/
    eco_pop_bel_pov_lin-economy-population-below-poverty-line. Data source
    reported as CIA World Factbook 18 December 2003 to 18 December 2008.

12 Center for American Progress Task Force on Poverty, April 2007. "From
    Poverty to Prosperity: A National Strategy to Cut Poverty in Half."

13 "The Progress Report." Center for American Progress Action Fund,
    April 16, 2008.

14 C. K. Prahalad, *The Fortune at the Bottom of the Pyramid: Eradicating Poverty
    Through Profits* (Upper Saddle River, NJ: Wharton School Publishing-Pearson,
    2005). No one has done more than Prahalad to open the eyes of businesses to
    the immense and neglected market of billions living in poverty. They need
    many of the same products, and Prahalad argues forcefully that by innovating,
    packaging, quantity, or use, most products can be made affordable by this large
    market of eager consumers. Businesses that ignore his message do so at their
    own peril.

15 Prahalad, op. cit.

2

Examining a Barrel of Current Solutions

"The greatest good you can do for another is not just share your riches, but to reveal to him his own."

—Benjamin Disraeli

Many people have thought long and hard about how to help the poor escape from the crushing burden of poverty. They recognize that poverty takes many forms and therefore requires a War Against Poverty, a war to be conducted on many fronts.

The proposed solutions vary with interpretations of what causes people to be poor. Major factors contributing to poverty were outlined in Chapter 1, "Why Poverty Hurts Everyone." Of interest here are the many explanations that have been offered to account for the persistence of poverty throughout human history, including the following:

- There will always be some people with handicaps such as low intelligence, low energy, poor health, or addictions that condemn them to a life of poverty.
- A great number of families give birth to more children than they can afford, which has the effect of impoverishing them.
- A culture of poverty settles into a set of people who fail to adopt the values and norms of mainstream society.

- Poverty is the result of the breakdown of families where children are born out of wedlock with no support from the male partner.
- Poverty persists because of a failure of social institutions to provide good education, marketable skills, good housing, and positive role models.
- Poverty is the result of caste and class and racial and ethnic discrimination that limits the opportunities available to those groups.
- Poverty is the result of an economy unable to generate a sufficient number of good-paying jobs in the face of a changing needed skill mix and deindustrialization.
- Poverty is the result of natural disasters (earthquakes, hurricanes, and poor harvests) and wars.
- Poverty is the result of the overconcentration of wealth in the hands of the few and the institutions and laws that favor and protect the wealthy.
- Poverty is the result of weak governance and corruption that retard economic growth and development.

Each explanation has its adherents and implies quite different policies and solutions. No wonder there is so much controversy and disagreement over proposed antipoverty programs. Tools for fighting poverty include such disparate methods as advocacy, social work, education, legislation, voluntary service, charity, and community organizing.

Major Strategies Proposed for Reducing Poverty

Experts who have studied the causes and conditions of poverty have come up with four major and quite different strategic paths to reducing poverty: economic growth strategy, redistribution strategy, massive foreign aid, and population control.

Economic Growth Strategy

Many see the task of poverty reduction as lying in building up the rate of economic development through sound investments and job creation. For example, between 2000 and 2006 Brazil and Mexico experienced significant economic growth. As a result, a new lower middle class has been emerging in these countries. People have a little more money to spend, and it is driving the growth of a mass consumer market. Clearly, increasing the rate of economic growth will help reduce the number of poor living below the poverty line.

This strategy of employing measures to increase the pace of economic development would provide some help to the poor. But it is never clear how much of the created wealth would trickle down to the poor. In the case of China, its rapid rate of economic development has truly lifted millions of people out of poverty. The millions of jobs created by building factories and apartment buildings have drawn many poor rural people into urban areas such as Beijing and Shanghai and have given them work and pay. At the same time, it has increased the number of billionaires in China who have retained a lot of the created wealth as a reward for the risks they have taken. Economic growth by itself does not normally tap into and reduce the extreme poor in the absence of further measures, such as building more schools and health facilities to serve them.

Redistribution Strategy

Others say that a second strategy must be implemented—namely, making sure that the rich assume a larger burden in helping to create needed schools, health facilities, and other institutions and services to help the poor improve their lot in life. Rapid economic growth combined with some redistribution features would work well together. Of course, if the wealth tax is too high, it could discourage risk-taking and investment and therefore reduce the rate of economic growth. Clearly the interests of the rich and the poor must be carefully balanced.

Massive Foreign Aid Assistance

This strategy argues that poor countries could never grow their economies fast enough or manage enough redistribution to help most of their poor. These poor countries, it is believed, need major injections of foreign aid from the rich countries to provide relief and trigger economic development.

This third strategy, that of massive foreign aid, has been strongly advocated by Jeffrey Sachs. He would want the world's wealthier nations to launch massive foreign aid programs (similar to the Marshall Plan) to give the poor the means to escape poverty.

Yet a number of critics contend that this would amount to a temporary and only partial attack on the problem, not one likely to be sustainable or practically adopted by wealthy countries. Furthermore, it is unclear who constitutes the set of "wealthy" nations. The United States, with a national debt of $10 trillion (2009), not to mention insufficient health and social security programs, has many of its own needs to cover. The European Union also has massive debt. Nor is China ready to take on more debt to help the United States participate in a Marshall Plan. The 2008 financial meltdown makes it even less possible to imagine the West giving massive aid to some of the poorest countries in the world.

William Easterly, Paul Collier, and other critics even suggest that foreign aid in some cases has done more harm than good.[1] First, it has created more dependency on the part of the poor, because they are rescued from having to work hard to find a more permanent solution to their problems. Critics argue that aid to the poor creates a "culture of poverty" that continues from generation to generation. Second, foreign aid in the form of free food distribution hurts the farmers in those poor countries, who work hard to grow food but no longer earn enough when that same food is distributed freely. Third, much of foreign aid never reaches the intended poor recipients. William Easterly charges in his book *The White Man's Burden* that the $23 trillion of foreign aid doled out over the last five decades reached tyrants in Zaire, Sudan, and Pakistan who rarely brought the 12-cent medicine and other supplies to children and other poor. Paul Collier in his book *The Bottom Billion* cites a study that tracked money released by Chad's Ministry of Finance to fund rural health clinics. Because of corrupt officials, only one percent reached its intended destination. Collier charges that those who lay the plans for dispensing the money have little experience or control over how it gets distributed.

Population Control

Others point out that poor families give birth to proportionately more children than rich families, which has the effect of keeping them poor. They call for national measures to influence the poor to have fewer children. These measures can range from encouraging the use of birth control pills and condoms, to providing incentives and payments to women to remain nonpregnant, to the extreme of legally limiting families to having only one child, as in the case of China. Thus, the measures can range from voluntary to involuntary. Those who advocate voluntary measures prefer to use the term "family planning" rather than "birth control." Birthrates can be brought down by voluntary social marketing methods, as vividly demonstrated by a case in Thailand, where Dr. Mechai Viravaidya popularizes condoms and other birth planning methods to lower the birthrate as well as infection from HIV/AIDS (see Chapter 4, "Segmenting the Poverty Marketplace").

A number of large-scale social factors tend to slow down the rate of population growth. As women get more education, as they find more job opportunities, as they give birth later in life, and as they move to urban areas, all these factors tend to reduce the rate of population growth.

The Need for a Multilateral Strategy

We believe that no antipoverty program can be effective by employing only one of these four strategies. Successful antipoverty programs require a mix of efforts and investments. An immediate need is to improve sanitation and safe drinking water to reduce the chance of disease or thirst. Funds must more generally go into improving health care facilities and programs to stem the spread of tuberculosis, malaria, HIV/AIDS, and other deadly diseases. To minimize food shortages, money must be invested in improving agricultural output through better seeds and fertilizers. Investments must also be made to improve infrastructure in terms of better roads, energy, transportation, and communication. A more long-term but high-return investment avenue is better education through more and better schooling available to poor boys and girls to help them acquire basic and vocational skills to earn a living. Each locality with concentrations of poor people must decide on the investments that will make the most sense given their own resources and efforts and what they may be able to attract from government and other donors.

Funding Organizations Active in Fighting Poverty

Several organizations are lending financial support to fund poverty-reduction programs. This section describes some of the leading organizations and individuals.

The United Nations Takes Up the Cause of Poverty Reduction

In the year 2000, the United Nations outlined its multilateral plan for reducing world poverty. Acting on a UN Millennium Declaration in 2000, the United Nations formulated the Millennium Development Goals (MDG).[2] The United Nations established a series of eight goals with eighteen accompanying targets, designed to significantly reduce poverty levels by 2015. Only one goal addresses income; the other seven deal with improving the human and social conditions of the poor. The United Nations Millennium Development Goals are described in the following sidebar.

United Nations Millennium Development Goals (MDG) and Targets for 2015

Goal 1. Eradicate extreme poverty and hunger.

Target 1. Reduce by half the proportion of people whose income is less than one dollar a day (1990–2015).

Target 2. Reduce by half the proportion of people who suffer from hunger (1990–2015).

Goal 2. Achieve universal primary education.

Target 3. Ensure that, by 2015, children everywhere, boys and girls alike, will be able to complete a full course of primary schooling.

Goal 3. Promote gender equality and empower women.

Target 4. Eliminate gender disparity in primary and secondary education, preferably by 2005, and to all levels of education no later than 2015.

Goal 4. Reduce child mortality.

Target 5. Reduce by two thirds, between 1990 and 2015, the under-five mortality rate.

Goal 5. Improve maternal health.

Target 6. Reduce by three quarters, between 1990 and 2015, the maternal mortality ratio.

Goal 6. Combat HIV/AIDS, malaria, and other diseases.

Target 7.   Have halted by 2015 and begun to reverse the spread of HIV/AIDS.

Target 8.   Have halted by 2015 and begun to reverse the incidence of malaria and other major diseases.

Goal 7. Ensure environmental sustainability.

Target 9.   Integrate the principles of sustainable development into country policies and programs, and reverse the losses of environmental resources.

Target 10.   Reduce by half the proportion of people without sustainable access to safe drinking water and basic sanitation by 2015.

Target 11.   Have achieved by 2020 a significant improvement in the lives of at least 100 million slum dwellers.

Goal 8. Build a global partnership for development.

Target 12.   Develop further an open rule-based, predictable, nondiscriminatory trading and financial system. It includes a commitment to good governance, development, and poverty reduction, both nationally and internationally.

Target 13.   Address the special needs of the least-developed countries. Includes tariff and quota-free access for the least-developed countries' exports, enhanced programs of debt relief for HIPCs and cancellation of official bilateral debt, and more generous ODA for countries committed to poverty reduction.

Target 14.   Address the special needs of landlocked countries and small island developing states (through the Program of Action for the Sustainable Development of Small Island Developing States and the outcome of the twenty-second special session of the General Assembly).

Target 15.   Deal comprehensively with the debt problems of developing countries through national and international measures in order to make debt sustainable in the long run.

> *Target 16.* In cooperation with developing countries, develop and implement strategies for decent and productive work for youth.
>
> *Target 17.* In cooperation with pharmaceutical companies, provide access to affordable essential drugs in developing countries.
>
> *Target 18.* In cooperation with the private sector, make available the benefits of new technologies.

Clearly, the UN Millennium Development Goals Program takes into account a great number of the factors that contribute to poverty. Unfortunately, the amount of progress in implementing and achieving these worthwhile goals is lagging. In May 2005, UN Secretary General Kofi Annan warned that there is a danger that many poor countries will not meet many, or even most, of the MDG.[3] Deaths from childbirth are increasing in the risky areas, average incomes gained only marginally in some regions and fell in others, and hunger increased from 1997 to 2002. Gender equity, primary school enrollment, staying in school, and most of the other goals remain elusive and are unlikely to be achieved by the target date of 2015.

The World Bank

The World Bank has been an active force in rallying efforts to measure, fund, and implement poverty reduction around the world. A great amount of new and changing information about poverty can be found on its website, Poverty Net.[4] Among the topics covered on Poverty Net are poverty analysis, poverty mapping, poverty monitoring, poverty reduction strategies, empowerment, moving out of poverty, and many others. Many useful books and articles are cited for researchers and other interested people.

The Global Fund to Fight AIDS, Tuberculosis, and Malaria

The idea for a Global Fund to fight poverty was proposed in 2001 in an article by Amir Attaran and Jeffrey Sachs. They called for a new funding stream of $7.5 billion to make grants, not loans, to the poorest countries.[5] The money would be donated by governments.

In January 2002, The Global Fund to Fight AIDS, Tuberculosis and Malaria was finally established with the aim of substantially increasing global financing for intervening in three worldwide diseases. These diseases kill over 6 million people each year.

The Global Fund was set up as a foundation that works as a public-private charity. It is not part of the United Nations World Health Organization or the World Bank, both of which also contribute money to fight these diseases. The Global Fund serves as a financing mechanism rather than an implementing agency. It has a Technical Review Panel that reviews and awards funds to deserving grant applications. It renews grants only after rigorous review of results achieved.

The Global Fund has already committed $10 billion in 136 countries to fight these diseases. In August 2006, the Gates Foundation contributed $500 million to the Global Fund, calling the fund "one of the most important health initiatives in the world."

The Project Red Campaign

In January 2006, the rock star Bono, along with Bobby Shriver, a nephew of John F. Kennedy, started the project Red campaign, which combines consumerism with altruism. Proceeds from this campaign go to the Global Fund. Red is an organization that charges companies a license fee to label one or more of their products "Red" and contribute to the fundraising effort to help the poor. Among the companies that have purchased licenses are Dell, Apple, American Express, Converse, Hallmark, The Gap, and Motorola. For example:

- American Express has issued a Red card (in Britain only) and will turn over 1% of total spending to the Global Fund.
- Apple has issued a special edition of the iPod and will turn over a portion of the retail price to the Global Fund.
- Dell will contribute $80 for each desktop computer sold and $50 for each laptop sold.
- Motorola will contribute $8.50 for each red MotoRazr phone sold.
- The Gap will contribute 50% of net profits from sales of its Red clothing line.

Red is an upgraded version of "cause marketing," which started in 1983 when American Express said it would donate a penny to restoring the Statue of Liberty for every cardholder purchase.[6] This led to a 45% increase in American Express card applications and a 27% increase in the card's usage. This project raised $1.7 million for the restoration. Since that time, several companies have run separate cause-marketing campaigns. But Red represents a new level involving many companies licensing the color Red. The benefit to the companies is that they can advertise their corporate social responsibility. Some critics have complained that Red companies have spent more on advertising their support of Red than the amount raised by Red. Red campaign officials acknowledge that the companies may have spent $50 million on advertising while contributing $25 million.

To date, Red funds have been used to administer antiretroviral treatments to over 300,000 people and have provided more than 300,000 HIV-positive pregnant women with counseling and treatment.[7] To cite a specific case, the Treatment and Research AIDS Center in Kigali, Rwanda was almost unable to cope with the huge influx of mothers needing treatment. Doctors would see patients and send them home knowing they would die without medication. Today, thanks to the American shopper, money has come from Red to help support their services to those afflicted with HIV.

The Bill & Melinda Gates Foundation

One of the most exciting recent funding developments was the establishment in 2000 of the Bill & Melinda Gates Foundation. Its assets of $37.6 billion make it the world's largest foundation.[8] Warren Buffett contributed another $3.4 billion and plans to contribute much more later. The Foundation has already disbursed $14.4 billion.

The Gateses decided to focus their grant areas rather than issue grants for all causes. They asked two questions: Which problems affect the most people? and Which have been neglected in the past? They decided to focus on five major areas:

- Reducing the world's deadliest diseases—AIDS, malaria, and tuberculosis
- Funding vaccinations and immunizations
- Offering microfinance to the poor
- Improving agricultural productivity through a green revolution for Africa
- Improving public high school education in the United States

The Gates Foundation doesn't work alone. It has allied with Rockefeller, Michael and Susan Dell, Hewlett, and other charitable foundations. The Gates Foundation helped start the GAVI Alliance (formerly called the Global Alliance for Vaccines and Immunization) with a contribution of $1.5 billion. GAVI is supported by seventeen donor governments plus the European Union. It has distributed vaccines (tetanus, hepatitis B, and yellow fever) to 138 million children in 70 of the world's poorest countries, saving lives by avoiding more than two million premature deaths.

Fifty Current Specific Measures to Help the Poor

There is a long history of countries adopting different specific measures to help the poor. They range from emergency aid programs, to safety net and social protection programs, to social equity schemes, to empowerment programs.

The starting point are short-run relief measures by the Red Cross, CARE, and others in third-world countries to aid populations hit by natural disasters. They are called *emergency aid programs* and consist of

- Cash transfers
- Direct feeding programs
- Free food distribution
- Price subsidies
- Public works programs

The principal purpose of these interventions is to protect the poor, especially the extreme poor, from the aftermath of natural disasters such as earthquakes, typhoons, floods, cyclones, and drought.

In other parts of the third world, especially Africa and South Asia, shocks and dislocations also came from civil war and conflicts. Post-conflict social safety nets were introduced and were categorized under what became known as the *Triple R Framework*:[9]

- Relief institutions and services
- Rehabilitation assistance
- Reconciliation and peace-building assistance

The need for "safety nets" moved beyond the period during and after natural and man-made shocks. It became apparent that the poor needed protection from the deteriorating conditions of their daily lives. Therefore, "social services programs" came to include poverty solutions such as the following:[10]

- Social security systems for those working in the informal sector
- Services for school dropouts and street children
- Workfare (emergency work relief) programs
- Microfinance and self-employment programs
- Maternal and child health services
- Psychosocial care for affected families
- Assistance for the elderly and disabled

A promising example of a social services program was recently begun in Latin America. In Brazil, it is called *Bolsa Familia* (Family Fund). It gives a cash payment of $54 to poor families who earn less than $68 per month, provided that their children attend school and take part in government vaccination programs.[11] Each family receives a debit card that is refilled every month, unless the family has not met the conditions. Those who do not meet the conditions a few times are suspended. About 11 million families now receive the benefit. This has led to higher school attendance and more vaccinations. Hopefully the children will be better educated than their parents and will have more opportunities.

In Western countries, particularly the United States, "social services" include food stamps, scholarships, and health care for uninsured, Medicaid, and other vulnerable populations.[12] For these target beneficiaries, social services include the following:

- Ambulatory care
- Hospital emergency room and inpatient services
- Health services for substance abuse, disabilities, and mental illness
- Assistive care services with ordinary and instrumental activities of daily living
- Medication assistance and health support

Then in the 1990s, *social protection services* and solutions took over. These services actually included safety-net measures, but they also covered longer-term solutions. They were not only protective (coming after a shock) but also preventive in character. According to the International Food Policy Research Institute: "Social protections are not only programs aimed at reducing the impact of shocks and coping with their aftermath, but also interventions designed to prevent shocks and destitution in the first place."[13] They include "all public and private initiatives that provide income or consumption transfers to the poor, protect the vulnerable against livelihood risks, and enhance the social status and rights of the marginalized; and so with the overall objective of reducing the economic and social vulnerability of poor, vulnerable and marginalized groups."[14]

In terms of services, these initiatives and "poverty solutions" take specific forms such as the following:

- Social assistance (or "old-style" social welfare) services such as
  - Disability benefits
  - Single-parent allowances
  - Social pensions for the elderly poor
- Social insurance schemes for
  - Pensions
  - Health insurance
  - Maternity benefits
  - Unemployment benefits and retrenchment packages, and funeral services
- Social services for the poor in need of special care:
  - Orphanages and reception centers for abandoned children
  - Institutions providing care for other people unable to provide for themselves
  - Feeding camps and settlement areas for refugees and "internally displaced persons"

- Social equity services for
  - Victims of domestic violence or sexual abuse
  - Marginalized minorities
  - Stigmatized groups

Toward the end of the last century and at the start of the new one, the idea of "empowerment solutions" came into prominence. It was the concept of Nobel Laureate in economics, Amartya Sen, that economic development is fundamentally "the expansion of individual freedom of choice" that inspired this shift toward empowering the poor as the key to a lasting end to poverty.[15]

At the start of the new millennium, the World Bank adopted empowerment as its primary strategy in "attacking poverty."[16] It is a poverty-reduction strategy aimed at "expanding the assets and capabilities of poor people to participate in, negotiate with, influence, control, and hold accountable institutions that affect their lives."[17]

The empowerment solutions encompassed such mechanisms as

- Material asset building assistance for
  - Expanding financial assets: savings and working capital
  - Expanding physical assets: land, housing, livestock, and others
- Human capability building assistance for
  - Education
  - Good health
  - Production
  - Other life-enhancing skills
- Social capability building assistance for
  - Organizing and mobilizing for collective problem-solving
  - Enhancing social capital, the norms and networks that enable collective action
  - Creating "bridge" relations to access new resources managed by other groups

- Empowerment support services and assistance, such as
  - Providing local agencies with the budget to support with information and staff the poor and their organizations for community-driven development (CDD) projects
  - Investing in citizen report cards on local government expenditures, follow-the-money surveys, and measurement of service delivery outcomes
  - Promoting dialogue between poor people's organizations, government officials and policy-makers, and the private sector to initiate pro-poor regulatory change
  - Providing graduated subsidies to broker new linkages between poor people and their organizations, on the one hand, and markets and formal financial systems on the other
  - Increasing poor people's access to information technology to improve their market access
  - Strengthening membership-based groups, organizations, and networks of the poor
  - Supporting judicial and legal reforms for improving poor people's physical and financial access to justice

These 50 poverty problem solutions have been proposed over the past three decades. Like laws, solutions have never been in short supply. That some or even many of them have worked in some places or for some period of time cannot be denied. But therein lies the problem: Poverty solutions have worked in some places but not in others, sometimes but not at other times, or over time.

The problem clearly is not a dearth of poverty initiatives but a lack of coordinated and collaborative programs and the problem of choosing the right programs to match the situation. Furthermore, some programs, if given insufficient thought, can have unintended consequences.

Unintended Consequences of Well-Intentioned Programs

Most programs designed to help the poor start with a "needs assessment" to gauge the knowledge, attitudes, beliefs, and practices (KABP) of the poor population to be helped. The needs assessment should guide the search for the appropriate interventions. Too often, however, the antipoverty agency just applies a standard intervention that ignores all the differences in each poverty group. This can happen with the use of the "rapid assessment method" (RAM)[18] in those cases where it is undertaken to lend "research" support to a predetermined set of interventions.

Regarding unintended consequences of antipoverty programs, consider the U.S. experience with poverty alleviation programs in recent times. During President Lyndon B. Johnson's administration in the 1960s, the United States launched the popular and well-intentioned Great Society programs, consisting of a number of measures previously mentioned. These programs, coupled with civil rights progress, created social support systems in federal, state, and local governments that employed a new middle class of formerly poor minority workers and bureaucrats. They eventually moved into the private sector. The antipoverty program was the foundation for an emerging black middle class.

In spite of some good created by these programs, they did not bring about the fully desired outcomes. The next 30 years saw increases in single-parent households, teen births, and education declines among the poor, and the program created a dependency on public assistance. Some parts of the program were subject to abuses and outright fraud. More importantly, the failure to actually improve the lives of the poor has led to yet another reform with the 1996 Welfare Reform Act. It too has not had the hoped-for outcomes, and a new underclass of working poor has emerged.

Similarly, many well-intentioned programs in other countries also have unintended consequences and outcomes. Some bear a striking similarity to the U.S. experience. For example, repeated food aid can interfere with, rather than encourage, local farmers. During a food crisis, the few farmers producing edible crops receive a premium for their output. This encourages further investment as the return provides the capital to invest. Massive food aid, often flown in by cargo planes, disrupts the markets, decreases the value of what local food is grown, and discourages farmers from investing. Food in neighboring countries also loses value and compounds the hunger problem. The populace develops a dependency on the aid rather than addressing the root causes of too little food: lack of good irrigation, inadequate distribution channels, corruption, and other problems. Food is often stolen and then resold by government officials. The Sudan has one of the worst records of starvation and food shortages of any African country. Gerard Prunier tells the compelling story of the unintended consequences of food aid during the 1984 famine in Sudan:

> When the market for rural-grown food evaporated following the free food, people poured into the cities, leaving their native villages empty. The cities became overburdened, food distribution was handled by a company with a record of inefficiency, and the vacated lands became targets for neighboring tribes seeking land. Surely nobody can continue to support repeated massive food drops when the situation repeats itself year after year, and this is not a solution, but a series of bandages over a gaping wound. Still, year after year, generous people are implored to contribute to the effort to feed the starving people in the Sudan; all the while, war is waged between neighbors.[19]

Why Marketing Thinking Must Be Added to the Poverty Solution

Our thesis is that antipoverty planners and implementers need a strategic marketing mind-set to direct their thinking and actions in the poverty solution arena. Applying strategic marketing is a proven methodology for solving problems in the commercial sector. It is also a proven methodology for solving problems in the social sector, such as helping people stop smoking, eat healthier foods, avoid sexual diseases and conception, and change other behaviors. The repeated success of marketing is attributable to a focused and singular concern: Who are the customers, and what do they need?

Marketing, properly applied, goes beyond the important contribution of C. K. Prahalad,[20] who has promoted meeting the wants of the poor as a profit opportunity. We applaud Prahalad for his brilliant work in promoting the poor as consumers of goods and the emphasis on business models as poverty solutions. Chapter 4, "Segmenting the Poverty Marketplace," and Chapter 12, "The Private Sector's Role in Poverty Reduction," discuss the many ways in which business can serve the interests of the poor at a profit.

As impactful as *The Fortune at the Bottom of the Pyramid* is, Stephen Smith[21] points out that reaching those with some disposable income, even $1 or $2 per day, has not been the problem. While Smith doesn't use marketing language, he reinforces the importance of marketing when serving the extreme poor and supports the argument for marketing as the best method for success. Before the extreme poor can consume anything, they need social capital, which consists of health, reduced infant mortality, protection from diseases, education to know how to use the assistance, and community connectivity. These are social and human development needs as opposed to dollar-denominated market needs.

As you will read in the next chapter, social marketing has a 30-year history of increasing social capital and implementing programs designed to meet fundamental and basic human needs.[22] The most pressing and fundamental need of the extreme poor is hope. Hope becomes reality when the target segment of the extreme poor believes the service provider has listened to them, understands the need, and has a planned implementation program that will stay around to complete the job. It all starts with the customer—bottom-up, not top-down.

Six Key Understandings About the Poor

Six taken-for-granted and sometimes unnoticed aspects of poverty must be appreciated if we are to do a better job of empowering the poor and helping them succeed.

The Poor Are a Heterogeneous Group

In any poverty-stricken country, the poor are the plurality and often the majority population. But not every one of them is poor in the same way. Some are *extremely and chronically poor*. Others are a bit above the extreme poor and are known as *moderate poor*. Still others are *borderline poor*, and another segment is only *relatively poor in relation to peer groups*. This means that if we are to effectively help the poor, we need to start by recognizing differences between and within each group.

The poor are made up of several differentially responsive segments. This means that we need to identify the major poverty segments and apply the appropriate procedures to help the poor in each segment escape from and stay out of poverty.

Different Poverty Segments Require Different Poverty-Alleviating Assistance

A quick but valid and cost-effective means of finding out what different poverty segments require for poverty alleviating assistance is market research. Poverty market research at the local level, both qualitative and quantitative, is critical to gaining insight into the right poverty-alleviating assistance to each segment.

The Poor Need the Help of All Institutions

Helping the poor escape from poverty is not solely a government responsibility. Effective and sustained poverty alleviation depends on action by a three-way partnership between government, nonprofit organizations, and businesses.

Synergy comes when the three work well together. In any sector or segment, synergy of results also occurs when the strength of one compensates for the weakness of the other or the two others.

Business, perhaps reluctant to invest in income-poor markets, has begun to see the *fortune at the bottom of the pyramid.* Corporations have long made philanthropic contributions, but now they are seeing the value of untapped and new markets. A single cell phone in a Sub-Saharan region can create a business opportunity for a small reseller of calls by the minute. In several African countries, cell phone sales are growing 150% a year, far in excess of saturated Western markets. Governments are eliminating import tariffs, and local microlenders are financing them through nonprofit agencies.

The Poor Differ in Their Perceptions of the Costs of Changing Their Behavior

In attempting to assist the poor in leaving their poverty status, it is necessary to gain insight into how the poor perceive the costs of changing their behavior and situation. Different poverty segments have differing costs for the poor in escaping poverty and staying out of poverty behaviors.

The needed insight is in understanding what for the poor in different segments can tip the balance in favor of poverty-escaping behavior.

The Poor Get Into and Out of Poverty and Back in Again

The poverty situation of the poor is not static, but dynamic. Through the right combination of outside help and personal effort, a poor person in the extreme poverty segment may successfully migrate into the less extreme condition of the overall poor segment. But after some months or a year or two and because of circumstances, the poverty escapee falls back into the originating extreme poor segment. Something similar recurs in many of the other poverty segments.

To offer the right bundle of solutions, poverty-escaping programs must understand the uncontrollable and controllable forces that cause people to transition back into poverty.

The True Face of Poverty Is a Localized Face

The poor are found at the local level. They can be engaged only in the locality where they live and work. It follows that the development and implementation of poverty solutions matters most at the local level.

At the local level, we meet the poor face-to-face. Antipoverty workers can live with the poor, listen to their stories (both sad and happy), eat with them, and make friends with them. This is an important step in poverty alleviation. Because the aid worker provides an intangible service, it is essential that mutual understanding and trust exist. In regions with high rates of illiteracy, the stories are often the only research methodology that works. Once this happens and gets repeated, making poverty history looks like a doable task.

At the national and macro level, the poor are a mass. There are just too many of them, and the problem looks immense. At the local level, the poor, even if they are many, are still countable. Poverty mapping has located them and counted them and now is monitoring them as they move into and out of poverty. It is at the local level that ending poverty becomes a real possibility.

Not What, But How

Knowing what has to be done is not the same as knowing how to implement programs and achieve successful outcomes that contribute to the alleviation of poverty. In Part II, "Applying Marketing Perspectives and Solutions," we expand on these six poverty aspects and realities. The chapters offer examples of and guidance for further segmentation, engagement of the critical agencies, research, targeting, positioning strategies, value exchanges, promotional and educational strategies, and success measures.

Summary

Many different explanations have been offered as to why poverty exists and persists. Different groups who fight for poverty reduction have seen the solution as lying in one of four major strategies: economic growth, income or wealth redistribution, massive foreign aid, or population control. But poverty reduction calls for a multilateral approach. This is exemplified by funding organizations such as the United Nations, World Bank, the Global Fund, the Project Red Campaign, and the Gates Foundation. We listed 50 different specific measures used by countries to provide safety nets, social services and protection, social equity, and empowerment strategies. Finally, we argued that adding a marketing mind-set, principles, and tools will help achieve a new level of effectiveness in planning and implementing poverty-reduction programs.

Endnotes

[1] See Clark C. Gibson, Krister Andersson, Elinor Ostrom, and Sujai Shivakumar, *The Samaritan's Dilemma: The Political Economy of Development Aid* (Oxford: Oxford University Press, 2005); William Easterly, *The White Man's Burden: Why the West's Efforts to Aid the Rest Have Done So Much Ill and So Little Good* (NY: Penguin, 2006); and Paul Collier, *The Bottom Billion* (Oxford: Oxford University Press, 2007).

[2] The Millennium Development Goals Report, 2006.

[3] The Millennium Development Goals Report, May 2005. Reporting on each of the goals indicates that progress is being made in portions of Asia where the total economies are growing. However, many other regions, Sub-Saharan Africa in particular, are losing ground.

[4] Poverty Net website as of September 5, 2008. http://web.worldbank.org/ WBSITE/EXTERNAL/TOPICS/EXTPOVERTY/0,,menuPK:336998~pagePK: 149018~piPK:149093~theSitePK:336992,00.html.

[5] See "The Global Fund Saves Lives." The Global Fund website.

[6] Hamish Pringle and Marjorie Thompson, *Brand Soul: How Cause-Related Marketing Builds Brands* (New York: John Wiley & Sons, 1999).

[7] Ron Nixon, "Little Green for (Red)," *New York Times*, February 6, 2008, pp. C1 and C5.

[8] Patricia Sellers, "Melinda Gates Goes Public," *Fortune*, January 21, 2008, pp. 44–56.

[9] Ramani Gunatilaka and P. A. Kiriwandeniya, "Protection for the Vulnerable." Workshop presentation for a Policy Framework for Poverty Reduction in Sri Lanka, October 1999.

[10] Michelle Adato, Akhter Ahmed, and Francie Lund, "Linking Safety Nets, Social Protection, and Poverty Reduction—Directions for Africa," a conference brief prepared for the conference on "Assuring Food and Nutrition Security in Africa by 2020: Prioritizing Actions, Strengthening Actors, and Facilitating Partnerships," Kampala, Uganda, April 1–3, 2004. Sourced from http://www. ifpri.org/2020africaconference and viewed March 7, 2005.

[11] See "Happy Families," *The Economist*, February 9, 2008, pp. 39–40.

[12] Grantmakers in Health Resource Center, *Shoring Up the Safety Net: Findings from the Grantmakers in Health Study of Philanthropic Strategies to Support Communities under Stress.* Sourced from http://www.gih.org/usr_doc/safety_ net_finding.pdf, viewed July 8, 2005; and Agency for Health Care Administration, Safety Net Project Background. Sourced from http://www.MyFlorida.com, viewed July 8, 2005.

[13] Adato, Ahmed, and Lund, op. cit.

[14] Jane Mpagi, *Social Protection in Uganda: A Study to Inform the Development of a Framework for Social Protection in the Context of the Poverty Eradication Action Plan.* Phase 1 Report, Social Protection Task Force, Uganda, October, 2002. Sourced from http://www.ids.ac.uk/ids/pvty/pdf-files/UgandaCh1-2.pdf, viewed July 8, 2005.

[15] Amartya Sen, *Development as Freedom* (New York: Knopf, 1999). Sen had earlier presented this concept of development in Amartya Sen, "Well-Being, Agency and Freedom: The Dewey Lectures 1984," The Journal of Philosophy, Vol. 82, No. 4: 1985, pp. 169–221.

[16] World Bank, *World Development Report 2000/2001: Attacking Poverty* (New York: Oxford University Press, 2000).

[17] Deepa Narayan, *Empowerment and Poverty Reduction: A Sourcebook* (Washington, D.C.: The World Bank, 2002), p. 14.

[18] See Bie Nio Ong, *Rapid Appraisal and Health Policy* (San Diego: Singular Publishing Group, 1996), and Taryn Vian, "Rapid Needs Assessment Following Cyclone Disaster in Madagascar." A paper presented at the 129th Annual Meeting of the American Public Health Association, October 24, 2001.

[19] G. Prunier, *Darfur: The Ambiguous Genocide*. Copyright © 2005 by Gérard Prunier. Published in North America by Cornell University Press. Prunier presents a more complete understanding of the often terrible consequences of ineffective aid. Roaming rebels, displaced families, and intervention by predatory neighbors can all be attributed to what is described as bungled attempts to assist rather than solve the problems.

[20] C.K. Prahalad, *The Fortune at the Bottom of the Pyramid: Eradicating Poverty Through Profits* (Upper Saddle River; NJ: Wharton School Publishing-Pearson, 2005).

[21] Stephen C. Smith, *Ending Global Poverty: A Guide to What Works* (New York: Palgrave-MacMillan, 2005).

[22] See P. Kotler and E. Roberto, 1989, "Social Marketing: Strategies for Changing Public Behavior," for extensive real-world examples of successful marketing campaigns to combat AIDS, illiteracy, and teenage pregnancy and to create positive social change. Also, see P. Kotler, E. Roberto, and N. Lee, *Social Marketing: Improving the Quality of Life*, 2nd edition (Thousand Oaks, CA: Sage, 2002) for additional examples, and P. Kotler and N. Lee, *Social Marketing: Influencing Behaviors for Good*, 3rd edition (Thousand Oaks, CA: Sage, 2008).

3

The Social Marketing Solution

"I imagine a future in which the random chance of where a child is born doesn't determine her odds of being happy and successful. I envision a different world in which suffering isn't automatically the lot of billions of people."

—Melinda Gates[1]

Consider the impact we would have on the number of people in poverty in various parts of the world if we could support and persuade more people to get immunized on time, put mosquito nets over their beds, take their tuberculosis medicines, use condoms, reduce saturated fats in their diets, quit smoking, breastfeed for six months, get screened for cancer, say no to drugs, use alcohol only in moderation, purify their water, access services for the homeless, and wash their hands often, for as long as it takes to sing "Happy Birthday" twice.

What would it mean if we were also successful in influencing more children to be prepared for their first year in school, and more teens to finish high school and then go on to college, to then get and keep a job, live within their means, and be prepared when bringing a child into the world?

What difference would it make if we had more volunteer tutors, mentors, and informed voters, and were better prepared as communities for natural disasters? And then picture, most importantly, perhaps, government agencies, nonprofit organizations, philanthropists, and corporations providing integrated support to make these behaviors more affordable, popular, and easy—everywhere in the world.

This is in fact is what social marketers do every day, around the world, as they *influence behaviors for good*.

What Is Involved in Trying to Change Someone's Behavior?

Many positive behaviors are not adopted for a variety of reasons. Some current behaviors are addictive and take a strong will to change. Some behaviors are spontaneous and repeated without much thought or educated concern. Some behavior changes involve costs or unpleasant efforts. Some lack a system or persons who will support or facilitate the behavior.

The purpose of social marketing is to develop constructive approaches to support desired behavior changes. The basic principle is to increase the audience's perception that the benefits of the new behavior outweigh the costs of adopting it. The new behavior must be seen as having higher value than the current behavior. For example, to get someone to consider giving up smoking, there are two broad approaches:

- Increase the perception of the benefits of the desired behavior (such as by emphasizing to young people how their breathing is better when they engage in sports and give up smoking)
- Increase the costs of the undesirable behavior (such as by raising the tax on cigarettes)

Social marketers, like their counterparts in commercial marketing, use the four Ps—product, price, place, and promotion—to encourage purchase or adoption of behaviors. They improve the attractiveness of the behavior and sometimes offer goods or services to support the behavior (product). They alter the price or cost of one behavior versus another (price). They make it easier to move into the new behavior (place). They promote the short-term and long-term benefits of the new behavior (promotion).

Commercial marketing, which has been so effective in getting people to improve their material life, uses a set of principles and practices that can be applied effectively in the social realm, as illustrated by the following scenario.

Picture a village in India that experiences a sudden outbreak of influenza. Suppose a vaccine exists that can stop the flu epidemic from spreading, especially if everyone in the village would show up and be vaccinated when the truck arrives with the vaccine. It is important to get 100% turnout for the vaccine. *The number of people in the village who show up for the vaccine will depend on the intensity of the marketing campaign.* Consider these possible levels of the marketing campaign, from weak to strong:

- Only send a marketing agent to visit each family and announce the day of the vaccination.
- Add to this: The agent asks if anyone in the family (such as a disabled person) will need help on that day to get to the site of the mass vaccination.
- Add to this: The agent describes to the family the strong benefits of getting the vaccination or the possible harm of catching the disease.
- Add to this: The agent mentions that there will be entertainment at the site of the vaccination.
- Add to this: The agent mentions that free food will be supplied at the site.
- Add to this: The agent mentions that each person who receives a vaccination will receive a gift (such as a transistor radio or some other item that has been donated by a corporate partner).

If the agent follows only the first step, chances are most of the villagers won't show up. Pure information rarely carries a motivational charge. Offering to help all the family members attend—children, the elderly, and the disabled—improves the turnout. Helping villagers vividly recognize the benefits of the vaccination will increase their intention to show up. Offering entertainment at the site will improve attendance, as will free food. Finally, if it is absolutely critical to get 100% turnout, it might also be important to give each person some gift they would find appealing.

Even this approach is only a limited marketing view of what it takes to draw a large turnout of people for a vaccination. It has the character of a "mass marketing" approach, as opposed to a "target marketing" approach. The agent has chosen to attract everyone with a similar package of benefits, assistance, entertainment, and gifts. But some villagers will not be persuaded by any of these inducements. People also differ in their readiness and willingness to respond. Some villagers may be against vaccinations, believing that vaccinations go against their religion. Other villagers may believe the vaccinations will be painful or ineffective. People carry different perceptions, attitudes, and beliefs that affect their behavior. Understanding this, a sophisticated marketing agent would not have developed his vaccination plan until he had interviewed people in the village and talked to the tribal leader to see what beliefs would facilitate the project and what beliefs would hinder it. And they may then employ different strategies with different segments.

Even this segmenting and targeting scenario is too limited a view of a sound social marketing approach. Our campaign describes only *downstream* social marketing—planning to change the behavior of the target "consumers." But *upstream* social marketing work also must be done, to alter the impact of larger factors and forces that will affect the campaign's success. Here are some examples connected with successfully vaccinating all the persons in a village:

- The marketing agent has to raise money to pay for the vaccines, instruments, facilities, marketing research, and promotion of the event. This calls for a market analysis of possible sources of funds—perhaps a government agency, donor companies, or nongovernment organizations (NGOs). The marketer may want to set up a vaccination campaign fundraising unit that identifies, visits, and solicits support from specific organizations and individuals who are likely to contribute.

- The marketing agent has to find a site where the vaccinations and activities can take place. Its location must be easily accessible. The agent may have to convince a specific farmer who has a large, empty field to make it available for that day.

- The marketing agent may have to contact an insurance company to gain favorable terms to cover any villagers who are hurt by the vaccinations or activities of that day.

Social marketing relies on understanding the target audience's needs, wants, perceptions, preferences, values, and barriers and turning this understanding into an effective plan to achieve the desired behavior outcomes, upstream as well as downstream. Without this understanding, many poverty workers with the best of intentions fail to achieve their objectives in reducing poverty. Simply telling someone that a new behavior would be good for him or her is not enough. Every cigarette package contains a warning that smoking is harmful to your health. We know that this is not enough. Social marketing supplies the steps usually missing in otherwise well-intentioned social betterment efforts.

What Is Social Marketing?[2]

Social marketing is a process that applies marketing principles and techniques to create, communicate, and deliver value in order to influence target audience behaviors that benefit society (public health, safety, the environment, and communities) as well as the target audience.[3]

Social marketing has made enormous strides since its founding in the early 1970s. It has had a profound positive impact on social issues such as family planning, tobacco usage, drunkenness, teen pregnancy, HIV/AIDS, immunizations, skin cancer, and literacy. Scores of social marketing campaigns deal with problems in industrial societies, such as obesity, lack of exercise, eating disorders, drinking and driving, seatbelts, gun storage, water conservation, litter, and energy conservation.

Social marketing as a term, however, is misunderstood or misused by many. There are several common misunderstandings to clear up:

- Don't confuse social marketing with social advertising. We have all seen well-meaning public campaigns for putting out campfires ("Smokey Bear"), getting a good education ("Go to college"), and not using drugs ("Just say no to drugs"). Social advertising is an important tool of social marketing. But social marketing goes well beyond simply promoting a cause. In fact, promoting the cause is the last step in developing a full social marketing campaign.

- Assure your colleagues, elected officials, and funders that social marketing is not another term for manipulation and hardselling. In fact, it is just the opposite, as it is rarely successful without a customer-driven, customer-sensitive approach.

- Understand that the term "social marketing" is not the same as "social networking" or "social media," although these are promotional tactics that social marketers may use.

- Know that a social marketing strategy may include providing subsidies for products such as mosquito nets and HIV drugs. But providing subsidies for products is not social marketing.

What Poverty-Related Issues Can Benefit from Social Marketing?

Table 3.1 presents 30 major poverty-related issues that can benefit from the application of social marketing principles and techniques. It is only a partial list, but it represents the major poverty causal factors that might be supported by social marketing efforts. Examples of downstream behaviors that contribute to alleviating the issue are also presented.

TABLE 3.1   Thirty Poverty-Related Issues That Social Marketing Can Impact Increasing Resilience to Economic Hardship and Decreasing Vulnerability to Poverty

Poverty-Related Issues That Social Marketing Might Help		One Behavior That Might Be Chosen for a Social Marketing Effort
Health	HIV/AIDS	Use condoms.
	Tuberculosis	Take all prescribed drugs as directed.
	Malaria	Put a mosquito net over the bed.
	Cancer	Have screenings for breast, prostate, and colon cancers.
	Heart disease	Engage in regular physical activity.
	Polio	Agree to have children inoculated.
	Nutrition	Breastfeed for at least the first six months.
	Safe drinking water	Sanitize water before drinking.
	Diarrhea among infants and toddlers	Accept oral rehydration therapy.
	Infectious diseases	Wash hands.
	Alcoholism and drug abuse	Seek treatment.
	Senior falls	Have a fall risk assessment.
	Sanitation	Secure and place functioning latrines.
	Essential medicines	Form partnerships to secure funding or subsidize costs.
	Mental health	Reduce stigma in communities.
Education	School preparedness	Make sure preschoolers are read to 20 minutes a day.
	Literacy	Eliminate gender inequalities.
	Finishing high school	Find a volunteer tutor for at-risk youth.
Family planning	Teen pregnancy	Postpone having sex.
	Inability to support large families	Empower women to make fertility choices.
Food supply	Agricultural productivity	Add soil nutrients.
Employment	Unemployment	Apply for microfinancing loans.
	Lack of job skills	Attend jobs skills training.

(continued)

TABLE 3.1   Continued

Poverty-Related Issues That Social Marketing Might Help		One Behavior That Might Be Chosen Chosen for a Social Marketing Effort
Financial management	Bankruptcy	Live within your means.
Natural disasters	Hurricanes	Follow evacuation requests.
Shelter	Homelessness	Access available services.
	Shelter	Help build a roof to keep out the rain.
Safety	Smoke	Install a chimney to remove smoke from a cookstove.
	Domestic violence	Call the domestic violence help line.
	Crime	Form neighborhood watch groups.

How Does Social Marketing Differ from Commercial Marketing, Nonprofit Marketing, and Marketing in the Public Sector?

There are several important differences between social and commercial marketing:

- In the case of commercial marketing, the marketing process aims to sell a tangible product or service. In the case of social marketing, the marketing process is used to sell a *desired behavior*.

- Not surprisingly, in the commercial sector, the primary aim is *financial gain*. In social marketing, the primary aim is *individual* or *societal gain*. Commercial marketers choose target audiences that will provide the greatest volume of profitable sales. In social marketing, segments are selected based on a different set of criteria, such as what will produce the greatest amount of behavior change. In both cases, however, marketers seek to gain the greatest returns for their investment of resources.

- Competitors are very different. The commercial marketer sees competitors as other *organizations offering similar goods and services*, or ones that satisfy similar needs. Social marketers see the *competition as the current or preferred behavior of the target audience* and the perceived benefits and costs of that behavior. This includes any organizations that sell or promote competing behaviors (such as the tobacco industry).

Social marketing is more difficult than commercial marketing. Consider the financial resources that the competition has available to make smoking look cool, to promote alcoholic beverages, to glamorize sexual promiscuity. And consider the challenges faced when trying to influence people to give up an addictive behavior (stop smoking), resist peer pressure (be sexually protected), go out of their way (avoid drinking contaminated water), hear bad news (get an HIV test), risk relationships (avoid taking hard drugs), or remember something (take pills three times a day).

Despite these differences, we also see many similarities between the social and commercial sector marketing models—ones that are key to any marketer's success:

- *A customer orientation is critical.* The marketer knows that the offer (product, price, place) needs to appeal to the target audience, solving a problem they have or satisfying a want or need.
- *Exchange theory is fundamental.* The target audience must perceive benefits that equal or exceed the perceived costs.[4] As Bill Smith at AED often exhorts, we should think of the social marketing paradigm as "Let's make a deal!"[5]
- *Marketing research is used throughout the process.* Only by researching and understanding the specific needs, desires, beliefs, and attitudes of target adopters can the marketer build effective strategies.
- *Audiences are segmented.* Strategies must be tailored to the unique wants, needs, resources, and current behavior of differing market segments.
- *All Four Ps are considered.* A winning strategy requires an integrated approach, one utilizing all the tools in the toolbox, not just relying on advertising and other persuasive communications.

- *Results are measured and used for improvement.* Feedback is valued and seen as "free advice" on how to do better next time.

Social marketing efforts are most often initiated and sponsored by those working in government agencies or nonprofit organizations. However, in the nonprofit sector, marketing is more often used to support utilization of the organization's services (such as tuberculosis testing), purchases of ancillary products and services (such as at museum stores), volunteer recruitment, advocacy efforts, and fundraising. In the government sector, marketing activities are also used to support utilization of government agency products and services (such as the post office and community clinics) and to engender citizen support and compliance. Thus, social marketing efforts are only one of many marketing activities conducted by those involved in nonprofit or public-sector marketing.

What Are the Main Principles of Social Marketing?

Focus on Behaviors

Similar to commercial-sector marketers, who sell goods and services, social marketers sell behaviors. Change agents typically want to influence target audiences to do one of four things:

- *Accept* a new behavior (such as putting a mosquito net over your bed)
- *Reject* a potentially undesirable behavior (such as starting smoking)
- *Modify* a current behavior (for example, for those with multiple sex partners, use a condom every time)
- *Abandon* an old, undesirable behavior (such as excessive alcohol use)

This may be the encouragement of a one-time behavior (such as getting tested for tuberculosis) or the establishment of a habit and the prompting of a repeated behavior (such as washing hands).

Although benchmarks may also be established for increasing knowledge and skills through education, and efforts may need to be made to alter existing beliefs, attitudes, or feelings, the bottom line for the social marketer is whether the target audience "buys" the behavior. For example, a specific behavior that substance abuse coalitions want to influence is for women to avoid alcohol during pregnancy. They recognize the need to inform women that alcohol may cause birth defects and convince them that this could happen to their baby. In the end, however, their measure of success will be whether the expectant mother abstains from drinking alcohol.

Recognize that Behavior Change Typically Is Voluntary

Perhaps the most challenging aspect of social marketing is that it relies heavily on voluntary compliance rather than legal, economic, or coercive forms of influence. And in many cases, the social marketers cannot promise a direct benefit or immediate payback in return for adopting the proposed behavior change. Remember the example of getting everyone in a village to voluntarily show up for a vaccination? Some believe that heavy reliance on individual voluntary behavior change is outdated and stress relying on other means, such as law or coercion. Those not showing up may have to pay a tax or lose schooling for their children or pay some other penalty. Social marketers prefer to encourage voluntary behavior change but may also advocate with other institutions (such as schools and laws) to use their influence as well when increased participation is seen as critical for a community.

Use Traditional Marketing Principles and Techniques

The most fundamental principle underlying marketing is to apply a *customer orientation overview* to understand market segments and each segment's potential needs, wants, beliefs, problems, concerns, and related behaviors. Marketers then select *target markets* they can best affect and satisfy. They establish clear *objectives and goals*. The product is *positioned* to appeal to the desires of the target market, and the game requires that marketers do this more effectively than the competition. They then use four major tools in the marketers' toolbox, the Four Ps, to influence target markets: product, price, place, and promotion, also called the *marketing mix*. Once a plan is implemented, *results are monitored and evaluated*, and strategies are altered as needed.

Select and Influence a Target Market

Marketers know that the marketplace is a collage of diverse populations, each having a distinct set of wants and needs. They know that what appeals to one individual may not appeal to another. Therefore, they divide the market into similar groups (market segments), measure the relative potential of each segment to meet organizational and marketing objectives, and then choose one or more segments (target markets) on which to concentrate their efforts and resources. For each target, a distinct mix of the Four Ps is developed, one designed to uniquely appeal to the targeted segment.

Considering again a more expanded view of social marketing, Robert Donovan and Nadine Henley, among others, advocate for also targeting individuals in communities who have the power to make institutional policy and legislative changes in social structures (such as school superintendents). These are upstream markets where efforts will move from (just) influencing an individual with a problem or potentially problematic behavior to influencing those who can facilitate individual behavior change.[6] The techniques remain the same.

Recognize that the Beneficiary Is the Individual, Group, or Society as a Whole—Not the Sponsoring Organization

Unlike commercial sector marketing, in which a major intended beneficiary are the company investors, the primary beneficiary of the social marketing program is the individual, a group, or society as a whole. The question many raise is, who determines whether the social change created by the campaign is beneficial? Although most causes supported by social marketing efforts tend to draw high consensus that the cause is good, this model can also be used by opponents who have the opposite view of what is good. Abortion is an example of an issue where both sides argue that they are on the "good" side and both use social marketing techniques to influence public behavior. Who, then, gets to define "good"? Donovan and Henley propose the UN Universal Declaration of Human Right (www.unhchr.ch) as a baseline with respect to the common good. Alan Andreasen suggests that the client or sponsor of the campaign gets to make that call. Craig Lefebvre says, "It is in the eye of the beholder."[7]

How Did the Social Marketing Concept Evolve?

When we think of social marketing as "influencing public behavior," it is clear that campaigning for voluntary behavior change is not a new phenomenon. Consider efforts to free slaves, abolish child labor, give women the right to vote, and recruit women into the workforce.

Launching the discipline formally more than 37 years ago, the term *social marketing* was introduced by Philip Kotler and Gerald Zaltman in a pioneering article in the *Journal of Marketing*. It described "the use of marketing principles and techniques to advance a social cause, idea, or behavior."[8] In the intervening decades, growing interest in and use of social marketing concepts, tools, and practices have spread from public health and safety to use by environmental and community advocates, as is evident from the partial list of seminal events, texts, and journal articles in the following sidebar.

Social Marketing: Seminal Events and Publications

1970s:
- 1971: A pioneering article, "Social Marketing: An Approach to Planned Social Change," in the *Journal of Marketing* by Philip Kotler and Gerald Zaltman coins the term "social marketing."

- More distinguished researchers and practitioners join the voice for the potential of social marketing, including Alan Andreasen (Georgetown University), James Mintz (Federal Department of Health, Canada) Bill Novelli (cofounder of Porter Novelli Associates), and William Smith (Academy for Educational Development).

1980s:
- World Bank, World Health Organization, and Centers for Disease Control start to use the term and promote interest in social marketing.

- 1981: An article in the *Journal of Marketing* by Paul Bloom and William Novelli reviews the first 10 years of social marketing. It highlights the lack of rigor in the application of marketing principles and techniques in critical areas of the field, including research, segmentation, and distribution channels.

- 1988: An article in the *Health Education Quarterly*, "Social Marketing and Public Health Intervention," by R. Craig Lefebvre and June Flora, gives social marketing widespread exposure in the field of public health.

- 1989: The book *Social Marketing: Strategies for Changing Public Behavior*, by Philip Kotler and Eduardo Roberto, lays out the application of marketing principles and techniques for influencing social change management. (Nancy Lee joins the authors, and two subsequent editions are published in 2002 and 2008.)

1990s:

- Academic programs are established, including the Center for Social Marketing at the University of Strathclyde in Glasgow and the Department of Community and Family Health at the University of South Florida.

- 1992: An article in the *American Psychologist* by J. Prochaska, C. DiClemente, and J. C. Norcross presents an organizing framework for achieving behavior change. It's considered by many as the most useful model developed to date.

- 1994: The publication *Social Marketing Quarterly* by Best Start, Inc. and The Department of Public Health, University of South Florida, is launched.

- 1995: The book *Marketing Social Change: Changing Behavior to Promote Health, Social Development, and the Environment*, by Alan Andreasen, makes a significant contribution to both the theory and practice of social marketing.

- 1999: The Social Marketing Institute is formed in Washington, D.C., with Alan Andreasen from Georgetown University as interim executive director.

- 1999: The book *Fostering Sustainable Behavior*, by Doug McKenzie-Mohr and William Smith, introduces community-based social marketing.

2000s:

- 2003: The book *Social Marketing: Principles and Practice* by Rob Donovan and Nadine Hadley was published in Australia.

- 2005: The National Social Marketing Centre is formed in London, England, headed by Jeff French and Clive Blair-Stevens.

- 2005: The 10th annual conference for Innovations in Social Marketing is held.

- 2006: The book *Social Marketing in the 21st Century*, by Alan Andreasen, describes an expanded role for social marketing.

- 2008: The 19th annual Social Marketing in Public Health conference is held.

- 2008: The first World Social Marketing Conference takes place in Brighton, England.

Source: *Social Marketing: Influencing Behaviors for Good* (Sage, 2008)

Bill Smith at AED pointed out that large-scale social marketing programs began in the 1970s:

> "The first large-scale social marketing programs were international—the early diarrheal disease work in El Salvador by Manoff, AED's work in Honduras, The Gambia, and then Egypt. Very soon after these efforts came the social marketing of contraceptives by PSI, the Futures Group, AED and others. Tens of millions of dollars have been invested in designing, conducting, and evaluating these social marketing efforts... From the very beginning they were product oriented and not message oriented. That is, the solution to a problem was found in social marketing of new products and services. Give-a-ways were never part of these early social marketing efforts. Products—condoms and contraceptives, ORS packets, etc, were physical products—with real costs, distribution channels, and promotion efforts. Price was discovered early on to ADD VALUE to products and some of the most interesting pricing studies among the poor have been done by these programs going back 30 years. But they are all but unknown by most 'public health' social marketers in the US."[9]

Who Does Social Marketing?

In most cases, social marketing principles and techniques are used by those on the front lines who are responsible for improving public health, preventing injuries, protecting the environment, and engendering community involvement. Rarely do they have a social marketing title. More often, they are program managers or are working in community relations or communication positions. Efforts usually involve multiple change agents who, as Robert Hornik points out, may or may not be acting in a consciously coordinated way.[10] Many international organizations are involved in social marketing activities, such as groups like the World Bank and units of the United Nations such as UNESCO and the World Health Organization. Most often organizations sponsoring these efforts in a country such as the United States are *public sector agencies*, national ones such as the Centers for Disease Control and Prevention (CDC), Departments of Health, Departments of Social and Human Services, the Environmental Protection Agency, the National Highway Traffic Safety Administration, the Departments of Wildlife and Fisheries, and local jurisdictions including public utilities, fire departments, schools, parks, and community health clinics.

Nonprofit organizations and foundations also get involved, more often supporting behaviors aligned with their agency's mission. Here are some examples:

- World Vision trains birth attendants in Ghana.
- The Academy for Educational Development (AED) partnered with the private sector to increase the use of insecticide-treated bed nets to prevent malaria.
- Population Services International (PSI) promotes multivitamins with iron and folic acid to women of reproductive age in developing countries.
- The Kaiser Family Foundation's Know HIV/AIDS campaign promotes testing.

What Are Other Ways to Impact Social Issues?

Social marketing clearly is not the only approach to impacting a social issue such as poverty, and social marketers are not the only ones who can influence the situation. Other forces and organizations, ones some people describe as upstream factors, can influence individual behaviors downstream—and even make personal change unnecessary. Included are technological innovations, scientific discoveries, improved infrastructures, new school policies and curricula, public education, and the media:

- *Technology.* In western Kenya, a fourth of the farmers in the Sauri district use a new technique to improve crops that involves planting nitrogen-fixing trees alongside maize and other food crops, providing a natural substitute for chemical fertilizers.[11]

- *Science.* Medical discoveries may eventually provide inoculations for certain cancers, such as one recently released for young girls to help prevent cervical cancer. And in 2006, researchers at the Mayo Clinic announced they felt they were close to discovering a shot that could help smokers quit (or even ensure that they do).[12]

- *Improved infrastructures and built environments.* Clean water in South Africa became more accessible in some communities when an entrepreneurial company came up with a device to replace hand pumps. The Play Pump™ water system is a type of merry-go-round that pumps groundwater from boreholes into a storage tank. With the children spinning the merry-go-round about 16 times a minute, it can produce about 1,400 liters of water per hour, easily enough to meet the estimated 6 liters per person per day needed.

- *Schools.* School district policies and offerings can contribute significantly in all social arenas: health (offering healthier options in school cafeterias and regularly scheduled physical activity classes), safety (requiring students to wear ID badges), environmental protection (providing recycling containers in each classroom), and community involvement (offering school gymnasiums for blood donation drives).

- *Education.* The line between social marketing and education is a clear one. Education serves as a useful tool for the social marketer, but one that does not work alone. Most often education is used to communicate information and/or build skills, but it does not give the same attention and rigor to creating and sustaining behavior change. It primarily applies only one of the four marketing tools—promotion. Many in the field agree that when the information is motivating and "new" (such as the finding that secondhand tobacco smoke increases the risk of sudden infant death syndrome), it can quickly move a market from inaction—even resistance—to action. Unfortunately, this is not typical. Consider the fact that warnings about tobacco use have been posted on cigarette packs for decades, yet the World Health Organization estimates that 29% of youth/adults (ages 15 and over) worldwide still smoke.[13]

• *Media*. News and entertainment media have a powerful influence on individual behaviors because they shape values, are relied on for current events and trends, and create social norms. Many argue, for example, that the casual and sensational attitude of movies and television toward sex has had a major contribution to the problems we see among young people today.[14] On the flip side, the media was a powerful factor influencing people to donate time and resources to victims of Hurricane Katrina.

What Is the Social Marketer's Role in Influencing Upstream Factors?

Many believe that to date we have been placing too much of the burden for improving the status of social issues on individual behavior change and that social marketers should direct some of their efforts to influence upstream factors. We agree.

Alan Andreasen in his book *Social Marketing in the 21st Century* describes this expanded role for social marketing well:

> "Social marketing is about making the world a better place for everyone—not just for investors or foundation executives. And, as we argue throughout this book, the same basic principles that can induce a 12-year-old in Bangkok or Leningrad to get a Big Mac and a caregiver in Indonesia to start using oral dehydration solutions for diarrhea can also be used to influence politicians, media figures, community activists, law officers and judges, foundation officials, and other individuals whose actions are needed to bring about widespread, longlasting positive social change."[15]

Consider the issue of the spread of HIV/AIDS. Downstream, social marketers focus on decreasing risky behaviors (such as unprotected sex) and increasing timely testing (such as during pregnancy).

If they moved their attention upstream, they would notice groups and organizations and corporations and community leaders and policy makers who could make this change a little easier or a little more likely, ones who could be a target market for a social marketing effort. Social marketers could advocate with others to influence pharmaceutical companies to make testing for HIV/AIDS quicker and more accessible. They could work with physician groups to create protocols to ask patients whether they have had unprotected sex, and, if so, encourage them to get an HIV/AIDS test. They would advocate with offices of public instruction to include curricula on HIV/AIDS in middle schools. They would support needle exchange programs. They would provide the media with trends and personal stories, maybe even pitch a story to producers of soap operas or situation comedies popular with the target audience. They might look for a corporate partner that would be interested in setting up testing at its retail location. They could organize meetings with community leaders such as ministers and directors of nonprofit organizations, even provide grants for them to allocate staff resources to community interventions. If they could, they would visit hair salons and barbershops, encouraging owners and staff to spread the word to their clients. They would testify before a senate committee to advocate for increased funding for research, condom availability, or free testing facilities.

The marketing process and principles are the same as ones used for influencing individuals, utilizing a customer orientation, marketing research, clear objectives and goals, positioning, a marketing mix, monitoring, and evaluation. Only the target market has changed.[16]

Summary

Social marketing is a process that applies marketing principles and techniques to create, communicate, and deliver value to influence target-audience behaviors that benefit society (public health, safety, the environment, and communities) as well as the target audience.[17]

Poverty-related issues that can benefit from social marketing applications include those that impact health, safety, education, family planning, food supply, employment, personal financial management, natural disasters, shelter, and gender inequality—all factors that when improved increase resilience to economic hardship and decrease vulnerability to poverty.

There are a few important differences between social marketing and commercial sector marketing. Social marketers are focused on selling a behavior, whereas commercial marketers are more focused on selling goods and services. Commercial sector marketers position their products against those of other companies, whereas the social marketer competes with the audience's current behavior and associated benefits. The primary benefit of a "sale" in social marketing is the welfare of an individual, group, or society, whereas in commercial marketing it is shareholder wealth.

There are many important similarities between the social and commercial marketing models:

- A customer orientation is critical.
- Exchange theory is fundamental.
- Marketing research is used throughout the process.
- Audiences are segmented.
- All the Four Ps are considered.
- Results are measured and used for improvement.

Principles for success are as follows:

- Focus on behaviors.
- Know that the behavior change typically is voluntary.
- Use traditional marketing principles and techniques.
- Select and influence a target market.
- Recognize that the beneficiary is the individual, group, or society as a whole.

Those engaged in social marketing activities include professionals in public sector agencies, nonprofit organizations, corporate marketing and community relations and advertising, public relations, and market research firms. A social marketing title is rare and is most likely to fall within the responsibility of a program manager, community relations, or communications professional.

Other approaches to changing behavior and impacting social issues include technological innovations, scientific discoveries, economic pressures, laws, improved infrastructures, changes in corporate business practices, new school policies and curricula, public education, and the media. Many agree that these factors and audiences are well within the purview, even responsibility, of social marketers to influence.

Endnotes

[1] Melinda Gates, keynote speaker, Seattle Biomedical Research Institute, April 30, 2008. Quote appeared on mailer promoting the event.

[2] Much of the text from the remainder of this chapter was adapted from Philip Kotler and Nancy R. Lee, *Social Marketing: Influencing Behaviors for Good*, 3rd edition (Thousand Oaks, CA: Sage, 2008).

[3] Kotler and Lee, op. cit., p. 7.

[4] R. P. Bagozzi, "Marketing as Exchange: A Theory of Transactions in the Marketplace," *American Behavioral Science*, March–April 1978, pp. 535–556.

[5] William Smith, "Social Marketing and Its Potential Contribution to a Modern Synthesis of Social Change," *Social Marketing Quarterly*, Volume VIII/Number 2, Summer 2002, p. 46.

[6] Rob Donovan and Nadine Henley, 2003. *Social Marketing: Principles and Practices I (Melbourne, Australia: IP Communications)*

[7] Social Marketing Listserve, 2006.

[8] "Social Marketing: An Approach to Planned Social Change" (1971) in the *Journal of Marketing* by Philip Kotler and Gerald Zaltman coined the term "social marketing."

[9] Email communication from Bill Smith, November 2007.

[10] Robert Hornik, "Some Complementary Ideas About Social Change," *Social Marketing Quarterly*, Volume VIII/Number 2, Summer 2002, p. 11.

[11] Jeffrey Sachs, *The End of Poverty: Economic Possibilities for Our Time* (New York: Penguin Press, 2005), p. 229.

[12] http://www.foxnews.com/printer_friendly_wires/2006Jul27/0,4675,Tobacco Vaccine,00.html.

[13] Statistics are for the year 2000 from the World Health Organization, Tobacco Free Initiative.

[14] Alan Andreasen and Philip Kotler, *Strategic Marketing for Nonprofit Organizations*, 6th edition (Prentice Hall, 2003), p. 490.

[15] Alan Andreasen, *Social Marketing in the 21st Century* (Thousand Oaks, CA: Sage, 2006), p. 11.

[16] Philip Kotler and Nancy Lee, *Marketing in the Public Sector: A Roadmap for Improved Performance* (Prentice Hall, 2006).

[17] Philip Kotler and Nancy R. Lee, *Social Marketing: Influencing Behaviors for Good*, 3rd edition (Thousand Oaks, CA: Sage, 2008).

Part II

Applying Marketing Perspectives and Solutions

4

Segmenting the Poverty Marketplace

"Everyone is poor in a different way."

—Anonymous

The first three chapters of this book made the case that a social marketing approach is often missing from the mix of poverty-reduction solutions. We believe, as pointed out, that this discipline has a unique and strategic role to play in moving people up and out of poverty and to help keep them from falling back.

Part II, "Applying Social Marketing Perspectives and Solutions," introduces and illustrates five tools that are familiar to commercial marketers. These chapters also describe applications for developing program plans and strategies that support poverty-reduction programs:

Chapter	Marketing Tool	Question This Tool Tackles
4	Segmenting the market	Who are potential market segments for our efforts?
5	Evaluating and choosing target market priorities	Who should we focus on first or most?
6	Determining desired behaviors	What do we want them to do?
7	Identifying barriers, benefits, and competitors	What do they think of the idea?
8	Developing a desired positioning and strategic marketing mix (the Four Ps)	What do they need to do this?

This chapter focuses on market segmentation. It defines and describes the process and then advocates for a micro versus macro segmentation approach, recognizing that the poverty marketplace is as vast and diverse as humanity itself. After all, the majority of us (more than 60%) are poor.

As with each of the chapters in the remainder of the book, we begin with an inspirational case story that illustrates principles and theories presented in the chapter. This chapter's case highlights efforts in Africa and Thailand to address the impact of HIV/AIDS on the poor. It shows how success in each case had its foundation in recognizing the need to identify homogeneous population groups and to develop strategies tailored to their unique set of wants, needs, and preferences.

HIV/AIDS:
Reversing the Tide Through Audience Segmentation Techniques

The effect of HIV/AIDS on poverty is profound, but often it is not fully appreciated or consistently measured. Illness reduces income and increases expenses. Caring for family members reduces productivity and increases social isolation. Loss of income often forces the sale of assets, including productive ones such as cattle, goats, and chickens, leaving households even more vulnerable. This loss of income and assets further disrupts social support networks and undermines the acceptance and effectiveness of intervention and outreach efforts.

The social marketer's role in HIV/AIDS is often downstream, focusing on influencing behaviors that stop the spread of the disease and encouraging early diagnosis and treatment. Our potential role upstream is to influence policy makers, NGOs, philanthropists, and private-sector organizations to provide support that makes these behaviors easier and more accessible, affordable, and acceptable.

We begin making strategic decisions by answering the first and most important question: *Who do we want to influence?* As you can see from the following list of *potential target audiences* for an HIV/AIDS campaign, what we ultimately want to influence a target audience to do depends on who they are:

- *Women in Mexico* whose husbands work in agricultural camps in Florida and have unprotected sex with prostitutes who frequent the camps

- *Children in Rwanda, South Africa*, who are HIV-positive and whose parents living with AIDS are too ill to take them to a clinic for antiretroviral drugs

- *Young gay men in Brazil* who smoke crack together and share needles for injecting cocaine

- *Sex workers in Nepal* who find it difficult to buy condoms late at night or around the dance restaurant where they work and are afraid to buy them during the day at the local pharmacy because they know the people who work there and would be embarrassed

- *Single African-American moms in the United States, ages 18 to 24*, who are having unprotected sex with boyfriends who are also having unprotected sex with gay men—and the women don't know about it

- *Men ages 30 to 40 in Botswana* who have more than five sexual partners, only one of whom is a steady girlfriend—the one they don't have protected sex with

The following two stories have encouraging endings, in part because country leaders started by answering this important first question.

Uganda: A Life Stage and Behavior-Related Segmentation Approach

Uganda has one of the world's earliest—and perhaps most dramatic—success stories in confronting AIDS. The prevalence of AIDS in the early 1990s was at 15%, falling to 6.5% by 2004. The decline was even greater among pregnant women (a key indicator of the epidemic's progress) in the capital city of Kampala, with the prevalence declining from a high of approximately 30% in 1993 to about 10% in 2004. And a survey conducted by the World Health Organization reported that casual sex encounters declined by well over 50% between 1989 and 1995.[1] Not surprisingly, Uganda's success has been the subject of intense study and analysis.

It appears that Uganda's decline in HIV prevalence was associated with the realization that reaching and persuading different population groups would require different interventions and messages appropriate to unique needs and abilities to respond. Different behaviors are promoted for very different markets:

- Young people who had not yet begun to have sex were cautioned to wait.

- Young people who had just begun to have sex were urged to return to secondary abstinence.

- Sexually active young adults were encouraged to reduce their number of partners.

- Married couples were encouraged to remain monogamous.

- Sex workers, and others engaged in the riskiest behaviors, were encouraged to correctly and consistently use condoms.

The balanced promotion of all of these behaviors is commonly known as the "ABC" approach. "A" stands for abstinence or delayed sexual initiation among youth, "B" is for being faithful or reducing the number of sexual partners, and "C" is for correct and consistent condom use for casual sexual activity and other high-risk situations.[2]

It should be noted (and this is expanded in Part III, "Ensuring an Integrated Approach") that a powerful segmentation scheme such as this one succeeds only if it is fully implemented. And full-scale implementation requires a high level of political commitment to HIV prevention and care and involves a wide range of partners in all sectors of society. This integrated approach and commitment of resources made possible critical elements in Uganda's program implementation. This included sex education programs in the schools to help teens negotiate postponing sex, same-day results for HIV tests to decrease the need to travel long distances, self-treatment kits for sexually transmitted diseases (shown to help prevent HIV infection and increase the use of condoms), and providing subsidized condoms and increased availability in remote locations.

Thailand: A Health Status Segmentation Strategy

Thailand's "Condom King," Senator Mechai Viravaidya, is founder and chair of the Population and Community Development Association (PDA), a leading public health nongovernmental organization in Bangkok, Thailand. In an interview published online in September 2007, he shared his views with Glenn Melnick, a professor at the University of Southern California:

> "As a youngster, I was taught by my parents, who were both physicians, that they expected something sensible out of having spent all this money on the education of their children, something that would make the world a little bit

better and would help a few people. Their admonition to me was that if people like you work only for money, who will help the poor?"[3]

He believed that what he did to help alleviate the spread of HIV/AIDS and to then empower those living with AIDS was necessary to help the disadvantaged people in his country, those who would be most vulnerable when the HIV/AIDS crisis first materialized in the late 1980s. He quoted a study in 1990 that estimated if nothing were done about the impending HIV epidemic, up to four million Thais could be infected by the year 2000, and 460,000 deaths from AIDS could be expected.

Initially, other Thai politicians refused to recognize AIDS as a problem. Publicizing it would potentially hurt one of their major industries: the sex trade. But Viravaidya warned those who managed the sex industry that it was in their interest to take every precaution against the spread of AIDS, or the industry would lose both its sex workers and its customers to the disease. The PDA ran programs to publicize and halt the spread of AIDS:

- Movies were shown to expose the fatality of the disease and to stigmatize those who spread it.

- Amway salespeople helped distribute literature about the disease and distribute condoms.

Targeting Those at Risk for HIV/AIDS

The key to stopping the spread of HIV/AIDS at this early stage was to develop an integrated public information campaign. Viravaidya was certain that it would take more than the government to accomplish such a massive outreach. The business, religious, and educational sectors needed to be included as critical partners. "Everyone joined." Gas stations and McDonald's restaurants gave out condoms; banks and insurance companies distributed printed AIDS information to their customers and the public. Cars passing through toll booths received AIDS information and condoms with their change. Radio and television stations were required to air 30-second AIDS education messages every hour. TV and radio stations that put correct AIDS information into their regular programming received subsidies. And Viravaidya was not shy about distributing condoms and promoting their use all on his own. "The condom," he would explain, "is a great friend. You can do many things with it.... You can use different colors on different days—yellow for Monday, pink for Tuesday, and black when you are mourning"[4] (see Figure 4.1).

FIGURE 4.1   Mechai Viravaidya, the Condom King, working hard to make condoms a social norm

Much has been achieved. The levels of HIV that were feared in the early 1990s have been checked, and the number of new HIV cases occurring annually has fallen. Most importantly, there is irrefutable evidence that the high-risk behaviors that facilitate HIV transmission have decreased. Commercial sex establishments have a 100% condom use policy that is vigorously enforced.

But Viravaidya believed more needed to be done, especially for a different market segment.

Helping Those with HIV/AIDS

While preventing transmission of HIV was essential to a successful HIV/AIDS control program, Viravaidya believed not enough was being done for people who were already living with HIV. More often than not, they lost their jobs, used up their savings, and returned to their village communities to be taken care of by their families. Others, not welcome, suffer from discrimination and have no way to make a living.

So in 2004, the PDA introduced a program called *Positive Partnerships* that lends money to HIV-positive persons as long as they find themselves a "buddy" for a small-business venture—someone who is not infected. Funded by the Pfizer Foundation in Thailand, the person who is not infected, often a friend or family member, is responsible for becoming a community ambassador for people living with HIV. "Buddies" talk to neighbors and community groups about the realities of HIV, trying to replace fear with facts.[5]

Since the official launch in 2004, about 750 partnerships have started, and 84% of them are repaying their loans on time, exceeding the rate of repayments within the general Thai banking system. And surveys of community members in the project areas indicate that anxiety levels around AIDS and the stigma against people living with HIV have dropped from 47% to about 14%.[6]

Viravaidya believes that people living with HIV are now seen as an asset in their community. They are a source of capital. They also are appreciated, because they are helping their community while spreading understanding and tolerance. "It's a truly magnificent project whereby people who are literally given up for dead and hopeless are now becoming a very key element in their communities.... It's just turning total defeat into a wonderful victory."

Steps in Determining Target Market Priorities

Determining targets for your campaign is a three-step process:

1. *Segment the market.* You should divide the larger population of initial interest for your campaign into smaller homogeneous groups. These groups should have something in common— something that makes them likely to respond similarly to your offer. This chapter defines four traditional variables that you can use to segment your market: demographic, geographic, psychographic, and behavior-related. We also describe a recommended approach when choosing from among these options.

2. *Evaluate the segments.* Next you evaluate each segment using a variety of factors that are described in detail in Chapter 5, "Evaluating and Choosing Target Market Priorities": segment size, problem incidence, problem severity, defenselessness of the segment, ability to reach the segment, readiness of the segment to change a behavior, incremental costs to reach and serve, likely responsiveness to the marketing mix tools (Four Ps), and organizational capabilities.

3. *Choose target market priorities.* Ideally, you then will be able to choose one or a few segments as target markets for your

campaign. Importantly, you will be able to demonstrate that you made this decision after identifying the most relevant segments to consider and then conducting a thorough and objective evaluation of each segment based on stringent and relevant criteria.

The Traditional Theory and Practice of Market Segmentation

A brief explanation (or review for some) and description of the traditional commercial marketer's view of market segmentation will be helpful prior to exploring its application to the poverty marketplace.

Market segmentation is the subdividing of a market (population) into distinct subsets of similar potential customers (individuals).[7] A *market segment* is a group of customers who share a similar set of needs, wants, and preferences.[8] A *target market* is a segment you decide you want to focus on and influence.

The rationale for segmentation is straightforward. Marketers want to persuade a target market to "buy" their product. To accomplish this most successfully, they develop an offer (product, price, place, promotion) that is uniquely designed to appeal to the wants, needs, and preferences of a specific, desirable group—an offer they hope will be more tempting than that of the competition. Some organizations have a *concentrated marketing strategy*, developing products to appeal to only a few market segments (such as Enterprise, offering rental cars to people whose cars have been wrecked or stolen). Others appeal to a variety of segments with a variety of offers, using a *differentiated approach* (such as Starbucks). A few have an *undifferentiated approach*, treating the market as an aggregate, focusing on what is common in the needs of most people rather than on what is different (such as Google).[9]

There are four major segmentation variables: demographic, geographic, psychographic, and behavior-related (see Table 4.1):

- *Demographic* variables are the most familiar, dividing a population into groups based on factors such as age, family size, family life cycle, gender, income, occupation, education, religion, race, generation, and nationality. This is a popular way to segment the market because it creates groups that are easier for the marketer to define, research, reach, and monitor.

- *Geographic* variables are also common; they refer to where a segment lives, works, or travels.

- *Psychographic* variables distinguish groups on the basis of less-definitive factors such as personality characteristics, cultural norms, values, and lifestyle. We all know others with whom we share a similar demographic and geographic profile, yet we have differing wants, needs, preferences, leisure activities, books we like to read, and candidates we vote for.

- *Behavior* segmentation divides the market on the basis of knowledge, attitudes, and behaviors relative to the product being sold. Variables include occasions for usage, benefits sought, and buyer readiness. Some consider these the most "inspiring" characteristics because they provide the marketer with rich insights into potential windows of opportunity. In fact, some segmentation strategies start with dividing a market into those most ready to buy. Then they develop detailed profiles of this segment, examining how this group differs from others in terms of demographic, geographic, and psychographic characteristics.

In reality, marketers rarely limit their segmentation to the use of only one segmentation scheme. More often, they use a combination of variables that provide a rich profile of a segment, distinguishing the buyer not only by clear preferences, but also by associated demographics and media habits.[10]

TABLE 4.1   Major Traditional Segmentation Variables

Major Segmentation Variable	Specific Categories	Sample Classifications (Commercial Marketing, United States)
Demographics	Age	Under 6, 6 to 11, 12 to 17, 18 to 34, 35 to 49, 50 to 64, 65 and over
	Gender	Male, female
	Family size	1, 2 or 3, 4 or 5, 5 or more
	Family life cycle	Young, single; young, married, no children; young, married, youngest child under age 6
	Life stage	Going through a divorce, going into a second marriage, taking care of an older parent, buying a home for the first time, and so on
	Income	Under $10,000, $10,000 to $30,000, $30,000 to $50,000, $50,000 to $100,000, $100,000 and over
	Occupation	Professional and technical, manager, elected official, technician, service worker, maintenance, clerical staff, sales, farmer, student, homemaker, unemployed, retired
	Education	Grade school or less, some high school, high school graduate, some college, college graduate, graduate degree
	Religion	Catholic, Protestant, Jewish, Muslim, Buddhist, Hindu, other
	Race	White, Black, Asian, Hispanic
	Nationality	North American, South American, British, French, German, Italian, Japanese, Pacific Islander, Mexican, African
	Social class	Lower lowers, upper lowers, working class, middle class, upper class
	Generation	Silent Generation, Baby Boomers, Generation X, Generation Y, Millennials
Geographic	Region	Northeast, Southeast, North Central, South Central, Northwest, Southwest
	Density	Rural, suburban, urban
	Workplace	Work site with more than 100 employees, work site with fewer than 100 employees, home office

Major Segmentation Variable	Specific Categories	Sample Classifications (Commercial Marketing, United States)
Psychographic	Lifestyle	Achievers, strivers, strugglers
	Personality	Compulsive, gregarious, authoritarian, ambitious
	Innovation	Innovators, early adopters, early majority, late majority, laggards
Behavioral	Occasion	Use product regularly, use product only on special occasions
	Benefits	Quality, service, economy, convenience, speed
	User status	Nonuser, ex-user, potential user, first-time user, regular user
	User rate	Light user, medium user, heavy user
	Loyalty status	None, medium, strong, absolute
	Buyer readiness	Unaware, aware, informed, interested, desirous, intending to buy
	Attitude toward product/category	Enthusiastic, positive, indifferent, negative, hostile

Adapted from Keller and Kotler, *Marketing Management*, 12th edition, p. 248.

Segmenting by Level of Poverty

Let's start this poverty-related segmentation discussion by defining four groups: the Extreme Poverty Market, Moderate Poverty Market, Relative Poverty Market, and Vulnerable to Poverty, as shown in Figure 4.2. The arrows, starting on the left, represent the poverty reduction strategy that social marketers can contribute to:

- Moving those in *extreme* poverty to *moderate* poverty
- Moving those in *moderate* poverty to *relative* poverty
- Moving those in *relative* poverty out of poverty (but they are still vulnerable)

- Making sure that those who are *out of but vulnerable to* poverty don't enter (again)

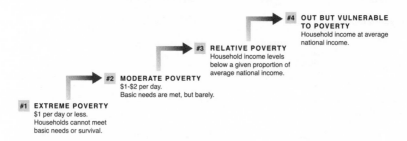

FIGURE 4.2   Poverty markets applying income segmentation

By now, hopefully it is obvious that these four markets are heterogeneous, composed of hundreds, if not thousands, of unique groups of individuals with varying demographic, geographic, psychographic, and behavior characteristics. To illustrate, consider not only the uniqueness of each of these single market segments described in Table 4.2, but also the differing desirable behaviors and strategies that are needed to inspire their adoption. Assume once more a focus on segmentation for HIV/AIDS-related efforts.

TABLE 4.2   Unique Market Segments for HIV/AIDS Progams

	Extreme Poverty	Moderate Poverty	Relative Poverty	Vulnerable to Poverty
HIV/AIDS Status	AIDS Infected when selling blood	HIV-positive	Not HIV-positive	Not HIV-positive
Geographics	China's Henan Province	Rural Cambodia	Haiti	New York City
Demographics	Male heads of household 30 to 50 years old Farmers Children living at home	Pregnant women 18 to 34 years old Married Low literacy	Children ages 10 to 12 living at home Attending school irregularly	Disabled veterans Ages 50 and over Unemployed Single

	Extreme Poverty	Moderate Poverty	Relative Poverty	Vulnerable to Poverty
Psychographics	Loves farming Reliable, trustworthy Wants to help his family	Subservient	Traditional beliefs in "magic rather than microbes" Honor voodoo priests	Hopeless Angry
Behavior-Related	Not taking antiretroviral drugs due to side effects or taking drugs, but not regularly	Unaware of HIV status	Sexually active Not using protection	Injection drug users

The Prevalence of and Problem with Macrosegmentation

As the term implies, macrosegmentation strategies assume "one size fits all"—or, at the most, a couple of sizes. And as an article in *The Economist* in July 2005 proclaimed and illustrated, years of mistakes have taught sponsors that "Grand macro-solutions often neglect the nagging micro-foundation."[11] They described one such example they titled "The Moral of Bednets," summarized as follows:

> At the World Economic Forum in Switzerland in January 2005, a speech on malaria by Tanzania's president which included the statistic that 150,000 African children were dying of malaria every month prompted Sharon Stone, the Hollywood actress, to stand up and pledge $10,000 for bednets on the spot. She then challenged her fellow audience members to do the same. In five minutes, around 30 others followed and raised $1,000,000—enough to buy 250,000 nets at $4 each.[12] Sadly, according to the article in *The Economist*, six months later this generosity is not likely to be instantly gratified. The problem is the strategy targeted a macro market (all those who would benefit from bednets) and did not

take into consideration the multiple diverse segments (the micro-foundation) that success would depend on: *suppliers, distributors,* and the *users* themselves. First, there were local entrepreneurs who were making bednets who would be put out of business by this free-for-all strategy. And governments didn't want this to happen as these commercial sellers would be needed in the future after this wave of funding had been depleted. Secondly, there were many additional established small distributors of bednets with micro-loans they would be forced to default on because of the free nets. Thirdly, the strategy assumes that recipients of the nets would install and then retreat them as required on a regular basis. There was no assurance this was the case, with one newspaper in Uganda reporting that a government official was warning (other) villagers not to turn their nets into wedding gowns![13]

As this example illustrates, before potential macro solutions are deployed in a marketplace, it is important to identify segments that will be key to success and then research their needs and potential reactions to your proposed strategy. This will often lead to a microsegmentation strategy that includes segments for end-user segments (often more than one), as well as others who might "make or break" the deal. This is the only way to help ensure that you will achieve well-intended consequences, as well as avoid unintended ones.

The Case for Microsegmentation

Stephen Smith illuminates the need for microsegmentation best when he says "Targeting the poor involves a multistep procedure. You cannot do anything for the ultra-poor if you cannot find them, or distinguish them from the moderately poor."[14] Smith, as others have, notes that the extreme poor have far different needs than those with even modest financial resources or skills. We believe these needs, when microsegmented, can be addressed with precision. We make the case for this approach first with a (virtual) visit to New York City's Health Department on Valentine's Day 2007, and then to the Hutongs of China:

New York City continues to be the epicenter of the HIV/AIDS epidemic in the United States, with only 3% of the country's population but 18% of the HIV/AIDS cases.[15] Over the past two decades, New York City's epidemic has increasingly affected *blacks* (44% of AIDS cases in 2003 versus 31% in 1987), *Latinos* (32% of AIDS cases in 2003 versus 25% in 1987), *women* (31% of AIDS cases in 2003 versus 12 % in 1987), and *the poor*. Within each of the groups are unique segments categorized by types of risk behaviors, including men who have unprotected sex with men (MSM), men who have unprotected sex with men and women (MSMW), men and women having unprotected sex with multiple concurrent partners, intravenous drug users who share needles, and high school students having unprotected sex.

Despite these odds and challenges, Mayor Michael Bloomberg wants to make NYC a national and global model for HIV/AIDS prevention, treatment, and care. And making condoms more accessible and more the norm for each of these segments is a cornerstone strategy.

New York City's condom initiative dates back to 1971, when the Health Department started distributing them through its clinics. The program expanded during the '80s to include community-based service organizations. Distribution increased more than seven-fold in June 2005, when the Department launched an Internet-based bulk ordering system.[16] Then, on February 14, 2007, the New York City Health Department unveiled the NYC Condom, becoming the first city in the nation with an official brand, and announced an expanded distribution system (see Figure 4.3). To reach targeted market segments, the city reached beyond "main street" distribution channels such as health centers and community service organizations (a macrosegmentation approach) to the "side streets," where very specific micro target markets shop, dine, do laundry, get their hair cut, and hang out.[17]

FIGURE 4.3   New York City's branded condom package (2007)

"Get Some" condoms are free, and campaign messages encourage citizens to "Get Yours. Grab a handful and go!" at hundreds of locations in the city, including *subways, barbershops, African hair braiding parlors, nail salons, delis, wine and liquor stores, laundromats, mini-marts, bathhouses, spas, tattoo parlors, theaters, bars, taverns, saloons, restaurants, ethnic cafes, health clubs, YMCAs, churches*—even *retail stores* such as Kenneth Cole. As co-chair of the condom campaign, Kenneth Cole believes "Any successful product has a strong brand, and condoms are no different." During the Valentine's Day press conference, Cole also unveiled a new line of T-shirts and boxer shorts, each sporting a condom-sized pocket and a discreet woven label reading "Safety Instructions: This garment and its contents should be worn whenever conceivable." And the message that "safer sex is better sex, whatever one's orientation" is central to the campaign.

And consider how easy the city is making it for more and more potential distribution sites to come onboard. A New York City establishment can become a partner in the campaign simply by calling 311 or visiting the website at www.nyccondom.org. The Health Department will then deliver free NYC Condoms in bulk and replenish them as needed. These expanded efforts were expected to increase the number from 2.5 million per year to some 18 million per year. In fact, it has increased to 39 million per year![18]

Now consider this additional example of microsegmentation, this time in China and this time carried out by a private-sector company, using a strategy that can be used by antipoverty workers as well:

A global pharmaceutical company entered China in 1995. Its entry market plan looked at China's total market of 1.2 billion people and reasoned that reaching just one quarter of them would result in unprecedented success. Going after the market using a broad, undifferentiated approach did bring sales, but after nine months sales peaked and began to decline. Efforts to rally the sales force were ineffective. The company began to examine the methods of other companies, perhaps better attuned to the purchasing patterns in China. They found that established and successful companies were not using mass marketing but rather a finely tuned process of block-by-block, street-by-street penetration targeting "Hutongs." These are communities of residential streets lined on both sides by courtyards shared by many families. These communal gathering places provide valuable word-of-mouth promotion as a family excited about a product shares that enthusiasm with the other families who then try the product. This strategy of targeting microsegments resulted in repeat purchasing behavior, and "company sales quadrupled in one year."[19]

We can find support for microsegmentation at the national government level as well.

Again, China, for example, has enjoyed unprecedented growth in economic terms, averaging nearly 8% a year for well over a decade. To manage its social and economic development services, in the early

1990s the central government began segmenting 1.2 billion people by occupation and residential locations. This resulted in the identification of six distinct market segments:[20]

- Urban residents: 350 million, 28.4%
- Farmer families: 290 million, 23.6%
- Farmers: 250 million, 20.3%
- Town and village workers and enterprises: 120 million, 9.8%
- Families of workers in town and village enterprises: 120 million, 9.8%
- Migratory workers and families: 100 million, 8.1%

The large size of these segments makes the effort appear at first to be a macrosegmentation effort. It would be if the government had stopped there, but it didn't. It then broke these larger segments into smaller, more homogeneous ones that could be targeted for resources essential for well-being. By 1995 the Chinese government had identified 380 development zones (DZs) with detailed profiles of the people living there, including what skills they possessed. Matching the available labor supply and skills enabled China to attract international investment from companies that were eager to serve these now more clearly identified targets. For example, the profile of Xinjiang Province stressed its advantage for hosting foreign companies going into agricultural ventures. Qinhai Province was better for developing natural resources, and Shaanxi Province was attractive for more high-tech development companies.

In this segmenting example, the government had a big-picture strategy called "Jie Gui" (the integration of China into the global economy) and used marketing thinking to implement it. A strong case can be made that this has been far more effective than massive aid and relief projects would have ever been and that the result is greater self-sufficiency and a sustainable economy. So we can say that China reduced the number of inadequately fed and clothed poor from 250 million in 1978 to 29 million in 2003.[21] Perhaps presciently, Kotler,

Fahey, and Jatusripitak in 1985 said "when this giant finally awakens and stirs, every other country will have to scramble for position. China is already moving rapidly in the direction of liberalizing its economy and decentralizing many businesses."[22] Decentralizing the production centers was another form of segmentation that China employed as it brought the workplace to the most qualified workers.

The segmentation process continued, moving to ever smaller and well-defined targets. For example, profiling the rural versus urban population by income growth and residential construction revealed more useful information. Rural residents were experiencing higher income growth than urban residents, and rural construction was three times higher than in urban areas. By segmenting the population, skill sets, resources, and markets, China appears to have avoided the rush to cities and shantytowns experienced by other developing countries.

Recommended Segmentation Strategies for Social Marketing Campaigns

At this point, we have introduced the rationale for segmentation and major segmentation variables used to "sort" individuals into homogeneous groups: demographic, geographic, psychographic, and behavior-related. We have also made a strong case for creating micro segments within macro markets, because failed approaches are often rooted in deploying a one-size-fits-all strategy.

Assuming, then, a microsegmentation intent, what variables are best utilized to create these potential target markets? (Remember, we will evaluate and prioritize these potential segments later.)

For social marketing campaigns, we recommend using the behavior-related segmentation variables as the primary basis for creating segments. After all, by definition social marketing campaigns focus on changing current knowledge, attitudes, and practices relative to a desired behavior. After you identify these segments that differ according to current behaviors, you then develop a rich description of each segment, providing demographic, geographic, and psychographic characteristics to assist in evaluating and prioritizing segments.

To illustrate this process, assume that you are a state health department in the United States, charged with reducing the increasing prevalence of HIV/AIDS among African-American women. Assume further that increased routine testing is the focus of your social marketing campaign. Table 4.3 presents a segmentation grid that you would want to complete, using behavior-related variables first. As you review this table, consider how powerful this information will be in determining specific target market segments within this broader population. Even though it is unlikely that those getting tested at the recommended levels will be a target priority for a campaign, it will be very beneficial to examine the characteristics of this "doers" segment compared with the three "nondoers."

TABLE 4.3 Segmentation Scheme for Evaluating and Choosing Priority Markets for HIV/AIDS Testing

Increasing HIV/AIDS Testing Among African-American Women

Sexual Activity	Sexually active: multiple partners last year			
Level of Protection	Not using condoms on a regular basis			
Behaviors Relative to Testing	Never tested	Got tested more than a year ago	Getting tested, but only once a year	Getting tested for HIV/AIDS three to six months after having unprotected sex (the desired behavior)
Size				
Demographics				
Geographics				
Psychographics				
Additional Relevant Behavior-Related Variables (such as Healthcare Coverage)				

Additional Considerations When Choosing Segmentation Variables

Although you should consider behavior-related segmentation variables first, there may also be valid reasons to choose an alternative primary base. Your strategy may be influenced more substantially by the change agent and/or the poverty issue you are addressing.

Segmentation Strategies Depend on the Change Agent

We see understandable and perhaps natural differences in segmentation approaches between government organizations (GOs), nongovernment organizations (NGOs), and the business sector.

GOs are most likely to use income levels to initially segment the market and then describe these broader groups using additional demographics (employment status, ethnicity, household size, age) and geographics (region, urban versus rural). This approach makes sense, because this type of citizen data is the most accessible to public agencies and can be used most reliably to monitor and track progress. In the United States, for example, in 2006, 36.5 million people were living in poverty, with poverty status determined by total income levels relative to family size and ages of family members. Poverty rates are then reported and tracked by race, age, and region of the country.

NGOs, on the other hand, are more likely to first segment a marketplace by mission-critical factors. The Bill and Melinda Gates Foundation's Agricultural Development initiative focuses on increasing crop productivity on *small farms* in Sub-Saharan Africa and South Asia by introducing new seed varieties, irrigation, fertilizer, and training for farmers. Population Services International's (PSI) Maternal Health program focuses on *home births*, providing clean delivery kits that include a sterile razor to cut the umbilical cord and a clean clamp or cord tie to prevent tetanus and other infections. And the Carter

Center's River Blindness Program focuses on the eleven countries that have the *greatest incidence of this parasitic disease* transmitted by the bites of small blackflies.

The business sector is more likely to segment the poverty market by the potential for product sales and usage. For example, Casas Bahia in Brazil is a retail store chain selling home furniture, TV sets, refrigerators, and other home appliances specifically to the poor.[23] In its marketing operations, it geographically segments the total market, by regions and within each region by states. In each local market, Casas Bahia segments the market into five socioeconomic classes: A, B, C, D, and E. Classes D and E are the poverty market segments, with Class D counting the moderate poor and Class E being the extreme poor. These segments are profiled by population size and by ownership of household durable goods.

Table 4.4 presents the national population sizes of the five socioeconomic class segments. Table 4.5 shows the ownership ratios for selected household durables among the five socioeconomic class segments nationwide.

TABLE 4.4   The Stratification of the Brazilian Population in 2002

Socioeconomic Class	Family Income (in MW°)	Population Size (in Millions)	Household Population (in Millions)	Household Size
E	0 to 2 times	54.3	7.6	7.1
D	2 to 4 times	44.2	9.4	4.7
C	4 to 10 times	48.9	12.6	4.0
B	10 to 25 times	21.6	5.4	4.0
A	More than 25 times	7.3	2.5	2.9

°MW = minimum wage (R$200/month)
Source: C. K. Prahalad, *The Fortune at the Bottom of the Pyramid* (Upper Saddle River, NJ: Pearson Education Published as Wharton School Publishing, 2005), p.119.

TABLE 4.5 Ownership Ratios for Selected Household Durables and Facilities

Items	Percentage of Segments Owning/Having Item			
	Segment E	Segment D	Segment C	Segments A and B
Number of toilets per household				
0	36%	14%	5%	1%
1	60%	77%	74%	39%
2	4%	8%	18%	34%
3	0%	1%	3%	18%
4 or more	0%	0%	1%	8%
Garbage pickup	60%	80%	90%	96%
Electricity	87%	96%	99%	100%
Phone	11%	28%	51%	86%
Microwave	3%	9%	22%	58%
Refrigerator/freezer	62%	88%	96%	99%
Radio	78%	88%	93%	97%
Television	72%	90%	96%	99%

Source: C. K. Prahalad, *The Fortune at the Bottom of the Pyramid* (Upper Saddle River, NJ: Pearson Education Published as Wharton School Publishing, 2005), p.121.

Notice in Table 4.5 that the highest ownership of household durables among the extreme poor is for radio and TV. This is above having the convenience of toilets and refrigerators. The extreme poor of Brazil apparently place a higher priority on home entertainment than drinks served cold, food stored in refrigerators, and the convenience of disposing of their human waste in toilets.

Segmentation Strategies Depend on the Social Marketing Issue

Factors that social marketers use to create potential target market segments vary significantly by the social issue they are addressing. As you can see from the following examples, there is often an initial major segmenting variable, followed by secondary variables. Segments are then further described according to additional characteristics:

- Tuberculosis segmentation efforts might begin by looking at a combination of the *severity* of the disease and *related behaviors*, grouping those who are infected but not diagnosed; those who are diagnosed but not getting treatment; those who are taking medications but not on a regular basis; and those who have become drug-resistant and live in close quarters with other family members.

- Tobacco prevention programs are most often interested in the *youth population*, but within this segment they have differing approaches for middle school youth than for college students. Cessation programs are often organized around *health status*, with special efforts aimed at pregnant women, those who are obese, and those with heart problems.

- Homeless populations may differ most by *how long* they have been homeless and whether there are *children in the family*. These larger groups are then further profiled and potentially subdivided by relevant demographics including age, ethnicity, physical and mental health status, and potential employment skills.

- Education-related issues for those in poverty or at risk of poverty often focus on *literacy levels*, identifying segments that would benefit from potential outreach and interventions. As California Governor Arnold Schwarzenegger recently pointed out, economic studies show that Mexican immigrants in that state who speak English fluently earn 50% more than those who don't.[24]

- Employment improvement strategies are often tailored to market segments based on current *employment status* and *job skills*. It makes sense that different strategies would be needed for the working poor than for the unemployed. And within the working-poor segment, there are different needs and approaches for married couples with young children under the age of 5 than for a single mom with teenagers. And among the unemployed, we might group individuals according to job skills and where in the community they live.

Keep in mind that the groups created by these segmentation exercises only represent potential target markets. This prepares you to take the next step—evaluating segments and then selecting or prioritizing segments for campaign efforts and/or resource allocation. These topics are covered in the next chapter.

Summary

Market segmentation is the subdividing of a market (population) into distinct subsets of similar potential customers (individuals).[25] A *market segment* is a group of customers who share a similar set of needs, wants, and preferences.[26] A *target market* is a segment you decide you want to focus on and influence.

Three steps are involved in determining target market priorities: segmentation, evaluation, and choosing.

Four major variables are used to segment the market: demographic, geographic, psychographic, and behavior-related. For social marketing campaigns, we recommend using behavior-related variables as a primary base, and then describing these segments using the other three major variables. In reality, which variables are used to place individuals into more homogeneous groups may vary by who the change agent is for the effort. Differing approaches could be used for government organizations (GOs), nongovernment organizations (NGOs), and the business sector. It may also depend on the poverty issue of focus for the campaign.

Macrosegmentation assumes a "one size fits all" strategy, which often leads to disappointing results. Not only does it ignore people's different wants, needs, and preferences, but it also ignores the need to develop strategies that can "make or break the deal" for your target market.

Endnotes

1   USAID HIV/AIDS, "The ABCs of HIV Prevention." Retrieved April 2, 2008 from http://www.usaid.gov/our_work/global_health/aids/News/ abcfactsheet.html.

2   Ibid.

3   Health Affairs—Web Exclusive, September 25, 2007, "Interview: From Family Planning to HIV/AIDS Prevention to Poverty Alleviation: A Conversation with Mechai Viravaidya," Glenn A. Melnick, gmelnick@usc.edu.

4   Ibid.

5   UNAIDS. "'Positive partnerships' break down AIDS-discrimination Thailand." 2006 Feature Stories. Retrieved April 2, 2008 from http://www.unaids.org/ en/KnowledgeCentre/Resources/FeatureStories/archive/2006/20060330- thailand.asp.

6   Ibid.

7   P. Kotler, *Marketing Management* (3rd edition) (Englewood Cliffs, NJ: Prentice Hall, 1976), p. 144.

8   P. Kotler and K. Keller, *Marketing Management* (12th edition) (Englewood Cliffs, NJ: Prentice Hall, 2006), p. 248.

9   P. Kotler, *Marketing Management* (3rd edition), p. 151.

10 P. Kotler, *Marketing Management* (3rd edition), p. 144.

11 This conclusion was drawn from "Special Report: The $25 billion question— Aid to Africa," *The Economist*, July 2, 2005.

12 *New York Times*, January 29, 2005, nytimes.com.

13 *The Economist*, op. cit.

14 Stephen C. Smith, *Ending Global Poverty: A Guide to What Works*, 2005 (New York: Palgrave/Macmillan) reproduced with permission of Palgrave Macmillan.

15 Report of the New York City Commission on HIV/AIDS, October 31, 2005.

16 Ibid.

17 "Health Department Launches the Nation's First Official City Condom." Press Release, NYC Department of Health and Mental Hygiene, February 14, 2007.

18 Ibid.

19 Michael Fairbanks, "Changing the Mind of a Nation: Elements in a Process of Creating Prosperity," in Lawrence Harrison and Samuel Huntington, eds., *Culture Matters: How Values Shape Human Progress* (New York: Basic Books, 2000), p. 271.

20 Michael Fairbanks, op. cit., p. 281.

21 http://www.worldbank.org/devoutreach/oct04/article.asp?id=267.

22 P. Kotler, L. Fahey, and S. Jatusripitak, *The New Competition: What Theory Z Didn't Tell You About Marketing* (Englewood Cliffs, NJ: Prentice-Hall, 1985).

23 A case study in C. K. Prahalad, *The Fortune at the Bottom of the Pyramid* (Upper Saddle River, NJ: Pearson Education, 2005) pp. 117–146.

24 *The Week*, April 4, 2008, p. 10.

25 P. Kotler, *Marketing Management* (3rd edition), p. 144.

26 P. Kotler and K. Keller, *Marketing Management* (12th edition), p. 248.

5

Evaluating and Choosing
Target Market Priorities

"As a young boy walked along the beach at dawn, he noticed an older man picking up starfish and tossing them into the sea. Catching up with the man, the boy asked why he was doing this. The older man explained that the stranded starfish would die if left in the morning sun.

"'But the beach goes on for several miles, and there are millions of starfish,' exclaimed the boy. 'How can you possibly make a difference?'

"The old man looked at the starfish in his hand and, as he threw it safely back into the sea, said to the young boy, 'I will make a difference to that one.'"

—Adapted from *The Star Thrower* by Loren Eiseley[1]

Choosing target market priorities is a difficult, if not painful, assignment, especially when it comes to poverty. As with the starfish, what happens to the ones you don't "pick up"? Where is the satisfaction in only making a dent with a few, when so many are left behind? Others recognize that they can't help everyone. When they tried this approach in the past, they ended up not really helping anyone.

We think the reality is that most organizations do in fact identify and choose priority markets for their efforts. What is often missing, though, is the use of rigorous analytical models to accomplish this.

Not only do we believe this will make you and others "feel better," we trust this is the best approach for doing the most good in moving the most people up and out of poverty. It will also help ensure that you will achieve the greatest return on your investment.

At this point in your planning, you have identified several potential groups for the focus of your efforts. The task now is to prioritize them, perhaps choosing only one or two for near-term resource allocation. This chapter presents several models that have been used to evaluate potential target market segments, enabling you to then establish these priorities.

We'll use the issue of homelessness to illustrate most of these models. We'll begin with a case story from the Bill & Melinda Gates Foundation that exemplifies the need for and success with this prioritization approach.

Sound Families:
A Bill & Melinda Gates Foundation Homeless
Initiative in Washington State

"I have lived here (Seattle) all my life, and it is no honor to be known for how many mothers in our community put their children to bed in the backseats of their cars.... Our city takes pride in what Seattleites have accomplished. We made the home computer a standard appliance. We made virtually every book in the universe available with a few keystrokes. We even convinced you to spend $4 on a cup of coffee. But one thing we haven't done is provide the most basic shelter for all our families.... And that is our shame."[2]

—William H. Gates, Sr.
National Conference on Ending Family Homelessness
February 7, 2008

The Bill & Melinda Gates Foundation is well known for its work in education and global health. But an initiative launched in 2000 has been an effort on a much smaller scale to address an issue closer to home—keeping kids from growing up in cars and shelters and on the streets by helping parents secure stable housing and move toward self-sufficiency. This case story describes why the Foundation made this homeless segment a priority, what strategies they used to help move this group into real homes, and how things turned out.

Background and Segment Options

On any given night in the United States, approximately 540,000 people are homeless. In Washington State alone, 22,045 individuals were counted as homeless one night in January 2007. Over the course of a year, the total number of homeless persons in the state is estimated to be 40,000 to 50,000 or more.[3] Based on standardized counting systems used by the state, we also know more about this macro market and the micro segments within (see Table 5.1).

TABLE 5.1   Subpopulations of the Homeless Population[4]

Homeless Subpopulations	Total in Shelters	Percentage
People with substance use disorders	3,070	19.8%
People with mental health disorders	2,729	17.6%
Survivors of domestic violence	2,482	16.0%
People with physical disabilities	1,359	8.8%
Veterans	1,165	7.5%
People with co-occurring substance use and mental health problems	1,097	7.0%
Unaccompanied youth	431	2.8%
Seniors	243	1.6%
Persons with HIV/AIDS	188	1.2%
Agricultural workers	23	.2%
Chronically homeless	2,706	17.5%
Total	**15,493**	**100%**

Source: Washington State Community and Economic Development, January 2007

Many people are surprised to learn that almost half (46%) of those who are homeless are families with children (see Table 5.2). Although the majority of these families at any given time are in emergency or temporary shelters, more than a thousand are not.

TABLE 5.2   Homeless Families with Children in Washington State: Point-in-Time Count of Homeless People, 2007[5]

	Sheltered	Unsheltered	Total	Percentage
Homeless individuals	7,124	4,835	11,959	54%
Persons in homeless families with children	8,827	1,259	10,086	46%
Total	15,951	6,094	22,045	100%
Homeless families with children	3,236	462	3,698	N/A

Source: Washington State Community and Economic Development, January 2007

A New Foundation Priority

The sheer size of the homeless population in Washington State and the fact that families with children were one of the fastest-growing homeless populations caught the Foundation's attention in 2000. Other factors (segment characteristics) then solidified this commitment. Consider the likelihood that children moving around constantly in search of shelter will fall behind in school, and that they will struggle to build reliable social networks which are essential to growing up to be confident, trusting adults. The parent or parents in these families face added challenges, finding it hard to work at the same time that they are caring for their children and trying to hold the family together. The societal impact grows even more significant when you consider the increased risk that these families will break up and these children will end up in foster care.

Objectives, Goals, and Strategies

In order to determine how to best help families move beyond homelessness, the Foundation studied national findings and listened to local partners. They learned two key facts: Many families in Washington State lack affordable housing, and families need more than a roof over their heads. They need a range of closely linked support services to help bring real stability to their lives and, most importantly, move toward self-sufficiency.

The Bill & Melinda Gates Foundation, in coordination with public sector partners from the Puget Sound region, Washington State, and the federal government, launched the Sound Families Initiative in 2000 with the ambitious goal of tripling the supply of transitional housing with support services for homeless families in Pierce, King, and Snohomish counties— three of the most densely populated counties in western Washington. Sound Families was started with a $40 million commitment from the Foundation, and over the next seven years, private and public entities invested more than $200 million in additional funds to address family homelessness. The goal was to build 1,500 units of service-enriched transitional housing, tripling the amount in the three counties that make up the Puget Sound region of Washington State. In keeping with the Foundation's investment philosophy, priority grants would be for grantees who would bring long-term, broad-based solutions to homelessness for families through community-based partnerships. And consistent with their objective of eventual self-sufficiency, this housing would need to be combined with social services that would help homeless families both move on and decrease their chances of returning to homelessness. Grantees would respond to requests for proposals that were to be issued biannually over several years and selected through a competitive process.

The initiative supported what is called service-enriched housing, an innovative approach to homelessness that combines affordable housing and social services, to help homeless families move toward self-sufficiency and decrease their chances of returning to homelessness. This provides homeless families with a home for up to two years and social services to help them prepare for a stable and self-sufficient future—services that address the underlying causes of homelessness. Families were assigned a case manager to help them access a wide range of services designed to meet specific needs, including domestic-abuse counseling, alcohol and drug treatment, a GED program, job training, job searching, and child care.

Partnerships were the foundation for success and would rely heavily on collaborative relationships among nonprofit and for-profit housing developers, property managers, service providers, and local housing authorities. Grants were provided to nonprofit organizations such as YWCAs, working with government agencies at various levels and relied in part on state tax credits; federal housing subsidies; and a patchwork of local, state, and federal funding (see Figure 5.1).

Outcomes

In December 2007, an evaluation of the Sound Families Initiative was prepared for the Bill & Melinda Gates Foundation by the Northwest Institute for Children and Families at the University of Washington's School of Social Work. It provided a closer look at these families' lives during and after their supportive transitional housing.

FIGURE 5.1 Typical scene at Sound Families housing
Photo courtesy of the Bill & Melinda Gates Foundation/Jennifer Loomis

It was reported that by 2007, 1,445 units were funded, serving almost 1,500 families with more than 2,700 children, with the average length of stay at just over 12 months (see Figures 5.2 and 5.3). It described the demographics of the families:[6]

- 85% were headed by single caregivers, typically a single mother.
- Half the families had one child living with them, one fourth had two, and one fourth had three or more children.
- The average age of primary caregivers was 31 years, and the average child age was 6.5 years.
- Half of primary caregivers were Caucasian/non-Hispanic; one fourth were African-American; and one fourth were Hispanic/Latino, American Indian, Asian-American, Native Hawaiian, or multiracial.

- 70% of primary caregivers had at least a high school diploma or GED when entering the program.
- 64% of families had been homeless before, some four or more times.
- 44% came from an emergency shelter and 30% from relatives' or friends' homes.
- Several precipitating causes of homelessness were reported by case managers. They included lack of affordable housing or a living wage, loss of income, and domestic violence.

Importantly, relative to the program's objectives, two thirds (68%) of all exiting families moved into permanent, non-time-restricted housing after an average of 12.3 months in the housing program. This rate was even higher among the families who successfully completed the service-enriched aspects of the program, with 89% moving on to permanent housing. A majority of these families were able to maintain the permanent housing over time. Additional good news included the finding that full-time employment tripled from entry to exit.[7]

Encouraged by the overall gains made by Sound Families, the Washington State Legislature created the Washington Families Fund in 2004, a first-of-its-kind, public-private partnership devoted to long-term funding for service-enriched affordable housing for families throughout the state. As of November 2008, $9.3 million has been awarded to 28 partnerships statewide, creating 389 units of service-enriched housing.

FIGURE 5.2   One of the Sound Families enjoying their new home
Photo courtesy of the Bill & Melinda Gates Foundation/Karie Hamilton

FIGURE 5.3   Another one of the Sound Families enjoying their new home
Photo courtesy of the Bill & Melinda Gates Foundation/Jennifer Loomis

Models for Evaluating Segments

Five potential models to evaluate and prioritize segments are described in the following sections, starting with one that uses a single analytical factor and progressing to those using multiple factors for decision-making:

- Using levels of poverty
- Using a triage model
- Using the stages-of-change model
- Using multiple factors
- Using poverty mapping

The concluding section of the chapter discusses considerations for choosing from among these models.

Using Levels of Poverty

This seemingly simplistic model uses only one criterion for evaluating and then choosing market segment priorities—level of poverty. For each of the micro-markets identified in a segmentation exercise, estimates of levels of poverty are developed and presented for consideration. This model is illustrated hypothetically in Table 5.3 for homeless families in a state. Providing this data to an organization such as the Bill & Melinda Gates Foundation would be useful in prioritizing market segments for future initiatives. As discussed in Chapter 4, "Segmenting the Poverty Marketplace," this data can be inspirational. You can imagine different approaches and types of assistance for a single mom in extreme poverty than for a family with both parents who are out of, but vulnerable to, poverty.

Moving on to choosing target priorities based on the numbers and potential long-term impact, program managers might decide that this large group of 4,000 families who are vulnerable to slipping (back) into poverty would be a viable primary market for focus. This segment would then need to be further analyzed to identify unique subgroups, potentially then resulting in a target priority within this group (such as parents who are non-English-speaking).

TABLE 5.3   Hypothetical Distribution of Homeless Families and Individuals in a State

	Single Parent and Children	Both Parents and Children
Size	5,000	5,000
Out But Vulnerable	1,000	4,000
	20%	80%
Relative Poverty	500	500
	10%	10%
Moderate Poverty	500	400
	10%	8%
Extreme Poverty	3,000	100
	60%	2%
	100%	**100%**

Using a Triage Model

As its name suggests, the triage model applies a medical model to evaluating potential market segments for poverty efforts based on three criteria:

- The number and percentage of people in the segment who are *poor*
- The number and percentage of people in the segment who are likely to escape the vicious poverty cycle in the *shortest period of time* and *requiring the fewest resources*
- The probability that this segment will *stay out of poverty*

To illustrate its application, we first turn our attention to a garbage dump in the Philippines and then to nearby coastal fishing villages. We'll then discuss application of the triage model to helping decide which segment should be a priority for the country's poverty relief funds.

Segment 1: The Scavengers

It may be hard for many people to imagine, but living off of garbage is the daily reality for the thousands who have dug through the 130-foot mountain of garbage outside Manila in the Philippines. Every day, well before dawn, hundreds of residents who live in the nearby slums make their way to the gates of Payatas, the city's biggest garbage dump, which ironically translates into "Promised Land." Teams of scavengers, wearing headlamps and carrying wicker baskets, search each truckload of fresh trash for items they can refurbish or recycle and then sell (see Figure 5.4).

FIGURE 5.4   A mangangalahig, or scavenger, atop the 130-foot garbage mountain at the Payatas Dump, Quezon City, Philippines
Photo: © Matthew Power, 2006

Cottage industries thrive as thousands, including children, sort through the baskets that are then brought back to the slums (see Figure 5.5). Treasures include foam rubber that is washed and dried before being glued into strips to make mattresses; piles of discarded backpacks that will be washed, repaired, and sold in markets in the poorer districts of Manila; and paper that, when dried, can be sold to recycling agents. The community is poor, but close. Their hope is that by having the whole family working (even those as young as four years old), they will each make two U.S. dollars a day, about twice the national mean income.[8]

FIGURE 5.5   An 8-year-old scavenger at a waste transfer station on the Manila waterfront
Photo: © Matthew Power, 2006

A study by the Asian Development Bank in 2005 estimated that about 150,000 residents are dependent, in one way or another, on the city's 500 tons of household garbage that are collected each day. This same study found that less than 10% of the city's garbage is recycled. Many city leaders are concerned about the health and well-being of these scavengers, as well as the fact that there was no comprehensive, overall waste management plan to deal better with the city's waste.[9]

Segment 2: The Fishermen

Fishermen and their families in coastal communities are among the poorest sectors of Philippine society. Multiple factors threaten their livelihood, including overfishing, destructive fishing, and pollution caused by discharges from canning companies, personal care and beauty product makers, and other manufacturing establishments. The presence of large commercial fishing vessels eliminates the option of catching fish further out to sea. And to add to this challenge there has been a dramatic rise in the numbers seeking to fish for a living, due to the poor state of land resources, with prime agricultural lands diminishing due to land conversion.[10]

First, we acknowledge that country leaders would be interested in creating strategies to support both segments, and are doing just that. Our hypothetical discussion here, however, is what if you were asked to decide which segment should be focused on first, or most? Would the triage model help? As shown in Table 5.4, based on hypothetical scoring, it might be easy to argue that the fishermen need the most poverty relief attention in the near term and that resources should be allocated for providing job training for new industries, increased food subsidizes, healthcare, and temporary housing. Longer-term strategies could seek to reverse the depletion of coastal resources and engage citizens in their stewardship. And perhaps the best thing to do for the scavengers is to create policies that help legitimize their industrious actions, give them a more formal role, not allow children to work, and add more rigorous health standards in the environment.[11]

TABLE 5.4 Hypothetical Comparison of Two Segments Using the Triage Model

	Segment 1: The Scavengers	Segment 2: The Fishermen
Number who are poor	Lower levels	Higher levels
Number who are likely to escape poverty in the shortest time (requiring the fewest resources)	Similar levels	Similar levels
Probability that this segment will stay out of poverty	Lower levels	Higher levels

Using the Stages-of-Change Model[12]

The stages-of-change model is also called the *transtheoretical model*. It was originally developed by Prochaska and DiClemente in the early 1980s.[13] It has been tested and refined over the past two decades. In a book published in 1994, *Changing for Good*, Prochaska, Norcross, and DiClemente describe six stages that people go through to change their behavior.[14] Four of these stages are presented in this section—those relevant to most poverty-related issues.

We'll continue with this chapter's focus on homelessness to illustrate each stage. Let's assume that the focus is on families that have children and two parents being screened for transitional housing. Assume further that there is space for only one in 10 applicants. Also, funders are most interested in admitting those who will attend regular job counseling sessions and apply for a full-time job within a month of moving into their housing (the desired behavior).

- *Precontemplation.* "People at this stage usually have no intention of changing their behavior, and typically deny having a problem."[15] In the case of an effort to influence a parent to attend job counseling and apply for a job, this segment is not really serious about it. They've tried before and have little faith that they'll find a job they want or that will pay enough. They'd rather continue to get public assistance than work in the types of jobs they would readily qualify for, and they think the job counseling is a waste of time.

- *Contemplation.* "People acknowledge that they have a problem and begin to think seriously about solving it."[16] Or they may have a want or desire, and have been thinking about fulfilling it. This segment wants a job, and they think the job counseling is a good idea for most people, but they are concerned they will fail. Because their situation is so unique, they worry that the counseling won't help. They may offer excuses when invited to attend, and may not follow up on job opportunities because they fear rejection.

- *Preparation/In Action.* "Most people in the Preparation Stage are (now) planning to take action ... and are making the final adjustments before they begin to change their behavior."[17] Those in this segment are interested in attending the counseling sessions and look forward to the process, but most of it is new for them. They are very likely to attend the classes. They've even put the classes on their calendar in case they get into the transitional housing unit they have applied for.

- *Maintenance.* "During Maintenance (individuals) work to consolidate the gains attained during the action and other stages and struggle to prevent lapses and relapse."[18] This segment has already started applying for jobs and has a few good potential offers. They are looking forward to the counseling sessions because they think the counseling will give them a chance to get an even better job—one that pays more, has better hours, and offers opportunities for advancement.

Many social marketers generally find two of these four segments the most attractive, based on the perceived rate of return on investment of resources to influence behaviors: *Contemplators* and those who are *Preparing/In Action*. Those in Contemplation are open to the behaviors we have in mind (attending counseling sessions and applying for jobs) and don't require the same motivational and "mind-changing" efforts as those in Precontemplation. And certainly those in Preparation/In Action have demonstrated their interest and will benefit from encouragement and a little hand-holding. You could argue from a prioritization perspective that those in Maintenance are also a lower priority for resource allocation because they need less of your attention (such as reminder calls) to ensure that they will follow through on their intentions for employment.

Using Multiple Factors

Professor Alan Andreasen at Georgetown University cites nine factors for evaluating segments relative to each other and then using the results to systematically prioritize market segments.[19] In the following list, these factors have been adapted to be most relevant for poverty-related issues, with typical questions that might be asked to establish each measure. To illustrate each factor, we'll again use the issue of homelessness and offer questions that should be considered to arrive at a score for each segment, for each criterion:

1. *Segment size. How many people are in this segment? What percentage of the population do they represent?*

   For each of the segments under consideration for initiatives, how many people are homeless, and what percentage of the homeless population in the country do they represent?

2. *Problem incidence. How many people in this segment are either engaged in the "problem-related behavior" or not engaged in the "desired behavior"?*

   For each segment, what is the average length of time they have been homeless, and how often? What percentage are accessing emergency or transitional shelter versus living unsheltered?

3. *Problem severity. What are levels of poverty in this segment?*

   How poor is this homeless group? What percentage of each segment are in extreme poverty, moderate poverty, relative poverty and are vulnerable to falling back into poverty?

4. *Defenselessness. To what extent can this segment "take care of themselves" versus needing help from others?*

How do the segments compare relative to health status, education, job skills, income, and other personal resources such as family support? Which group is perceived as being the most likely to succeed without your help?

5. *Reachability. Is this an audience that can be easily identified and reached?*

Can the homeless people in this segment be found efficiently and communicated with effectively? Are they homogeneous enough that they will respond to similar strategies and interventions?

6. *Readiness to change. How "ready, willing, and able" to respond are those in this segment?*

What are the estimated percentages of those in Precontemplation, Contemplation, Preparation/In Action, and Maintenance? Or, which groups are perceived to have the fewest numbers in Precontemplation?

7. *Incremental costs to reach and serve. How do estimated costs to reach and influence this segment compare with those for other segments?*

For each of the homeless segments, do existing services currently reach the segments that could be used, or would serving this segment require additional capacity or even new services?

8. *Responsiveness to marketing mix. How responsive is this market likely to be to social marketing strategies (product, price, place, and promotion)?*

Will this segment welcome services such as job training, anger management, drug and alcohol treatment, and mental health counseling? Will they respond positively to potential available incentives such as free meals? Can they access these services, or are there significant cognitive, language, transportation, or other barriers to successful influence?

9. *Organizational capabilities. How extensive is our staff expertise or availability to outside resources to assist in the development and implementation of activities for this market?*

What resources will be needed to serve this segment? Will this require reaching out to other individual and partners in order to adequately serve the market? How likely is it that these resources can be secured?

We recognize that the availability of data to answer these questions for all segments with precision is indeed idyllic, and that researching and developing these estimates is a rigorous exercise. Consider, however, the rewards that can be experienced, as shared in the case story in the following sidebar.

Whatcom County Coalition for the Homeless: Evaluating and Prioritizing Market Segments

Greg Winter
Cornerstone Strategies

Following passage of Washington State's Homeless Housing and Assistance Act in 2005, the Whatcom County Coalition for the Homeless reexamined its existing strategies and concluded that its work was fragmented—focused on *managing* but not *ending* homelessness.

As called for in the revised 2008 Whatcom County 10-Year Plan to End Homelessness, this project proposes a shift in focus from emergency response strategies to prevention and long-term housing. This systems-change approach, affecting all homeless subpopulations, increases the efficiencies of the existing homeless housing infrastructure, which consists of low-rent housing, transitional housing, and emergency shelter. At the same time, it saves money by diverting some individuals from high-cost institutional facilities.

Descriptions of Segments

The old way of managing homelessness frequently served homeless households based on demographic characteristics of interest to particular nonprofit service providers (domestic violence survivors, families with young children, youth). The community's desire to serve *all* subpopulations within the new system presented a challenge to program planners charged with projecting service costs. Using the same old demographic categories would be easy—that's how the needs assessments had always been done—but that method had two drawbacks. First, it emphasized the same kind of "favored subpopulations" that the Coalition wanted to avoid in the future. And second, it ignored the large variance in housing stability barriers that exists within any of those subgroups.

A more useful and practical approach to segmenting the homeless services market was to categorize the homeless by their level of housing barriers. This has the benefit of dividing the market based on the relative costs of interventions, which facilitates service planning and accurate cost forecasting. Whatcom County's Homeless Services Center uses the following segmentation scheme to design and deliver services:

- The *At Risk* segment is at imminent risk of homelessness (eviction) but is not yet homeless. Members of this segment have typically experienced a setback, such as an illness that prevents them from working, family breakup, or other loss of income that has prevented them from paying their rent. Intervening with one-time financial assistance is often all that is needed to prevent an episode of homelessness.

- The *Homeless with Hope* segment is currently homeless but has only low-to-moderate housing barriers. For example, they have job skills but have experienced long-term unemployment. They may be doubling up with another household or living in an emergency shelter or in transitional housing. Secondary intervention consists of shallow, short-term rent assistance and a modest amount of case management to help these households retain their new permanent housing.

- The *Chronically Homeless* segment has severe housing barriers. Most suffer from one or more disabling conditions, including severe mental illness and chemical dependency. They are either unsheltered or living in emergency shelter.

Tertiary intervention for this segment includes deep longer-term rent subsidy, engagement with mainstream services (such as Medicaid), and intensive case management. Because of this segment's high use of expensive public services (jails, hospital emergency departments), the high intervention costs may be more than offset by public cost savings due to reduced reliance on these more expensive public services.

In Table 5.5, these segments are analyzed using Andreasen's nine factors. A scale from 1 to 5 is used, with 5 indicating that this segment is very appealing as a target for this characteristic.

TABLE 5.5   Whatcom County, Washington State: An Evaluation of Homeless Market Segments for Prioritization

	At Risk	Homeless with Hope	Chronically Homeless
	300	1,200	150
Segment Size			
5 = Largest 1 = Smallest	3	5	3
Problem Incidence			
5 = Low rate of homelessness 1 = High rate of homelessness	1	3	5
Problem Severity			
5 = Extreme poverty 1 = At risk for poverty	2	3	5
Defenselessness			
5 = Need our help the most 1 = Need our help the least	2	3	5
Reachability			
5 = High likelihood we can reach them 1 = Low likelihood we can reach them	4	5	3
Readiness to Change			
5 = High percentage of readiness 1 = Low percentage of readiness	5	4	3

(continued)

TABLE 5.5   Continued

	At Risk	Homeless with Hope	Chronically Homeless
	300	1,200	150
Incremental Costs to Reach and Serve			
5 = Low incremental costs			
1 = High incremental costs	3	2	5
Responsiveness to Potential Interventions			
5 = High likelihood			
1 = Low likelihood	5	4	3
Organizational Capabilities			
5 = Can serve with existing resources			
1 = Will need additional resources	5	3	3
Average Score	**3.3**	**3.6**	**3.9**

The individual evaluation elements highlight the advantages, disadvantages, and challenges associated with serving each segment. Strong reasons to serve the At Risk segment include high readiness to change, low cost to serve, high response to intervention, and existing organizational capacity to provide appropriate interventions. Homeless with Hope households comprise the largest market segment, and they are easy to reach. Chronically Homeless individuals are extremely poor and relatively defenseless. The high incremental cost of serving this segment, however, is offset by the reduced public costs of alternative services such as crisis response, incarceration, and emergency room visits.

These last factors associated with the Chronically Homeless segment led program planners to allocate a disproportionate share of available resources to serving this group. This segment comprises only 9% of the households served annually; however, the community will invest 51% of available resources to provide them with stable housing and supportive services, as shown in Table 5.6.

TABLE 5.6 Whatcom County, Washington State: Homeless Services Resource Allocation Based on Market Segment Prioritization Analysis

Homeless Market Segment	Households Served Per Year	Annual Cost Per Household Served (Rent Subsidy Plus Case Management)	Total Annual Cost	Percentage of Annual Cost
At Risk	300	$600	$180,000	18%
Homeless with Hope	150	$2,000	$300,000	30%
Chronically Homeless	45	$11,300	$508,500	51%
Total	495	$13,900	$988,500	100%

Using Poverty Mapping

The World Bank describes *poverty mapping* as "the spatial representation and analysis of indicators of human well-being and poverty within a region."[20] Macro-market indicators (such as mean poverty levels in a geographic area) often hide important differences that distinguish micro-markets (such as neighborhoods). Poverty mapping analyzes available social and economic indicators for a geographic area to locate the poor, profile their conditions, and identify poverty-related determinants in that area. The results are often presented in a series of maps, accumulated from one year to the next. The time series can show how a certain locality's poverty situation is getting better or worse, or how one group of poor people in one locality is getting out of poverty, or how another may be sinking deeper. Once a geographic area (country, region, city, or village) has been mapped by poverty levels, you can more quickly pinpoint priority areas for intervention and development. And this tool becomes even more powerful when these poverty statistics are combined with data from other local assessments, ones related to access to services, and availability and condition of natural resources, transportation, and communication networks.

How Are Poverty Maps Built?

Assessment information comes from a variety of sources, including census data and household surveys that are used to provide indicators of income (such as income per capita) and well-being (such as life expectancy, child mortality, or literacy). An additional critical source of information is administrative or community data. For example, information on the transportation network in a village and its quality can be used to estimate the distance or travel time that communities face to reach essential goods and services such as schools, health centers, clean water, and markets. Other critical data sources, especially for determining appropriate interventions, include information on environmental factors such as rainfall and agricultural conditions, ones that can be used to develop monitoring systems and assess adequacy of food supplies. Sometimes these various indicators are then combined with other information systems to give an index of poverty or human development (such as the Human Development Index, a composite of life expectancy, literacy, and income).[21] Geographic Information Systems (GISs), made possible by computer software programs, are used to create the maps and allow the simultaneous analysis of information from a variety of sources, as long as they have common geographic location coordinates.[22]

What Are Poverty Maps Used For?

These maps are powerful visual tools for presenting complex information in a format that makes it easy to understand, especially for a nonspecialist audience. They can be used to help understand poverty determinants, because they can simultaneously display outcomes (income, incidence of diseases, school enrollment) and determinants (school locations, conditions of natural resources, availability of governmental services).

The following case story from Indonesia demonstrates how this disaggregated information was useful in identifying critical areas for focus and factors that then informed budget allocations, program design, and targeting.

Indonesia's Poverty Maps: Impacts and Lessons[23]

Highlights from Chapter 9 of the World Bank's 2007 Publication

"More Than a Pretty Picture: Using Poverty Maps to Design Better Policies and Interventions"

Chapter Authors: Yusuf Ahmad and Chor-Ching Goh

Indonesia is a large country with over 230 million people, the fourth most populous in the world (2007). Although the country was very successful in reducing poverty between 1960 and 1990, an estimated 37 million people were still living in extreme poverty in 1990, surviving on less than a dollar a day. By early 2000, the government was expressing immense interest in the poverty-mapping approach developed by a World Bank research team, combining existing information from a household survey with a population census to estimate and compare the economic welfare of small areas in the country.[24]

The mapping exercise relied on three sources of data: a 1999 socioeconomic household survey, the 2000 population census, and the 1999 village census. It was the first occasion on which all of these data sets were combined.

Impacts

Since their distribution in December 2004, these national poverty maps have been used in various applications by government agencies, donors, and nongovernment organizations. They helped the *Ministry of Finance* determine where unconditional cash transfers should be provided to the poor as a result of cutting fuel subsidies. They helped the *Ministry of Education* select beneficiary areas for its special programs, including the Skills-for-a-Living Program, the Mainstream Gender in Education Program, and the Prevention of Women Trafficking Program. They helped the *Ministry of Social*

Affairs and the *United Nations* cross-check information in their databases. They helped the *World Food Programme* select beneficiary areas using nutrition maps. And they helped the *World Bank* develop policy advice for the Indonesian government.

In addition to these specific impacts, the authors of this chapter indicated that many officials expressed that the poverty maps have highlighted the issue of poverty and energized the government to focus on poverty reduction.

Lessons Learned

The authors cited four lessons learned from Indonesia's experience:

- Consultation and effective dissemination are needed to dispel skepticism, foster dialogue, and encourage use.

- In fulfilling the goal of building local capacity, avoid creating parallel, potentially competing maps.

- Ensure the internal cohesion of the agency that produces the maps.

- Make potential users aware of the wide-ranging applications of poverty maps, and emphasize that poverty maps are complementary to (rather than a substitute for) other antipoverty information tools.[25]

Summary: Which Model Should Be Chosen?

This chapter introduced five models for evaluating segments, beginning with one using only one major factor, and progressing to those that are multifactorial in nature:

- Using levels of poverty
- Using a triage model
- Using the stages-of-change model
- Using multiple factors
- Using poverty mapping

We recommend using a Multiple Factors model, one similar to Andreasen's Nine Factors: size, problem incidence, problem severity, defenselessness, reachability, readiness to change, incremental costs, responsiveness, and organizational capabilities. Although these nine are likely to be applicable for most situations, you could certainly omit or add factors that are more relevant for your particular situation (such as a match for a grant priority). After that, we further recommend that you "map" the priority segments.

The Multiple Factors model requires additional data, which admittedly is difficult to pinpoint in many cases, and analysis is more rigorous, often requiring more time and resources to complete. However, this model has many benefits. You and others can be sure you have considered a comprehensive list of decision criteria. You can present strong arguments for priority segments, because you back decisions with objective data. This quantification also helps with resource allocation, often the most controversial issue, especially for public agencies.

After that, we recommend that you then use the Poverty Mapping model to locate and track the priority segments. This model makes it easier to communicate your strategies with decision makers and colleagues, because it gives you a quick understanding of where you will focus your efforts in a geographic area. We also like the fact that you can simultaneously overlay environmental factors and other poverty determinants on the map, providing inspiration for strategies you might need to employ (such as improving access to healthcare). Finally, you can track and then hopefully report (literally show) progress, again in a strong visual way, to funders, colleagues, and decision makers.

Endnotes

1 L. Eiseley. Adapted text from *The Star Thrower* (1978, Times Books, Random House). Hardcover: ISBN 0-8129-0746-9.

2 Bill & Melinda Gates Foundation. Newsroom. February 7, 2008. "National Conference on Ending Family Homelessness." Seattle, Washington. Prepared remarks by William H. Gates, Sr.

3 State of Washington Department of Community Trade and Economic Development. Homeless Management Information Systems. Retrieved May 9, 2008 from http://www.cted.wa.gov/site/890/default.aspx.

4 Ibid.

5 Ibid.

6 "Evaluation of the Sound Families Initiative: Final Findings Summary: A Closer Look at Families' Lives During and After Supportive Transitional Housing." December 2007. Prepared for the Bill & Melinda Gates Foundation by the Northwest Institute for Children and Families at the University of Washington's School of Social Work. p. 4.

7 "Evaluation of the Sound Families Initiative: Final Findings Summary: A Closer Look at Families' Lives During and After Supportive Transitional Housing," p. 5.

8 "Living on Earth: Garbage Mountain." January 19, 2007. Retrieved May 18, 2008 from http://www.loe.org/shows/segments.htm?programID=07-P13-00003&segmentID=6.

9 Agence France-Presse (AFP), The Terra Daily. "Manila's Garbage Dump Offers Lifeline For Poor." Retrieved May 18, 2008 from http://www.terradaily.com/reports/Manilas_Garbage_Dump_Offers_Lifeline_For_Poor.html.

10 OVER SEAS, An Online Magazine for Sustainable Seas, June 1999, Vol. 2, No. 6. Retrieved May 16, 2008 from http://www.oneocean.org/overseas/jun99/dar.html.

11 "Living on Earth: Garbage Mountain."

12 P. Kotler and N. Lee, *Social Marketing: Influencing Behaviors for Good* (Thousand Oaks, California: Sage Publications, 2008), p. 128–129.

13 J. Prochaska and C. DiClemente (1983). "Stages and Processes of Self-Change of Smoking: Toward an Integrative Model of Change." *Journal of Consulting and Clinical Psychology*, 51, 390–395.

14 J. Prochaska, J. Norcross, and C. DiClemente, *Changing for Good* (New York: Avon Books, 1994), p. 40–56.

15 Ibid, p. 40–41.

16 Ibid.

17 Ibid, p. 41–43.

18 Ibid, p. 44.

[19] A.R. Andreasen, *Marketing Social Change: Changing Behavior to Promote Health, Social Development, and the Environment* (San Francisco: Jossey-Bass, 1995), p. 177–179.

[20] World Bank Poverty Analysis. "What Can Poverty Maps Be Used For?" Retrieved May 19, 2008 from http://web.worldbank.org/WBSITE/EXTERNAL/TOPICS/EXTPOVERTY/EXTPA/0,,contentMDK:20239110~menuPK:462100~pagePK:148956~piPK:216618~theSitePK:430367,00.html.

[21] World Bank. "More Than a Pretty Picture: Using Poverty Maps to Design Better Policies and Interventions." Retrieved May 20, 2008 from http://web.worldbank.org/WBSITE/EXTERNAL/TOPICS/EXTPOVERTY/EXTPA/0,,contentMDK:21517522~isCURL:Y~menuPK:462078~pagePK:148956~piPK:216618~theSitePK:430367,00.html and "Poverty Mapping. What Are Poverty Maps?" Retrieved May 20, 2008 from http://www.povertymap.net/whatare.cfm.

[22] World Bank Poverty Analysis. "What Can Poverty Maps Be Used For?" Retrieved May 19, 2008 from http://web.worldbank.org/WBSITE/EXTERNAL/TOPICS/EXTPOVERTY/EXTPA/0,,contentMDK:20239110~menuPK:462100~pagePK:148956~piPK:216618~theSitePK:430367,00.html.

[23] World Bank Poverty Analysis. "Indonesia's Poverty Maps: Impacts and Lessons." August 2007. Yusuf Ahmad and Chor-Ching Goh. Chapter 9, p. 177–187. Retrieved May 19, 2008 from http://siteresources.worldbank.org/INTPGI/Resources/342674-1092157888460/493860-1192739384563/10412-09_p177-187.pdf.

[24] Chris Elbers, Jean Lanjouw, and Peter Lanjouw (2003). "Micro-Level Estimation of Poverty and Inequality." *Econometrica* 71 (1): 355–64.

[25] World Bank Poverty Analysis. "Indonesia's Poverty Maps: Impacts and Lessons." Chapter 9, p. 184–186.

6

Determining Desired Behavior Changes

"Like slavery and apartheid, poverty is not natural. It is man-made, and it can be overcome and eradicated by the actions of human beings. And overcoming poverty is not a gesture of charity. It is an act of justice. It is the protection of a fundamental human right—the right to dignity and a decent life. While poverty persists, there is no true freedom."

—Nelson Mandela[1]

Assume for a moment that your target audience for a poverty-reduction effort is sitting before you in a room. You have selected them carefully. Of all the possible groups you could have invited, this one seems the most ready for action, representative of a group you can reach, and one that can influence others. Your research and evaluation efforts also indicate that for the poverty issue you are focusing on, they are a good match for your organization's expertise, resources, and distribution channels.

The question before you now—one the group is eager to hear about as well—is, what do you want to influence them to do? In social marketing, these are the desired behaviors you will focus on—actions that, once taken, will have a positive impact on your target audience and the poverty issue you are addressing.

In this chapter, our poverty issue of focus is family planning. We begin with two case stories from Population Services International

(PSI), one from Pakistan and the other from Romania. Each represents the power of "handpicking" desired behaviors for your target audiences, ones selected based on as rigorous an evaluation as you conducted to find priority target audiences in the first place.

> ## Family Planning:
> ## A Poverty-Reduction Solution
> ## Case Stories from Population Services
> ## International (PSI)
>
> "Gulbibi (living in Pakistan) was married at the age of 16. By the time she was 26, she had been pregnant five times, suffered one miscarriage, and given birth to four children. Gulbibi is illiterate, and so are her husband and all their relatives and ancestors as far back as anyone can recall. They migrated to the city two years ago in search of opportunity and better living conditions, yet they could only afford to live in a slum."[2]
>
> According to the United Nations Family Planning Association (UNFPA), like Gulbibi, at least 200 million women in the world want to use safe and effective family planning methods. But they are unable to do so because they lack access to information and services, or they do not have the support of their husbands and communities.[3] Providing these family planning services is an important poverty-reduction solution. When couples can choose the number, timing, and spacing of their children, they are better able to adequately feed their families, educate their children, reduce healthcare costs, and maintain good jobs.
>
> Although the use of contraceptives by married women worldwide increased from 10% in the 1960s to 60% in 2003, the use of modern contraception has not risen in the past decade, and fertility rates are as high as seven births per woman in some

countries.[4] And, according to the UN, the current trajectory is likely to take us from a worldwide population of 6.6 billion to 9 billion or more by 2050. Almost all of this increase will take place in the less-developed countries, whose populations are expected to reach 7.8 billion in 2050, a 47% increase. By contrast, projections are that the population of the more-developed countries will remain around 1.2 billion.[5]

Improved access to modern and natural family planning options is the goal of all PSI family planning programs. Starting with one condom social marketing project in Kenya in 1973, PSI's family planning programs have expanded to include a range of oral and injectable contraceptives, IUDs, emergency contraceptives, vasectomies, and natural family planning methods, such as the Standard Days Method using CycleBeads. In 2007, PSI programs provided 12.2 million couples years of protection against pregnancy, averting an estimated 2.6 million unintended pregnancies and 13,400 maternal deaths.[6]

The following sections showcase two PSI success stories—one in Pakistan and the other in Romania.

PSI Pakistan: Green Star Training, "Lady Doctors," and Others[7]

Gulbibi's story, told earlier, does have a happy ending. She eventually convinced her husband that they could not afford to have any more children for a while. He agreed that she should visit a neighborhood health clinic, one with a Green Star on the sign, which she had heard meant they offered quality family planning services (see Figure 6.1). She returned home with an effective method for birth spacing and told others about it—an important and credible social influence, because many couples in Pakistan were poorly informed about family planning.

FIGURE 6.1   Pakistan: The Green Star Network of clinics provide birth spacing options.

In 1991 PSI established a nonprofit NGO, Social Marketing Pakistan. Together they designed and launched the Green Star Network, with a mission to improve the quality of life among people throughout Pakistan by increasing access to and use of health products, services, and information, particularly in the lower socioeconomic population groups. Contraceptive choices and access to information and services were limited; 76% of women were illiterate, and contraceptive use was low, with fewer than 17% of couples using any modern method at the time (the early 1990s). The Network focuses on existing clinics and pharmacies and works with them to be even more viable for family planning by expanding the number of services they offer and increasing the numbers of clients. From the beginning, the Green Star social marketing program had five components:

- *Medical training.* The Green Star Network has four types of providers, each receiving unique, targeted training. Green Star #1 is composed of *female doctors* who participate in an intensive 40-hour course on all contraceptive methods. Green Star #2 concentrates a one-day training session on *male physicians* to motivate their male patients to use contraceptives, to talk with their wives about contraception, to take responsibility for family planning, and to support their wives when they choose a method. This addresses the conservative cultural environment in which men typically discuss family planning only with other men. Green Star #3 involves *pharmacists* in a half-day training, increasing their skills in speaking knowledgeably about the contraceptive methods they carry. Green Star #4 focuses on *female health visitors* who make home calls or run small clinics in the poorest neighborhoods. They receive a one-day training in reproductive health, counseling, and nonclinical contraceptive techniques.
- *Reliable supply.* Subsidies from program donors make it possible to provide international-quality contraceptive pills, injectable contraceptives, IUDs, and condoms at prices that are affordable for low-income clients.
- *Public education.* Demand for Green Star reproductive health services and products is created through mass-media promotion of family planning and reproductive health services featuring the Green Star logo. The logo, promoted as the symbol of high-quality, affordable family planning products and services, is placed on signboards of certified clinics and pharmacies and also appears on the packaging of its four contraceptive products. Program staff members also reach directly into communities, organizing neighborhood meetings in which a broad range of reproductive health issues is addressed.
- *Technical support and quality control.* Green Star instructors make regular visits to Green Star clinics to follow up

on service quality and product availability. A medical detailing force also visits Green Star doctors and pharmacists.

- *Program evaluation.* The program has conducted a series of evaluations that assess improvements in quality of care, increases in service delivery, and program impact.

The Green Star Network has achieved concrete results in three very important measures: increased sales of contraceptives, increased number of clients, and improved quality of family planning services. An evaluation early in Green Star's development indicated that among Green Star female doctors, over 90% of clinics had oral contraceptives, injectables, and IUDs available. Doctors discussed three or more birth spacing methods with more than 85% of PSI researchers posing as patients, and over 75% of doctors discussed how to use the contraceptive method chosen.

By 2008, the Green Star Social Marketing Program (the current name for the NGO) was providing 27% of all modern contraception being practiced in Pakistan, making it the largest private source. And government policy requires that Green Star Social Marketing and the Green Star network continue to grow.[8]

PSI Romania: Giving Romanian Factory Workers the Facts

The "Among Us Women" (AUW) initiative is helping the Romanian government educate women of reproductive age by providing them with voluntary family planning and reproductive health information. The program targets factory workers in an effort to influence them to make informed decisions about their choices for contraception. (As will be pointed out later in this chapter, desired behaviors, such as the one illustrated here, may be prevention-related behaviors targeting those at risk for poverty, or poverty-escaping behaviors.)

Since its inception in 2002, the campaign has addressed formative research conducted in 1999 that identified that one of the
major barriers to acceptance and consistent use of modern
contraceptives was incorrect information. One of the most
common myths, for example, was that the birth control pill
would cause facial hair and cancer. To address such misperceptions and demystify reproductive health issues, the AUW
campaign was launched, funded by the U.S. Agency for International Development (USAID) through John Snow Inc. (JSI)
through 2006. The campaign conducts dialogue sessions facili-
tated by a female health worker, in places that have a high con-
centration of female workers, including textile and shoe
factories, bakeries, technical schools, and other production factories located in urban areas throughout Romania. At the close
of the sessions, reproductive health counselors provide refer-
rals to doctors and clinics. Participants are given the "Women's
Health Guide," which details information on contraceptive
methods and other reproductive health issues, and offers condoms and prizes for responding to questions (see Figure 6.2).

**FIGURE 6.2   Female workers listen to a PSI/Romania health
worker at an "Among Us Women" session.**

Each AUW interpersonal communication facilitator conducts an average of 20 workshops per month, with an average of 17 women in each workshop. It has proven to be a cost-efficient means to target and reach women of reproductive age; with the AUW, program costs are $3.90 per woman reached. The methodology of reaching groups of women in the workplace has allowed PSI to reach over 180,000 women in 80 factories with interactive sessions. Outcome surveys have shown that these sessions increase participants' overall knowledge of reproductive health choices and modern contraceptive use.

To measure actual impact on contraceptive use, in 2004 JSI and PSI implemented a quantitative survey in Bucharest to determine if the AUW program was effective in increasing the female factory workers' knowledge of modern contraception and changing their behaviors regarding family planning. The study design consisted of 226 women from two factories completing a self-administered questionnaire before the session and then four months after they completed the session. A control group consisting of 258 women from a third factory completed an identical questionnaire that was used for comparison with the intervention group. JSI concluded that "the results of this study suggest that AUW factory sessions have been successful in changing women's knowledge and behavior regarding modern contraceptive methods, with reported use of contraceptives among women who attended the sessions increasing from 60% to 70%."[9]

What Are Desired Behaviors?

Desired behaviors are ones we want to influence a target audience to "buy"—to *accept, reject, modify,* or *abandon* (see Table 6.1). Behaviors to accept are ones the target audience is not currently doing, that you'd like them to start doing. Those to reject are ones the target audience is not currently engaged in, and you want to persuade them to continue "abstaining." A modification to a behavior is applicable when your target audience is engaged in the desired behavior, but not at the ideal level. Abandoning refers to current (undesirable) behaviors you want your target audience to stop doing.

TABLE 6.1   Types of Desired Behaviors

Type of Behavior	Poverty Issue	Desired Behavior
Accept	Homelessness	Attend weekly job training workshops.
Reject	Health	Don't start smoking.
Modify	HIV/AIDS	Use condoms with your steady girl-friend, not only with sex workers.
Abandon	Literacy	Eliminate gender inequities by allowing girls to attend school.

In Table 6.1, notice how singular, specific, and measurable the behaviors appear. Notice as well how the behavior, once performed, has the potential to contribute to the poverty-related issue. You probably can imagine multiple additional behaviors that would also contribute to this poverty-related issue. The rationale for calling attention to these three behavior characteristics is strong:

- *Singular.* Even if you have several behaviors you want to influence your target audience to adopt, you will be most effective when you focus on one, or at least present them one at a time. This may be all your target audience can or wants to hear and take on, as with the homeless example in Table 6.1, where you want the target audience to attend job training workshops. After attending the training, you can move on to influencing them to apply for jobs.

- *Specific.* The behavior should be specific, as in the example in Table 6.1, where the desired behavior is to "Use condoms with your steady girlfriend, not only with sex workers." It could have just said "Use condoms," but in this case campaign planners know the target audience is using condoms with sex workers on a regular basis, but not with their steady girlfriend.

- *Measurable.* The behavior should be one that the target audience will know they have performed and that you will be able
to measure. Target audiences and evaluators, for example, can
measure and report on the number of people in a given region
or country who are not smoking and can then compare this
with the numbers in prior years. They would not, however, be
able to measure, track, and report on the number of people
who were "protecting their heart."

Desired behaviors, sometimes also called "calls to action," vary by
target audience (see Table 6.2). They can be illustrated well with our
chapter's focus on family planning, identifying the (next) step you
might want a target audience to take. It should be noted that these
desired behaviors are not campaign slogans or final copy for messages. They are simply the intended, desired behavior your strategies
will be designed to influence.

TABLE 6.2   Desired Behaviors Vary by Target Audience

Target Audience	Potential Desired Behavior
Parents of preteen girls	Talk to your daughter about postponing sex.
Young single women	Use condoms with every sexual encounter.
Married women in Pakistan	Visit a health clinic with the Green Star sign.
Married women in the U.S.	Talk with your doctor about using contraceptives.
Private-sector partners	Print family planning messages on your product's label.
Funders	Provide funding for family planning products in developing countries.
Healthcare visitors	Ask about myths about contraception, and dispel them.
Physicians	Share options available for contraceptives.
Pharmacists	Explain the advantages and disadvantages of contraceptive options.
Policy makers	Allocate funding for family planning services for low-income families.

And thinking again about our intent to move people up and out of
poverty, desired behaviors also vary by stage of poverty:

- *Poverty staying behaviors.* These behaviors are ones that most likely contributed to the poverty situation in the first place and, if not abandoned, will likely "keep them there." Typical ones you will work to eradicate might include those related to domestic violence, drug and alcohol abuse, mismanaging credit, unwanted pregnancies, and nonproductive farming practices.

- *Poverty escaping behaviors.* These behaviors are more typically new ones for the target audience, ones you want them to adopt. For farmers in Africa, desired behaviors might be to start using new fertilizers and irrigation systems to improve crop productivity. For the impoverished fishermen in the Philippines mentioned in Chapter 5, "Evaluating and Choosing Target Market Priorities," it may be to apply for jobs recently created by the government to begin restoring the habitats that have been degraded by siltation and pollution. For those living in the United States who are non-English-speaking, the behavior would likely be related to attending language classes.

- *Poverty prevention behaviors.* Modification and maintenance-related behaviors are most relevant here, encouraging those diagnosed with tuberculosis to complete their drug regimen, high school youth to stay in school, those engaged in risky sexual behaviors to have an HIV/AIDS test every three to six months, young families to spend within their means, and those who are obese to increase their physical activity and decrease their consumption of high-calorie and high-fat foods.

Behavior Change Theories

When selecting behaviors for the focus of a campaign or program effort, several models and theories can help guide your decision-making because they help assess how receptive your market will be to the behavior and how much might be required to achieve adoption. Models and theories described in this chapter include the following:

- Stages of Change/Transtheoretical Model
- Theory of Planned Behavior/Reasoned Action

- Health Belief Model
- Social Norms Theory
- Diffusion of Innovations
- Ecological Framework

At the conclusion of this section, we pull together themes from this collection. This can serve as a reference guide when you're trying to decide what behaviors you will be the most successful in persuading your target audience to adopt.

Stages of Change/Transtheoretical Model

The *stages of change* model, also referred to as the *transtheoretical model*, was presented in depth in Chapter 5. As a brief summary, it was originally developed by Prochaska and DiClemente in the early 1980s, and it identifies six stages that people go through in the behavior change process. A condensed version of the model described earlier includes four of those stages. This time we'll use a family planning effort in Honduras to illustrate the model. The desired behavior is for couples who don't want to use traditional contraceptives to use the Standard Days Method (SDM). SDM was developed by researchers at the Institute for Reproductive Health at Georgetown University School of Medicine. It helps couples recognize when they are most fertile, helping them avoid having unprotected sex during fertile periods. Many women who practice SDM use what are called CycleBeads to help them keep track of the days in their menstrual cycle.[10] Couples could be grouped into one of four stages:

- *Precontemplation* is the stage where people have little or no intention of changing their behavior or don't think their current behavior is a problem. Relative to SDM, these couples are not at all concerned about having another child. In fact, they look forward to it.
- *Contemplation* is the stage where people are considering changing, but they have considerations or concerns and have therefore not acted. These couples have heard about SDM

recently and like the idea, but they are concerned that it sounds complicated and doubt whether they could figure it out. They are also concerned about what their church leader's reaction might be.

- *Preparation/In Action* is the stage where people have decided they have a problem or see a potential benefit in a behavior change and are planning to take action. They may have even taken some initial steps in the desired direction. Relative to SDM, the women have made appointments at a local health clinic to learn more about this method.

- *Maintenance* is the stage where people are performing the desired behavior at the desired level, and the only typical concern is preventing relapses. These couples have been using SDM for several months and are pleased with its results. Once in awhile, they argue that it's hard to abstain for that length of time.

Once the sizes of these groups were estimated, program planners might decide to conduct formative research with the contemplators to learn more about perceptions, barriers, and what might motivate them to take the next step.

This theory will be most useful to you in campaigns where a sizable portion of the market is either contemplating the desired behavior (or at least is open to it) or has decided they will engage in the behavior and are preparing to do so. By contrast, if the vast majority of the "non-doers" are in precontemplation (unaware of and/or uninterested in the behavior), this model is less likely to provide insights that will inspire strategies.

Theory of Planned Behavior/Reasoned Action

The Theory of Planned Behavior, developed in 1980 by Ajzen and Fishbein, is an extension of the Theory of Reasoned Action, developed in 1975. It suggests that the best predictor of a person's behavior is his or her *intention* to perform the behavior. This intention is determined by three things: the person's attitude toward the behavior, subjective norms, and perceived behavioral control. As shown in Figure 6.3, this attitude toward the behavior is influenced by behavior beliefs, which refers to the person's favorable (or not) attitude toward the behavior. The second predictor, subjective norm, refers to the perceived social pressure to perform the behavior, determined by the extent to which "important others" for the target audience would approve (or disapprove) of performing a given behavior. And the third antecedent of intention, the degree of perceived behavioral control, refers to the perceived ease (or difficulty) of performing the behavior.[11]

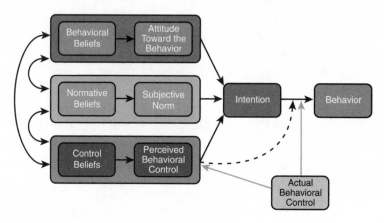

FIGURE 6.3   The Theory of Planned Behavior

Source: Ajzen, I. http://people.umass.edu/aizen/

Stated simply, a target audience is most likely to adopt a behavior when they have a positive attitude toward it, perceive that "important others" would approve, and believe they will be successful in performing it.

Illustrative example: Launched in India in 1995, the Small Family by Choice Project was designed by the Family Planning Association of India (FPAI) and funded by the International Planned Parenthood Foundation. The Project covered three districts in Madhya and a fourth in Raisen, with a population of nearly four million people in 3,900 villages. The thrust of the Project was to impact the acceptance of family planning, with a focus on increasing the use of contraceptives.

In line with the Theory of Planned Behavior, the project clearly targeted existing beliefs regarding family planning, created new norms for where babies were born, and increased perceived control by increasing access to and improving quality of health services. The project was launched at a meeting of 500 women in Bhopal, where women were encouraged to postpone marriage until after the age of 18 and to think about planning to have their babies in a hospital or health center rather than at home. (At the time, 80% of deliveries in the region were taking place at home.) They were also encouraged to demand better health care service from their government. An evaluation in 2004 showed that contraceptive prevalence rates increased from 36% at the start of the project to 61% ten years later. This had a tremendous catalytic effect on influencing the state government to establish community delivery rooms.[12]

This theory will be most useful in guiding your selection of behaviors when, as illustrated in this example, the following points are true:

- You have research on or insights into your target audience that indicate they have a positive attitude or feelings about the desired behavior.
- They believe they have the resources and skills to perform the behavior.
- Important others in their lives are also positive about the behavior.

You will eventually develop strategies that capitalize on these influential factors. By contrast, a behavior that your target audience is uninterested in, or perceives they don't have the resources or skills to perform, has little chance of success. This is especially true when social networks are also negatively inclined.

The Health Belief Model

The Health Belief Model (HBM), described in Table 6.3, is a psychological-emphasis model that attempts to explain as well as predict health behaviors. Developed by social psychologists at the U.S. Public Health Service in the 1950s, the model postulates that several conditions will impact the likelihood that a target audience will adopt a behavior. Since then, the HBM has evolved, with key variables identified by Rosenstock, Strecher, and Becker in the early 1990s. Some cite two limitations to the model. First, it relates largely to cognitive factors, predisposing a person to a health behavior, and it does not take into consideration other environmental or economic barriers that may influence their adoption. Secondly, it does not specifically incorporate the influence of social norms and peer influences on people's decisions regarding their health behaviors.[13]

TABLE 6.3   Health Belief Model

Concept	Definition	Family Planning Application
Perceived susceptibility	What are the chances that I am at risk?	What are the chances I'll get pregnant?
Perceived severity	Even if I am at risk, how concerned am I with the potential health condition?	How concerned am I about having (another) baby?
Perceived benefits	How effective do I believe the desired behavior would be in reducing the threat of the illness?	Do the contraceptives work?
Perceived barriers	Do I believe that potential negative consequences might result from taking the action?	Will the contraceptives cause cancer? Will my husband be angry?
Cues to action	Do I notice any physical symptoms? Do I see anything in my environment that encourages me to take action?	Does my village have any health clinics with the Green Star logo that tells me family planning services are offered there?
Self efficacy	How confident am I that I can perform the desired behavior?	Will I be able to follow the instructions accurately?

As shown in Table 6.3, this theory "forces" the development of a rich description of what your target audience is probably thinking and feeling about the behavior you have in mind. By investigating their position on each of these factors, you can know what you are up against, as well as what you need to do to successfully influence them. By contrast, as noted, it does not focus on external factors that may also be critical to behavior adoption—factors such as resources, access, and the influence of important others.

Social Norms Theory

The social norms approach, first suggested by H. Wesley Perkins and Alan Berkowitz in 1986, states that our behavior is influenced greatly by incorrect perceptions of how other members of our social groups think and act. For example, college freshmen often overestimate the extent to which students on campus drink and smoke. The social norms theory predicts that these overestimations of problem behavior increase the likelihood that these students will then engage in these risky behaviors. Similarly, underestimations of healthy behaviors discourage individuals from engaging in them. Thus, a focus on correcting misperceptions of group norms is likely to result in decreased problem behavior or increased prevalence of healthy behaviors. According to Berkowitz and Perkins, "these peer influences are based more on what we think others believe and do (the *perceived norm*) than on their real beliefs and actions (the *actual norm*). This gap between 'perceived' and 'actual' is called a *misperception*, and its effect on behavior provides the basis for the social norms approach. Presenting correct information about peer group norms in a believable fashion is hypothesized to reduce perceived peer pressure and increase the likelihood that individuals will express preexisting attitudes and beliefs that are health-promoting."[14]

Illustrative example: In 2004, Planned Parenthood of New York City launched a community campaign targeting parents of teens ages 11 to 17, intending to help young people avoid sexual risk-taking, including early intercourse. Focus groups with parents in the target community were conducted to identify specific practices that parents were currently using to help protect their teens from sexual risk-taking. This information then informed the development of a parent survey, which was conducted with a randomly selected sample of parents to determine actual and perceived norms for each of the identified parenting practices. As shown in Table 6.4, the survey identified large and pervasive misperceptions about parenting-related norms. For example, respondents guessed that only about a third of parents had talked with their teens about STDs, when in fact the vast majority (80%) indicated they had done this. This then informed the development of social norms marketing campaigns promoting positive parenting practices. At the core of the campaign were messages intended to establish with parents who were not engaged in these conversations with their children that these practices were "okay" to have. In fact, they are "the norm."[15]

TABLE 6.4   Parent Survey to Determine Actual Versus Perceived Norms

"What percent of parents do you think always..."	Perceived	Actual
Meet their teen's closest friends	20%	65%
Don't allow their teen to go to parties at homes where they know there won't be any parents	25%	78%
Talk to their teen about the dangers of sexually transmitted diseases	33%	80%
Talk to their teen about what might happen if she got pregnant/he got someone pregnant	30%	70%
Praise their teen when he or she makes good choices	37%	87%
Tell their teen how much they care about him or her	37%	90%

This theory is clearly most applicable when your target market is in the "minority"—when the majority of others within this population of focus are engaged in the desired behavior. This then naturally leads to a strategy that corrects misperceptions of the norm and capitalizes on its popularity. By contrast, when a behavior you are considering is not yet "popular," this theory will not provide significant inspiration when you're developing your campaign strategy.

Diffusion of Innovations Model

In his comprehensive book *Diffusion of Innovations, 5th Edition* (2003), Everett Rogers defines diffusion as the process by which (1) an innovation (2) is communicated through certain channels (3) over time (4) among the members of a social system. Innovation diffusion research suggests that different types of adopters accept an innovation at different points in time. Five groups have been identified:

- *Innovators* are motivated by a need for novelty and a need to be different.
- *Early adopters* are drawn by the product's intrinsic value.
- *Early majority* perceive the spread of a product and decide to go along with it, out of their need to match and imitate.
- *Late majority* jump on the bandwagon after realizing that "most" are doing it.
- *Laggards* finally follow suit as the product attains popularity and broad acceptance.

As illustrated by the bell curve shown in Figure 6.4, adoption begins with the (typically) small group of innovators, is picked up by the early adopters, and then by the larger early majority group, followed by the late majority, and, eventually, over time, the laggards. The adoption curve becomes an S curve when cumulative adoption over time is plotted.[16]

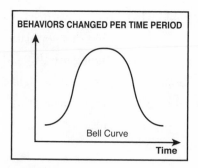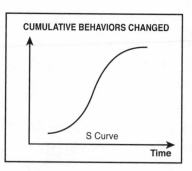

FIGURE 6.4   Diffusion of Innovations adoption curves

Illustrative example: Honduras, the second-largest country in Central America, has steadily and significantly decreased its total fertility rate in recent years, from an average of 5.6 children per woman in 1987 to 3.3 in 2005. Honduras has also made impressive gains in its contraceptive prevalence rate, increasing from 41% in 1987 to 65% in 2005, creating an S curve, as shown in Figure 6.5. These historic gains resulted from successful interventions, including increasing access to IUDs, innovative information, education and communication strategies, training in contraception eligibility criteria, and appropriate counseling. And according to USAID, political will has contributed to this adoption, acknowledging the government of Honduras for its commitment to comply with a series of international conventions and treaties.[17]

This model, like the Stages of Change Model, is useful when a significant portion of the population of focus is in groups that you can influence—the early adopters and the early majority in this model. On the other hand, if the largest or dominant segments are the late majority and laggards, your success in getting this behavior adopted further in the near term is diminished. Therefore, using this model to guide the development of strategies will be less inspiring.

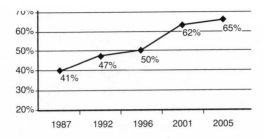

FIGURE 6.5   Contraceptive prevalence rate (all methods)
Source: USAID Demographic and Health Surveys

Ecological Model

A criticism of many theories and models of behavior change is that they emphasize the individual behavior change process and pay little attention to sociocultural and physical environmental influences on behavior—an ecological perspective. This approach places the importance and role of supportive environments on par with the development of personal skills.[18] Although several versions of ecological models exist, most have at least four major levels of behavior influence in common: *individual factors* (demographics, personality, genetics, skills, religious beliefs), *relationship factors* (friends, families, colleagues), *community factors* (schools, work sites, healthcare organizations, media), and *societal factors* (cultural norms, laws, governance). These models argue that the most powerful interventions are those that simultaneously influence these multiple levels, expected to lead to greater and longer-lasting behavioral changes. The key is to assess each of these levels of influence and determine what is needed that will provide the greatest influence on the desired behaviors.

Illustrative example: In the article "Ending Africa's Poverty Trap," Jeffrey Sachs and his coauthors outline a theory on Africa's poverty trap and point, in part, to structural conditions and history that have led to the trap (community and societal factors from the ecological model). These include "very high transport costs, small market size, low productivity agriculture, very high disease burden, adverse geopolitics and slow diffusion of technology from abroad." They then argue that what is needed is "a big push in public investments to produce a rapid step increase in Africa's underlying productivity, both rural and urban." They also urge that those African countries that are well-governed should be provided substantial increases in assistance to enable them to achieve the Millennium Goals for poverty reduction by the year 2015. The paper then lays out an investment strategy that focuses on *interventions*, broadly defined as the provision of goods, services, and infrastructure, "ones that could make enormous changes in productivity at rather low cost." Ones, we would add, that will support desired individual poverty-reduction behaviors (such as accessing family planning services).[19]

The advantage of using this ecological model for guidance is that it is so comprehensive that it forces you to explore multiple strategies to eventually influence the desired behavior. The potential bad news is that it may require you to implement these multiple strategies. These may be out of the normal purview of the social marketer's direct influence (such as the need for new roads to reach remote villages).

Themes from All Models[20]

To summarize behavior change interventions, Fishbein combined themes from most of the models presented in this chapter, providing a quick reference of options for understanding your target audience and then selecting the most appropriate behaviors for program focus. Generally speaking, it appears that behaviors that have the best chance of adoption are those that best meet the following criteria:

- The behavior is one that the target audience has a strong *positive intention* (or commitment) to perform (such as getting an IUD).
- There are *few or no environmental constraints* that make it impossible to perform the behavior (for example, affordable and accessible family planning services are available).
- The target audience has the *skills* necessary to perform the behavior (such as negotiating with their spouse regarding contraception).
- The target audience believes that the *advantages* (benefits, anticipated positive outcomes) of performing the behavior *outweigh the disadvantages* (costs, anticipated negative outcomes).
- The target audience believes there is more *social (normative) pressure* to perform the behavior than to not perform it (such as increasing the timing between the births of children).
- The target audience perceives that the behavior is more consistent than inconsistent with their *self-image* or that its performance does not violate personal standards (such as religious beliefs).
- The target audience's *emotional reaction* to performing the behavior is more positive than negative (such as condom use).
- The person perceives that he or she has the *ability* to perform the behavior under a number of different circumstances (such as using the natural Standard Days Method of contraception tied to menstrual cycles).

An Analytical Model for Selecting Behaviors

As you develop and consider potential behaviors to influence, the following five criteria will help you choose one(s) with the greatest potential for meaningful change, or at least assist you in prioritizing among those you have placed on your "short list":

- *Impact.* Assuming that target audiences adopt the behavior, what potential impact will it have on the poverty-reduction issue that your plan is focusing on (such as reducing unwanted pregnancies)? How does it compare with other potential behaviors under consideration for resource allocation? To determine this impact, we often rely on the expertise of scientists, sociologists, epidemiologists, and other technical experts regarding the effectiveness that this specific behavior will have (such as abstinence as a way to reduce teen pregnancies).

- *Demand.* How ready, willing, and able is your target audience to perform this behavior? Do any major internal or external barriers exist, either perceived or real? Do target audiences seem eager to do this? Do they have the skills and any required resources to perform the behavior (such as money to buy emergency contraceptives)?

- *Supply.* This criterion considers the extent to which other programs or organizations are already working to influence your target audience to adopt this behavior. If the market is "saturated" with others already doing "all that can be done" to influence this behavior, perhaps your support for a different behavior would be more beneficial to the poverty issue.

- *Support.* What level of support exists for this behavior from your key public? If it doesn't currently exist, will it be hard to build? This includes potential funders, policy makers, administrators, the media, and others who could influence your success. This criterion is distinct from demand, which is the extent to which your target audience is anticipated to support the behavior.

- *Organizational match.* Do you have the expertise and resources to influence this behavior? Is it compatible with your organization's mission and consistent with your organization's values and brand? Have you attempted something similar to this in the past and therefore have experience that you can leverage?

As illustrated in Table 6.5, each potential behavior being considered is evaluated on five factors, and then bottom-line scores are compared. This particular hypothetical example uses a rather subjective scale, with High, Medium, and Low and a corresponding score of

3, 2, or 1, respectively. As indicated, efforts to influence abstinence behaviors look most favorable for this school district, and emergency contraceptives are the least favorable.

TABLE 6.5   Hypothetical School District Evaluation of Potential Teen Pregnancy Prevention Behaviors to Support at Middle Schools

	Abstinence	Condoms	Contra-ceptives	Emergency Contra-ceptives
Impact (Preventing pregnancies)	High	Medium	High	Medium
Demand (Teen interest)	Low	High	Medium	Low
Supply (Whether other programs or organizations are already supporting the behavior)	Medium	Low	High	High
Support (From parents, school administrators, elected officials, community leaders)	High	Medium	Low	Low
Organizational Match (Ability of high schools to deliver or disseminate)	High	Medium	Low	Low
Overall Score	**12 points**	**10 points**	**10 points**	**8 points**

When more quantifiable data is available, you might be able to use a more objective rating such as an index or a more differentiating scale. To add even more rigor, you might want to weight one or more of the criteria. Referring to the middle school program to prevent teen pregnancies, for example, it would be most realistic to rate potential target audience demand as twice as important to you as support from others. In Table 6.5, this would increase the appeal of the condom behavior and significantly decrease the viability of the abstinence strategy.

In the end, we are most interested in choosing behaviors that will have a *positive impact* on the poverty issue, ones that our target audience is *(most) ready to adopt*, that are *not currently being handled* by other organizations, that our key public will *support*, and that are a good *match* for our organization. Consider the positive impact that the "Condom King" from Thailand, highlighted in Chapter 4, "Segmenting the Poverty Marketplace," had on influencing specific behaviors relative to family planning, as described in the following sidebar.

Gates Foundation Honors "The Condom King"

On May 29, 2007, the Bill & Melinda Gates Foundation announced that Thailand's Population and Community Development Association (PDA) had received the 2007 Gates Award for Global Health, in recognition of its pioneering work in family planning and HIV/AIDS prevention. This is the world's largest prize for international health. It aims to honor extraordinary efforts to improve health in developing countries. The prize honored Mechai Viravaidya, founder and chairman of the PDA. His organization has helped millions of Thais to live healthier lives by demonstrating that effective HIV prevention and family planning are possible in even the poorest communities.

In 1974, the average Thai family had seven children. Each child borne made the family poorer. Viravaidya saw too many births keeping Thailand stuck in poverty. He saw the answer as convincing mothers to use the Pill, and he developed innovative social marketing solutions:

- He renamed and publicized the birth control pill as "the family welfare pill."
- The Pill had to be prescribed by a doctor, but Thailand had too few doctors per hundred thousand people. So Viravaidya convinced the medical community that nurses should also be allowed to explain and prescribe the Pill.

- He used the Buddhist principle that life is suffering and said that the Pill would prevent a lot of suffering.

His whole premise was to make birth control popular and comfortable. Sex is a part of every living creative, and society has to acknowledge this.

Then Viravaidya recognized the condom as another potent solution. But condoms were not publicly discussed in Thailand. He decided to bring them into the open and discuss them everywhere. He turned to "edutainment" methods. To popularize the condom, he did the following:

- He held condom "balloon-blowing" contests with prizes for kids and adults, and he made sure that the media would take photos that he hoped would end up on page 1.

- He distributed condoms to shopkeepers, hairdressers, taxi drivers (many of whom were women), and hotels, and he recruited 320,000 rural teachers to talk about condoms and sex.

- Condoms were passed out or made available at tollbooths, in banks, and in hotels.

- One campaign featured a Captain Condom (looking like Superman) and Miss Condom.

- Publicity was given to a Cops and Rubbers program.

- An ad showed da Vinci's famous Mona Lisa with a condom on her arm.

- Fashion shows were run showing condoms in different colors.

- A special ad showing three condoms in three colors was prepared for the 2008 Olympics in China.

- Viravaidya showed other uses for condoms, such as putting them over the barrel of a gun to prevent sand from getting into the barrel. Each novel event supplied further publicity for the condom.

- He had monks bless condoms so that Thais would know there would be no ill effects from using them.

Then Viravaidya and the PDA turned to a third solution besides pills and condoms: vasectomies. He ran events to publicize the positive effects of having a vasectomy: that it was painless and would not produce children.

- The PDA ran a vasectomy contest, with the winner getting a million dollars.

- The PDA sponsored a Fourth of July vasectomy event held in a luxury hotel ballroom. The man could choose the music to hear during the procedure and afterwards had a choice of food to eat.

- The PDA ran a Father's Day Vasectomy event.

- The PDA purchased a tour bus. Those who could give evidence that they had had a vasectomy could ride the bus for free.

The PDA then turned to a fourth solution—motivating women not to get pregnant. The PDA offered nonpregnancy microcredits (to purchase pigs, chickens, and so on). The number of microcredits would increase each year that the woman remained unpregnant. The impact of all these efforts—the Pill, condoms, vasectomies, and nonpregnancy microcredits—was that the average number of children per family in Thailand went from 7 in 1974 to 3.3 in 2005. Thailand's population growth went from 3.2% a year in the 1970s to 1.2% in the mid-'90s (now it is 0.7%).

Summary

Desired behaviors, sometimes also referred to as "calls to action," are ones we want to influence a target audience to "buy"—to *accept*, *reject*, *modify*, or *abandon*. Those that are most effective are ones that are singular and specific in nature, making it easier for your target audience to perform and for you to then measure.

When you're selecting behaviors for the focus of a campaign or program effort, several models and theories can help guide your decision-making. They help you assess how receptive your market will be to the behavior and how much might be required to achieve adoption. These models and theories were described in this chapter:

- Stages of Change/Transtheoretical Model
- Theory of Planned Behavior/Reasoned Action
- Health Belief Model
- Social Norms Theory
- Diffusion of Innovations
- Ecological Framework

Behaviors that have the best chance of adoption are ones that the target audience has a strong *positive intention* to perform and that have *few or no environmental constraints*. The target audience has the *skills* necessary to perform the behavior, believes that the advantages outweigh the disadvantages, and believes that there is more *social (normative) pressure* to perform the behavior than to not perform it. They perceive that the behavior is more consistent than inconsistent with their *self-image*, and the *emotional reaction* to performing the behavior is more positive than negative. The person also perceives that he or she has the *ability* to perform the behavior under a number of different circumstances.

In the end, we are most interested in choosing behaviors that will have a *positive impact* on the poverty issue—ones that our target audience is *(most) ready to adopt* and that are *not currently being handled* by other organizations. They are also behaviors that our key public will *support* and are a good *match* for your organization.

Endnotes

[1] Nelson Mandela, speaking to a crowd in Trafalgar Square, London, February 2005, in support of the Make Poverty History Campaign.

[2] PSI. The Green Star Network, June 2000. Retrieved June 4, 2008 from http://www.psi.org.

[3] United Nations Family Planning Association (UNFPA). Retrieved June 4, 2008 from http://www.unfpa.org/rh/planning.htm.

[4] Rebecca H. Allen, MD, MPH, "The Role of Family Planning in Poverty Reduction," *Obstetrics & Gynecology*, Vol. 110, No. 5, November 2007, p. 999.

[5] UN News Service. "World population to reach 9.1 billion in 2050, UN projects," February 24, 2005.

[6] PSI. "Family Planning." Retrieved June 4, 2008 from http://www.psi.org/reproductive-health/.

[7] PSI. "The Green Star Network." June 2000. Retrieved June 4, 2008 from http://www.psi.org.

[8] Green Star Social Marketing. Retrieved June 5, 2008 from http://www.greenstar.org.pk/.

[9] Amy Lunch, MS. JSI research report. "Effects of the 'Among Us Women' Education Program in Factories in Bucharest, Romania."

[10] Institute for Reproductive Health, Georgetown University. "Honduras: Introducing the Standard Days Method into a Multi-Sector Family Planning Program," May 2003.

[11] I. Ajzen. *Attitudes, Personality, and Behavior*, 2nd ed. (Maidenhead, UK: Open University Press, 2005).

[12] Information & Knowledge for Optimal Health (INFO) Project, Johns Hopkins University. "Voices from the Field: Nina Puri." Retrieved June 9, 2008 from http://wwwinfoforhealth.org/practices/voices_from_field/ninapuri.shtml; Fulfilling People's Aspirations India. "Spot Light on Special Projects." Retrieved June 9, 2008 from http://fpaindia.org/sections/projects.html.

[13] Family Health International. "Behavior Change—A Summary of Four Major Theories." Retrieved June 9, 2008 from http://www.fhi.org/NR/rdonlyres/egdaxczahzns2exbwdfetxwj5b5bu3sj5sp5k6mkfhshai4mjmclf2lalzk2b6so7ixdrvnzlqnfqa/BCCSummaryFourMajorTheoriesenhv.pdf.

[14] Higher Education Center: The Social Norms Approach: Theory, Research and Annotated Bibliography. Retrieved June 9, 2008 from http://www.higheredcenter.org/socialnorms/theory/introduction.html.

[15] National Social Norms Institute at the University of Virginia. "A Community-Based Social Norms Campaign to Promote Positive Parenting Practices." Presenters: William Bacon, Ph.D., and Michele Bayley, Planned Parenthood of New York City. Retrieved June 9, 2008 from http://www.socialnorms.org/Resources/NC2004.php.

[16] Adapted with the permission of The Free Press, a Division of Simon & Schuster, Inc., from *Diffusion of Innovations, Fifth Edition* by Everett M. Rogers. Copyright © 1995, 2003 by Everett M. Rogers. Copyright © 1962, 1971, 1983 by The Free Press. All rights reserved.

[17] USAID/HONDURAS. State of the Practice Brief. "Moving Contraceptive Security Forward with Political Commitment and Financial Capital." October 2006. Retrieved June 9, 2008 from http://www.usaid.gov/.

[18] Behavior Change Theories and Models. Updated 2007 by Jim Grizzell, MBA, MA, Certified Health Education Specialist. Retrieved June 9, 2008 from http://www.csupomona.edu/~jvgrizzell/best_practices/bctheory.html# Ecological%20Approaches.

[19] Jeffrey Sachs, John W. McArthur, Guido Schmidt-Traub, Margaret Kruk, Chandrika Bahadur, Michael Faye, and Gordon McDord, "Ending Africa's Poverty Trap," Executive Summary May 10, 2004. Retrieved June 10, 2008 from http://www.unmillenniumproject.org/documents/BPEAEndingAfricasPoverty-TrapFINAL.pdf. Original article appeared in Brookings Papers on Economic Activity, Volume 35, 2004, p. 117–240, Brookings Institution.

[20] P. Kotler and N. Lee. *Social Marketing: Influencing Behaviors for Good*, 3rd edition (Thousand Oaks, CA: Sage Publications, 2008), p. 170–171. M. Fishbein, summarizing Bandura (1986, 1989, 1999) in *Developing Effective Behavior Change Intervention* (p. 3). As summarized by the Communication Initiative, Summary of Change Theories and Models. Slide 5.

7

Understanding Barriers, Benefits, and the Competition for Change

"I truly believe that compassion provides the basis of human survival."

—His Holiness, the 14th Dalai Lama

Return to the room with your target audience, even if only in your mind's eye. You've just shared what behaviors you would like them to consider adopting—ones such as participating in weekly job training workshops, allowing girls to attend school, visiting a health clinic for family planning counseling, or putting a mosquito net around their beds at night. The room is silent. People's faces have varied expressions. Some look puzzled. Some are frowning. Only a few are smiling. You recognize what a gift it would be to you if they would share their thoughts. For those who look puzzled, what are their questions? For those who are frowning, what are their concerns? And for those who are smiling, what are they imagining?

Their answers fall into categories that marketers and behavioral scientists refer to as perceived *barriers*, *benefits*, and the *competition*. Barriers are reasons your target audience does not want, might not want, or doesn't think they can adopt the behavior. These barriers may be real, or just perceived. Benefits are what they see in it for them to adopt the behavior, or what you might promise that would make it more likely that they would be motivated. Competitors are related behaviors (or organizations promoting them) that your target audience is currently engaged in, or prefers to do, instead of the ones you have in mind.

Taking the time and expending the resources to understand these audience perspectives is a *compassionate marketing approach*. It allows you to see what your request looks like from the "other side of the counter." Only then can you know what barriers you must remove or costs you must reduce. Only then can you know what benefits you need to highlight or features you need to add to the offer. Only then can you know who and what you are competing with, and what you must do to upstage or engage them.

Our opening case story introduces our poverty issue of focus for this chapter—agricultural productivity. In subsequent sections, we will further describe techniques for identifying audience barriers, benefits, and the competition.

Agricultural Productivity: The Promising Case in Malawi

"A food crisis grips the planet. Prices of rice, wheat, and other essentials skyrocket, leading to food shortage riots in a dozen countries and jolting governments and policy makers to rethink their ideas about commodities markets, biofuels, and agricultural production in the developing world... Within this haystack of gloom shines the needle of Malawi, where a government-led fertilizer subsidies program has produced two bountiful maize harvests, filling stomachs and cupboards across this formerly destitute sliver of southern Africa."[1]

—David Lepeska, Devex Correspondent
May 15, 2008

One of the central characteristics of the poor is that they are significantly rural. Because agriculture is the predominant provider of employment for the rural poor, agricultural productivity is likely to have a significant impact on poverty. Malawi has one of the highest population densities in Africa, with 85% of the population farming on small plots.[2] Soil degradation is widespread. As the country's population grew over the years, impoverished farmers could not let their land lie fallow, nor could they afford to fertilize it. As a result, their depleted plots yielded less and less food, and farmers fell deeper into poverty. After a disastrous corn harvest in 2005, almost a third (5 million) of Malawi's 13 million people needed emergency food aid.[3] Most agreed that having farmers use fertilizer and improved high-yield seeds was essential for raising farm productivity, and there were pressures on the government of Malawi to offer subsidies. But there were major barriers to this happening.

Major donors, such as the World Bank and others that Malawi depended on for aid, had serious concerns about universal subsidies. Instead, they stressed the importance of targeting only those who could not afford fertilizers, and they encouraged using research-based criteria to select fertilizers based on soil and rainfall conditions. They felt that strategies were needed to support and leverage broader private investments and should provide for exit options in the future. And the United States Agency for International Development (USAID) wanted to focus on the private sector for delivering fertilizer and seed, and it viewed subsidies as undermining that effort.

Since the food supply situation was grave, the Malawi government in 2005 reinstated and deepened subsidies (anyway). Fertilizer was distributed through a coupon-based distribution program to more than 1.3 million farm households. In 2006, approximately 1.5 million farmers received coupons for fertilizer, and 2 million received coupons for free maize seed. Over 50% of the budget of the Ministry of Agriculture and Food Security was allocated to pay these costs. And then, to address donor concerns, the Government of Malawi and the World Bank sponsored a Fertilizer Workshop, bringing all stakeholders to the table to discuss best practices on fertilizer and address the mistrust between the government and private-sector fertilizer suppliers. As a result, the government agreed to involve the private sector in developing its 2006–2007 subsidy strategy. Ultimately, 28% of the subsidized fertilizer was sold through private-sector outlets. And to revitalize fertilizer distribution in Malawi, USAID began developing a network of medium- and small-sized business dealers in fertilizer[4] (see Figure 7.1).

FIGURE 7.1   In Mchinji, Malawi, fertilizer is now accessible due to USAID's program—small bags and better prices—sold locally.

Source: Staff/International Center for Soil Fertility and Agricultural Development

In 2007, the government moved to increase public support for the program, giving people a more direct hand in determining who would receive subsidy coupons. In Chembe, for example, villagers gathered one morning in 2007 to decide who most needed fertilizer coupons in the next planting season. They had enough for only 19 of the 53 families in the village. In the end, with the leadership of the village chief, they came to an agreement, giving priority to families who were rearing children orphaned by AIDS and those caring for elders.[5]

In 2006 and 2007, farmers produced record-breaking corn harvests.[6] Child malnutrition dropped an impressive 80%, and the country exported 280,000 tons of maize, selling more corn to the World Food Program of the United Nations than any other country in southern Africa.[7] The harvest also helped the poor by lowering food prices and increasing wages for farm workers. And as David Lepeska reported further, these good times are likely to continue. "Despite the global economic downturn, the International Monetary Fund is forecasting nearly 8% growth for Malawi in 2008, as compared to 3.7% globally."[8]

Better than shipping food to various countries needing aid, the same money could be used to help the poor grow their own food. Malawi is an example of a country that took this route and doubled its food production in three years.

Barriers

We begin deepening our understanding of our target audiences' perspectives by exploring the nature of barriers, ways to identify them, and how they will be useful to you. Remaining sections in the chapter expand on similar topics for perceived benefits and the competition.

Types of Barriers

Barriers may be related to a variety of factors, including *internal* ones such as personal knowledge, beliefs, skills, and abilities related to the behavior. There are also likely to be *external* factors, including restraints created by existing infrastructures, technology, economics, and natural or cultural influences. They may be real ("Fertilizers and high-yield seeds will cost me more") or perceived ("I think the chemicals in the fertilizers might be dangerous"). In either case, they are always from the target market's perspective and often are something you need to address.

Table 7.1 presents examples of typical barrier categories, using the focus on agricultural productivity for illustration. Keep in mind that not every member of the target audience will have all, or even most, of these barriers. Additionally, not all barriers are "equal"; some are (way) more significant to your target audience than others.

TABLE 7.1 Examples of Potential Barriers for Small Farmers in Africa to Use Chemical Fertilizers and High-Yield Seeds

Type of Barrier	Example
Doubt or don't value the potential benefits	They won't help my crops that much.
Lack of understanding or knowing what this is about	How are these fertilizers and seeds different from the ones I am using now?
Self-efficacy—a concern with being able to perform the behavior or not having the know-how	Fertilizers are tricky and have to be done just right, or you could burn your crop.
Too much time, effort, energy	Switching to different seeds means I'll have to make all kinds of changes, like how I store and sow them.
Physical discomfort	Those fertilizers smell.
Concern with potential "side effects" or unintended consequences	The fertilizers are chemical-based. This could harm my livestock.
Reduced pleasure or pride	I feel better knowing that I improved my crops without aid from the government or donors.

Type of Barrier	Example
Costs too much	I have no extra money for new seeds or fertilizers.
Lack access, or not available to me	There is no place in our village to get them.
Not a norm, or others aren't doing it	This isn't how we farm in our village.
Concern with what others are doing or will think	What if I get a coupon but my neighbor doesn't? It wouldn't seem fair.

Identifying and Prioritizing Barriers

Identifying audience barriers should begin with exploring existing research, performing a literature review, and/or examining internal records and data. Your search may also warrant new qualitative and quantitative research efforts, especially when existing information does not apply to the specific behaviors you have in mind or markets you are targeting.

Existing Research or Data

This, of course, is the least costly and time-consuming option for gaining insights, if available. Search engines such as Google may quickly lead to journal articles, news stories, press releases, conference papers, or even a relevant YouTube video. For example, a simple search for "barriers for farmers to use fertilizers in Africa" yielded 628,000 potentially relevant articles in a third of a second. Queries to Listservs can also be quite productive. The Social Marketing Listserv, for example, managed by the Social Marketing Institute, has more than 1,700 members from more than 39 countries and is an active forum for queries on existing research studies.[9] Finally, an organization's own internal records and databases may provide informative, even anecdotal, comments that give you insights into target audience concerns and/or objections to proposed targeted behaviors.

Qualitative Research

Qualitative research generally refers to studies where sample sizes are typically small and are not reliably projected to the greater population. Since the focus for barriers research is often on just identifying and understanding them, this can be an efficient and effective technique. Focus groups, personal interviews, observation research, and ethnographic studies are common tools used for these purposes. Typical questions explored with target audiences might include asking "What are some of the reasons you haven't done this in the past?"; "What might get in the way of your doing this in the future?"; and "What other concerns do you have when thinking about doing this?"[10]

Quantitative Research

In some situations, it is important not only to identify barriers, but also to size and prioritize them, providing focus for strategic planning. In these cases, you may need to conduct quantitative studies, ones with larger sample sizes, rigorous sampling procedures, and controlled and organized environments. Common tools include telephone surveys, online surveys, and self-administered questionnaires.[11] Often a list of potential barriers will have been identified using existing or qualitative research, and then a quantitative survey can list (or present) each barrier, allowing the respondent to rate each on a scale in terms of its significance.

Using Insights on Barriers

This list of barriers will be your inspiration for what strategies you will incorporate in your marketing plan. As we will discuss in the next chapter, the marketer's toolbox has four traditional tools that you can use to create, communicate, and deliver value to your target audience—in return for the desired behavior. Conceptually, the process is a simple one. You consider each of the barriers, one at a time, and explore which one or more of the marketing tools (product, price, place, promotion) can potentially remove or lessen that barrier.

For example, one of the barriers for the farmers to using fertilizers and high-yield seeds presented in Table 7.1 was a concern with access. Bringing the fertilizers and seeds to the farmer or at least the nearby village (a "place" strategy) seemed essential. The farmers also saw the cost as a significant barrier, which implied that subsidies (a "price" strategy) would also "make or break the deal."

Benefits

Benefits, in contrast to barriers, are reasons your target audience wants, or might want, to adopt the behavior. They answer the question "What's in it for me?", often referred to as the WIFM factor. This marketing principle stresses the fact that consumers are always sizing the potential benefits when considering whether to "buy." And, as mentioned earlier when describing the Exchange Theory, they won't buy unless they see value equal to or greater than the costs they will pay.

Types of Benefits

Typical benefits that marketers appeal to are as follows:

- Health
- Safety
- Physical comfort and pleasure
- Entertainment
- Economic status
- Employment

- Relationships
- Self-esteem and recognition
- Growth and development
- Self-actualization
- Environmental protection
- Contribution to others and the community

Some are more relevant than others to poverty-related behaviors (such as economics and employment versus entertainment and self-actualization). What is relevant is that the target audience (the buyer) may have a very different benefit in mind that appeals to them than we (the sellers) do. Bill Smith at the Academy for Educational Development often cites the example of benefits sought for physical activity, illustrating the fact that benefits may not always be so obvious. "The whole world uses health as a benefit. (And yet) health, as we think of it in public health, isn't as important to consumers—even high-end consumers—as they claim that it is. What people care about is looking good (tight abdominals and buns). Health is often a synonym for sexy, young, and hot. That's why gym advertising increases before bathing suit time. There is not more disease when the weather heats up, just more personal exposure."[12]

For the example of subsidies for fertilizers described in the case story at the beginning of the chapter, major benefits included increased crops, revenue, and, potentially, decreased labor.

To illustrate types of benefits further, we now turn our attention to India and a different agricultural productivity issue—that of serious concerns with water supplies for irrigating crops. One strategy being used is to construct what are called check dams—small barriers built across the direction of water flow on shallow rivers and streams to harvest water (see Figures 7.2 and 7.3). These small dams retain excess water flow during monsoon rains in a small catchment area behind the dam wall structure. The water is later tapped for irrigation and livestock, during the dry season. Benefits to the rural poor and small farmers are numerous: *increased employment through increased working days, increased income through increased daily wages, security against hunger,* and *decreased need to migrate to another village.*[13] (Later in the chapter, we will compare how these benefits stack up against alternative strategies, one many consider the competition for check dams.)

FIGURE 7.2   Check dam: a work in progress.

Source: Vishal Himalaya Foundation

FIGURE 7.3   Check dam: work is completed.

Source: Vishal Himalaya Foundation

Identifying and Prioritizing Benefits

Techniques to identify benefits are similar to those used to discover barriers: reviewing existing research and data, pursuing qualitative efforts, and conducting quantitative surveys. Several questions help reveal true audience benefits: What are some of the reasons you might consider doing this? What could someone say to you, give you, or show you that might make you more likely to do this?

One technique that can help prioritize benefits is a doer/non-doer analysis. This approach can be used in both quantitative and qualitative surveys. It involves comparing perceived benefits (and additional variables) of those who perform the desired behavior with those who do not. Through this comparison, you gain insights into what factors may be important to both ensure and promote. Typical questions for such a survey include "What do you see as the advantages of doing this?" and "What would make it easier for you?" Table 7.2 presents a hypothetical example of the results from a survey, using the check dam example.

TABLE 7.2 Hypothetical Doer/Non-Doer Analysis of Check Dam Project Acceptance

	Responses from Village Leaders Accepting Check Dam Projects	Responses from Village Leaders Not Sure About Check Dam Projects
	"What do you see as the main advantages of your check dam?"	"What do you think would be the main advantages of having a check dam?"
Decreased need for migration to another village	80%	30%
More food for my villagers	70%	30%
Workers get higher wages per day	40%	25%
More people are employed more days throughout the year	30%	20%

Using Insights on Benefits

Knowing an audience's perceived benefits, especially their prioritization, gives you strategic direction when you're developing the marketing plan, especially for the communications component. Based on the responses in the hypothetical example in Table 7.2, those promoting check dams will want to emphasize the dams' potential to decrease the need for migration to other villages. They also will want to share that villages where dams have been installed have experienced greater food supplies for villagers. After all, these are what "current customers" are saying they have experienced and value most from the offer.

Finally, by also exploring what benefits, if added, would increase interest in the offer, you will have inspiration for additional elements of the marketing mix, including product enhancements (check dams with larger catchment areas), price (more volunteers helping to install the dams), and place (materials for the dam delivered to the village).

The Competition

Some people are surprised that social marketers spend time identifying, understanding, and developing strategies that will position the desired behaviors more favorably than the competition. "What competition?" they ask. Others recognize that without this exercise, we will have a tough time persuading young people to finish school, sex workers to use condoms with their customers, policy makers to fund check dams, parents to read to their children each day, a homeless veteran to attend job skills training, mothers to breastfeed exclusively for the first six months, villagers to purchase and install new latrines, women to postpone having another child, and food workers to wash their hands carefully after going to the bathroom. Without this exercise and informed competitive positioning, a target audience is likely to continue doing "what they've always done" or start doing something that "everyone else is doing," but not what you have in mind.

Types of Competitors

Three major types of competitors exist in social marketing:

- Behaviors the target audience would prefer to do or start doing instead of the one being promoted
- Behaviors they (and others) have been doing "forever" that they would have to give up
- Organizations and influential individuals who are sending messages that promote an alternative behavior or oppose the desired one

The job is toughest when all three competitive situations are present—one in which the target audience sees more benefits or fewer costs for the competing behavior, the alternative behavior is one they and others have been doing "forever," and organizations and others they listen to advocate for this alternative.

Table 7.3 illustrates the nature and range of competitors. A variety of behaviors are included, representing the range of potential solutions to major poverty-related issues. A quick scan of the column on the right gives you a sense of how tough the competition can be.

TABLE 7.3   The Competition for Desired Behaviors

Desired Behavior	Competition: Behaviors, Organizations, or Important Influential Others
Finish high school.	I play video games at night instead of doing homework.
Use a condom, even with your boyfriend.	My boyfriend's other girlfriends don't ask him to use condoms.
Fund check dams.	Large-scale dams and canal systems are more up to date.
Read to your child every day.	We watch television together as a family every night.

Desired Behavior	Competition: Behaviors, Organizations, or Important Influential Others
Attend job skills training.	I'd rather sleep in.
Breastfeed babies exclusively for six months.	This village has a taboo that prohibits sex while breastfeeding.
Purchase and place functioning latrines.	Pit latrines are already in place; they're free and work well.
Postpone having another child.	Having another child soon is important for helping on the farm.
Wash your hands before returning to work.	Wiping my hands on my apron has worked fine for 30 years.
Use high-yield seeds.	I've already bought seeds for this year's crop.

Identifying and Prioritizing Competitors

Qualitative research is often sufficient to at least identify the competition and related perceived benefits and costs. You can pose a few questions to your target audience:

- What do you do instead of (the desired behavior) or prefer to do?
- What do you like about doing this/the idea of doing this?
- What concerns do you have about doing this?
- Who else encourages you to do this (alternative behavior)?

Keep in mind that this process may reveal several competitors, not just one. Also keep in mind that you are not looking for barriers to adopting the behavior, although overlap or similarities may occur between the competitive and barriers "lists." The competition is distinct in that it represents alternative behaviors or those who advocate for them.

Using Insights on the Competition

The name of the marketing game is to change the ratio of benefits to costs, relative to the competition. For example, persuading farmers to use new high-yield seeds versus their traditional ones could include four tactical options:

- *Increasing benefits for the desired behavior* (such as having a neighboring farmer share the increase in corn this past year from using the new seed)
- *Decreasing the costs of the desired behavior* (such as bringing the new seeds to the village versus having to travel to pick them up)
- *Decreasing the benefits of the competing behaviors* (such as having the tribal leaders in the village explain why the old seed is no longer in the farmer's best interest)
- *Increasing the costs of the competing behavior* (such as having the traditional seed now available only in locations that will require the farmer to travel)

Table 7.4 shows a framework for organizing and analyzing the desired behavior (the middle column) relative to the competing one (the last column). How is this useful? How would you use this if you were in a position of advocating to potential funders to allocate resources to the check dams versus the larger-scale dams, canal systems, and other modern technologies? Your argument might be strengthened by referring to this list and stressing each of the benefits of the check dam and the corresponding costs of the alternative large-scale dams. Research and fact-finding efforts would be important to verifying sources and establishing credibility.

TABLE 7.4 Potential Benefits and Barriers Related to Irrigation Options in Rural India

	Desired Behavior: Check Dams	**Competing Behavior: Large-Scale Dams, Canal Systems, and Other Modern Technologies**
Benefits	Lower costs Less environmentally disruptive Less socially disruptive Less maintenance	More potential funding is available More leadership support The "modern" way

	Desired Behavior: Check Dams	Competing Behavior: Large-Scale Dams, Canal Systems, and Other Modern Technologies
Barriers/Costs	More locations are required Less funding is available	More maintenance is required Construction delays Increased rates of malaria Displacement of local populations Short life of many reservoirs

In the next chapter, we will focus on how these insights shape your marketing strategy—its product, price, place, and promotional elements.

Summary

This chapter emphasized how a deeper understanding of your target audiences' barriers, benefits, and the competition (relative to a desired behavior) will inspire your strategic thinking and planning.

Barriers are reasons your target audience does not want, might not want, or doesn't think they can adopt the behavior. They may be real or perceived, and may be based on internal and/or external factors. To identify them, begin by exploring existing research, reviewing publications and journal articles, and/or examining internal records and data. You also may need to conduct qualitative research more directly related to your unique target audience and quantitative research when it is important to prioritize the barriers to provide focus for strategic planning.

Benefits, in contrast to barriers, are reasons your target audience wants, or might want, to adopt the behavior. They address the WIFM factor—"What's in it for me?" Typical benefits include those related to health, safety, physical comfort/pleasure, entertainment, economics, employment, relationships, self-esteem, growth and development, self-actualization, environmental protection, and contribution to others and the community. Techniques to identify benefits are similar to those used to discover barriers.

Competition in social marketing includes the following:

- Behaviors your target audience would prefer to do instead of the one you have in mind
- Behaviors they (and others) have been doing "forever"
- Organizations and influential individuals who are sending messages that promote an alternative behavior or oppose the desired one

Four options for "beating the competition" include:

- Increasing the benefits of the desired behavior
- Decreasing the costs of the desired behavior
- Decreasing the benefits of the competing behaviors
- Increasing the costs of the competing behavior

We close the chapter with a final example from Cambodia, one that further illustrates these three distinctions and demonstrates their application to strategy.

Farm Field Schools in Cambodia: A Success Story from the United Nations[14]

Background

In Cambodia, poverty and food insecurity are interlinked. The majority of Cambodians work as subsistence farmers who depend on their own capacity to meet food requirements. About half are women. According to the World Bank, in 2004, 91% of the country's poor lived in rural areas, with agriculture the primary occupation for 72% of heads of household. Crop yields in Cambodia are among the lowest levels among East, Southeast, and South Asia regions, and rice dominates production in all regions.[15] Accelerating poverty reduction in Cambodia is largely about helping to raise this agricultural productivity and these incomes.

Barriers to Agricultural Productivity

Both internal and external factors have challenged farmers. Many lack skills, education, and confidence in their ability to deal with change. Infrastructure challenges such as poor irrigation facilities and soil fertility also exist. There are natural environmental challenges as well, including seasonal flooding and problems with pest control. The farmers' (natural) tendency and inclination have been to maintain their strong beliefs in traditional techniques.

Benefits of Agricultural Productivity

The desire to increase crop and livestock productivity is strong. It is seen as a way to increase food supplies, income, and time to then devote to land diversification.

Competition

Long-held traditional beliefs and practices compete with new technologies, including burning straw instead of the better practice of incorporating it into the soil, and planting crop varieties with long versus short maturity periods.

Strategies

In 2004, a Farmer Field School program was launched. It uses a community-based approach that begins with identifying the needs of poor farmers in a specific region and then developing a targeted learning curriculum. Farmers learn by doing, through detailed observations in the field, analyzing their observations, and presenting their results and conclusions to 25 to 30 fellow farmer "classmates." Subject matter revolves around agronomy, livestock, small-scale inland aquaculture, and irrigation. For example, Cheong Chuon, a chicken and frog farmer, learned that he could feed his chickens well and for less money by giving them earthworms and could feed his tadpoles termites from a termite mound. He was also helped to apply for a microloan that he used to buy more chickens and build a chicken house. He was able to repay the loan with his increased productivity.

Outcomes

5,063 farmers from six provinces benefited from the field schools. This standard model of the school, with its emphasis on learner-centered and experiential learning, initially used with rice systems, is now being adopted to improve a range of food crops.

Endnotes

1. David Lepeska, "The Promising Case of Malawi and the Future of Farm Output in Africa," May 15, 2008. Retrieved on July 21, 2008 from *devex Do Good. Do It Well* at http://www.devex.com/articles/the-promising-case-of-malawi-and-the-future-of-farm-output-in-africa.

2. USAID. "Making Fertilizer Accessible to Malawian Farmers." Retrieved on July 21, 2008 from USAID at http://www.usaid.gov/stories/malawi/fp_malawi_fertilizer.html.

3. Celia W. Dugger, "Ending Famine, Simply by Ignoring the Experts," December 2, 2007. Retrieved on July 21, 2008 from the *New York Times* at http://www.nytimes.com/2007/12/02/world/africa/02malawi.html?_r=1&ex=1197349200&en=6536a7a7f09d8f44&ei=5070&emc=eta1&oref=slogin.

4. The World Bank. "Malawi, fertilizer subsidies and the World Bank." Retrieved on July 21, 2008 from http://web.worldbank.org/WBSITE/EXTERNAL/COUNTRIES/AFRICAEXT/MALAWI.

5. Dugger, op. cit.

6. Dugger, op. cit.

7. Lepeska, op. cit.

8. Lepeska, op. cit.

9. Information on the Social Marketing Listserv can be obtained at http://www.social-marketing.org/.

10. Philip Kotler and Nancy R. Lee, *Social Marketing: Influencing Behaviors for Good* (Thousand Oaks, CA: Sage, 2008), pp. 81–82.

11. Ibid.

12. Kotler, Lee, op. cit. pp. 162–163.

13. "Check-Dams and Irrigation." Retrieved on July 23, 2008 from Development Alternatives: Sustainable Livelihoods at http://www.dainet.org/livelihoods/checkdams2.htm.

14 Food and Agriculture Organization of the United Nations. "Special Programme for Food Security: Cambodia Success Story." Retrieved on July 28, 2008 from http://www.fao.org/spfs/about-spfs/success-spfs/cambodia/en/.

15 The World Bank. "Cambodia: Halving Poverty by 2015?" Retrieved on July 28, 2008 from http://web.worldbank.org/WBSITE/EXTERNAL/COUNTRIES/ EASTASIAPACIFICEXT/CAMBODIAEXTN/0,,contentMDK:20815621~page PK:141137~piPK:141127~theSitePK:293856,00.html.

8

Developing a Desired Positioning and Strategic Marketing Mix

"I believe the genius of modern marketing is not the 4Ps, or audience research, or even exchange, but rather the management paradigm that studies, selects, balances, and manipulates the 4Ps to achieve behavior change. We keep shortening 'The Marketing Mix' to the 4Ps. And I would argue that it is the 'mix' that matters most. This is exactly what all the message campaigns miss—they never ask about the other 3Ps, and that is why so many of them fail."

—Bill Smith
Executive Vice President
Academy for Educational Development[1]

At this point in the planning process, you will have answered big questions. Who are the priority market segments for this effort? What behaviors do you want to influence? How does your target market feel about what you have in mind?

It's time to open the marketing toolbox. You'll find the four traditional Ps inside: product, price, place, and promotion. Our experience is that you will need all of them to create and deliver the value your target market expects in exchange for a new behavior. Our observation is similar to Bill Smith's. This doesn't happen often, primarily because many, if not most, practitioners think of marketing as promotion, not recognizing that, instead, it is a process that usually ends up with a promotion.

Yet, even before making decisions about your marketing mix, we recommend that you engage in one more exercise—that of determining a desired positioning for your offer. A desired positioning is how you want your target audience to view your offer, especially compared with that of competing offers (alternative behaviors in most social marketing settings). As described in this chapter, a simple positioning statement becomes a powerful, clarifying reference point when you choose a marketing mix strategy. It is the job of product, price, place, and promotion to help you achieve the position that you desire in your customers' minds.

Our opening case story highlights this positioning practice, as well as the poverty issue of focus in this chapter—malaria.

Sustainable Malaria Prevention: NetMark's Success Story in Africa

Approximately 40% of the world's population is living in areas at risk of malaria, a mosquito-borne disease that has devastating health and economic impact. Every year, between 350 and 500 million people become severely ill with malaria, and more than 1 million die, with most living in the world's poorest countries.[2] In Africa, it is the number one cause of death for pregnant mothers and children under 5 years of age. It accounts for 40% of public health expenditures in Africa, 30% to 40% of inpatient admissions, and up to 50% of outpatient visits in areas with high malaria transmission.[3] Economically, malaria cripples Africa with an estimated loss of US$12 billion each year, slowing economic growth on the continent by 1.3%. As a result, the GDP of African countries is 32% lower than it would be in the absence of malaria.[4]

The World Health Organization recommends insecticide-treated nets (ITNs) as the best way for families to protect themselves from malaria. They are proven to reduce the risk of infection by up to 45% and the risk of death by 30%.[5] In 2000, the United States Agency for International Development (USAID) initiated a five-year effort called "NetMark" to increase demand for and appropriate use, availability, and affordability of ITNs. In 2002, encouraged by positive results, funding for NetMark was extended.

This case story describes the program's rigorous application of social marketing principles, including the use of all Four Ps in the marketing mix.

Background, Purpose, and Program Focus

Managed by the Academy for Educational Development (AED), a nonprofit human and social development organization, NetMark developed public-private partnerships, including ones with commercial net and insecticide manufacturers and their African distributors. A special focus was given to reaching those most at risk (pregnant women and children; see Figure 8.1) and to creating a sustainable program—one that would survive long after funding disappeared. To accomplish this, AED developed an innovative, market-based approach called Full Market Impact™. It was founded on the premise that as demand grows within a competitive market, consumers benefit from improved quality, lower prices, and wider availability.

Consumer Research

Strategies were informed and inspired by the following:

- Extensive consumer research into knowledge of and beliefs about mosquitoes and malaria

- Beliefs and attitudes about the use of treated and untreated mosquito nets

- Levels of access to and affordability of nets, especially by the most vulnerable groups

- Consumer preferences regarding net size, shape, and color

FIGURE 8.1   NetMark educational session for pregnant women

Barriers to usage included the perceived high cost of nets, lack of variety in net size and shape, concern with safety, fear of potential adverse health effects from treated nets, and limited access. In Nigeria, for example, the vast majority (92%) of respondents said that the closest place they could purchase a net was an outdoor market and that the average time to get there would be approximately one hour by bus.[6] In terms of perceived benefits of the insect-treated nets, strong value was expressed for the nets' potential to actually kill mosquitoes, not just keep them away.

Positioning

Based on these barriers and perceived benefits, a positioning statement for the program might read as follows: "We want ITNs to be seen as the best way to protect your family from malaria. Unlike untreated nets, they actually kill mosquitoes."

Product

Product strategies focused on ensuring an adequate supply of the treated nets, and a quality product. Supplies were enhanced by coordinating commercial and institutional procurements and by providing technical and financial support to expand manufacturing capacity and quality. A "seal of quality" (shown in Figure 8.2) was developed to reassure consumers that products carrying the seal met international standards, including the use of WHO-recommended insecticides. Partners incorporated the seal into their packaging designs, which served to link their brand with the generic marketing campaign. And new technology was introduced to develop long-lasting nets—ones that did not require retreatment to remain effective.

FIGURE 8.2   The program's seal, assuring product quality

Price

NetMark worked to lower the price of the nets, as well as make them available for those who could not pay. NetMark successfully advocated for reducing taxes and tariffs in the interest of the public good in several countries. This was a stronger and more compelling messenger for policy makers than for-profit businesses could have been. By then engaging the commercial sector in promoting and selling nets to those who could afford to pay (see Figure 8.3), the limited resources available from the public sector were then used to offer discounted or free nets for those who truly could not afford to pay.

FIGURE 8.3   Commercial sign promoting the sale of ITNs

Place

Initially, NetMark chose distributor partners that carried other well-known international consumer packaged-goods brands. But NetMark found that the nets were not a priority for these large businesses, especially given the nets' size and bulk. Net-Mark then expanded distribution by including small businesses that would focus solely on nets and, as such, were more loyal and energetic market developers. International donors were encouraged to include these smaller enterprises in their funding allocations. Additional distribution channels were created by working with grassroots organizations for community-level distribution (see Figure 8.4) and by creating mobile channels, such as sales staff who would travel the country on motorcycles.

FIGURE 8.4   Rural sales of NetMark at a health clinic

Promotion

NetMark's communications campaign sought to build demand for the nets by informing the public about the dangers of malaria and the benefits of sleeping under treated nets. Two premier advertising agencies helped develop an advertising and communication campaign with regional and country-specific components. The initial tag line was "Mosquitoes KILL. KILL mosquitoes." In subsequent campaigns, the seal was linked with the message "Insecticide Treated Nets are the new way for Africa to live." The campaign included mass media (print, television, and radio) and special promotions such as wall murals, street theater, and road shows (see Figure 8.5).

FIGURE 8.5   The NetMark campaign goes on the road.

Outcomes

The NetMark project has shown that international and African companies are willing to invest in producing, marketing, and distributing treated nets when working in partnership with the public sector. A 2005 report cited the following accomplishments between 2000 and 2005:[7]

- Private-sector partners have invested more than US$18 million in developing the commercial treated net market in Africa.

- ITNs are protecting nearly 15 million more people from malaria.

- More than 100 million people have been educated about malaria, the importance of ITNs, and how to use the nets effectively.

- More than 350,000 pregnant women and children younger than 5 received discount vouchers, of which 243,000 were redeemed.

- Treated nets now cost from 30% to 75% less than untreated ones did in 2000 due to the competition fostered by NetMark.

- Before NetMark, few nets were treated with insecticide, which makes them twice as effective at preventing malaria. Now, 65% of nets owned in NetMark countries have been treated.

- The number of distributors increased from two in 1999 to 29 in 2005.

Positioning

Positioning is the act of designing the organization's actual and perceived offering in such a way that it lands on and occupies a distinctive place in the mind of the target market—where you want it to be.[8]

As you may recall, social marketers strive to create, communicate, and deliver value to a target market in exchange for performing a desired behavior. A positioning statement describes what you want your target market to think and feel when they hear about your offer. It establishes positive points of difference relative to the competition (alternative behaviors). It is developed with the profile of your target market in mind, including any unique demographic, geographic, psychographic, and behavior-related characteristics. It is inspired by findings from your research on perceived barriers and benefits of the behavior, as well as the competition. It is, as advertising executives Al Ries and Jack Trout describe it, a "battle for the mind" of your audience. We live in an overcommunicated society where "the average mind is already a dripping sponge that can only soak up more information at the expense of what's already there."[9]

Positioning involves implanting the brand's unique benefits and differentiation in customers' minds. "Thus, Tide is positioned as a powerful, all-purpose family detergent; Ivory Snow is positioned as the gentle detergent for fine washables and baby clothes. In the automobile market, Toyota Tercel and Subaru are positioned on economy, Mercedes and Cadillac on luxury, and Porsche and BMW on performance. Volvo positions powerfully on safety. Consumers are overloaded with information about products and services. They cannot reevaluate products every time they make a buying decision. To simplify the buying process, consumers organize products into categories—they "position" products, services, and companies in their minds."[10]

One fairly straightforward way to develop a positioning statement is to fill in the blanks of this sentence, or one similar to it:

We want (OUR TARGET MARKET) to see (OUR DESIRED BEHAVIOR) as (DESCRIPTIVE PHRASE) and as more important and beneficial than (COMPETING BEHAVIORS).[11]

Keep in mind this statement is for "internal use only." It is not the same as your messages for your target market, but it will guide their development. It should be shared with others working on your effort to develop your marketing mix strategy, helping to unify and strengthen decision making. Consider how agreement on the following statements would guide teams working toward a unified approach. Notice how different target markets require different positioning statements, even for one program effort such as that of NetMark:

- "We want *mothers* to see insecticide-treated nets (ITNs) as the best way to protect their families from malaria and a better choice than untreated nets, because these nets actually kill mosquitoes."

- "We want *commercial manufacturers* of ITNs to see Africa as a great market opportunity, one that can open up an entirely new and large consumer base. We also want them to believe that NetMark will work closely with them to create cutting-edge technology. NetMark also will help reduce taxes and tariffs so that prices can be lowered to reach this large base at the bottom of the pyramid."

- "We want *small business enterprises* in local communities to see focusing on sales and distribution of ITNs as a profitable venture. We also want them to realize that they will not be adversely affected by subsidized nets that the government will provide for those who can't pay."

- "We want *policy makers* to see lowering the taxes and tariffs for commercial partners for ITNs as being in the interest of the public good, and to know that local manufacturers cannot meet the need and expected demand for these nets. We also want policy makers to target subsidies for these nets to those in need who cannot pay."

As mentioned, inspiration for this descriptive phrase will come from the lists of barriers and benefits identified in your research. Ideally, this research would include a prioritization of barriers and benefits, giving you a clear sense of what factors would be most important to highlight. Keep in mind that you are searching for the "higher value"—the key benefits to be gained or costs that will be avoided by adopting the desired behavior.[12]

The Strategic Marketing Mix (The Four Ps)

This section describes in more detail the four traditional elements of the marketing mix, outlining decisions associated with each. A malaria success story will be used to highlight each. The sequence of the Four Ps is significant. Product is determined first, followed by price, because these influence decisions about place. And until all three of these strategies are known, you won't know the offer your communications will promote.

The First P: Product

A product is anything that can be offered to a market to satisfy a want or need. It isn't as many typically think, just a tangible offering like soap, tires, or hamburgers. It can be one of several types: a physical good, a service, an experience, an event, a person, a place, a property, an organization, information, or an idea.[13]

Poverty-reduction efforts include all types of products, as illustrated by the following examples:

- *Physical good.* Mosquito nets, condoms, check dams, high-yield seeds
- *Service.* Job counseling, family planning sessions, tobacco quit line
- *Experience.* Attend school with your child, visit a hospital's malaria ward
- *Event.* World Tuberculosis Day, evacuation training events
- *Person.* Village chiefs, a tuberculosis healthcare worker
- *Place.* Preferred sites for obtaining safe drinking water
- *Property.* A stall for selling crafts, a grain storage bin
- *Organization.* Family planning clinics, microlenders
- *Information.* How to feed earthworms to chickens and termites to tadpoles
- *Idea.* Wash hands long enough to sing "Happy Birthday" twice

Traditional marketing theory puts forward that from the customer's perspective, a product is more than its features, quality, name, and style. It identifies three product levels you should consider when developing your product: *core product, actual product,* and *augmented product* (see Figure 8.6).

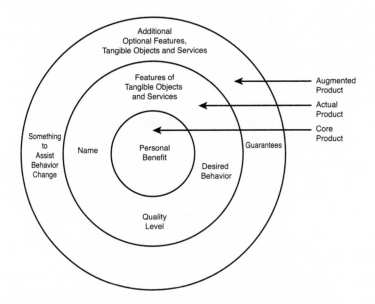

FIGURE 8.6   The Product Circle

Adapted from Kotler and Armstrong, *Principles of Marketing*, 9th edition, p. 294

The *core product,* at the center of the product platform, is the benefit the target market wants and expects in exchange for performing the behavior. It answers these questions: What's in it for the customers to perform the behavior? What benefits will they receive? What needs will the desired behavior satisfy? What problems will it solve that they care about? Keep in mind that each question should be asked from the customer's perspective, not the organization sponsoring the effort. The great Harvard marketing professor Theodore Levitt was known to have told his students, "People don't want to buy a quarter-inch drill (the actual product). They want a quarter-inch hole (the core product)!"[14]

The *actual product* is built around the core product. In commercial marketing, it is the tangible product or service, and its features, name, quality level, brand name, and packaging that have all been carefully selected to deliver the core benefit. For example, the Sony camcorder is an actual product. Its name, parts, styling, features, and packaging have all been combined carefully to deliver the core benefit—a convenient, high-quality way to capture important moments.[15] In social marketing, the actual product describes the features of the behavior you want to influence. Sometimes it is a behavior relative to using "someone else's" actual product: use condoms, eat five fruits and vegetables a day, switch to high-yield seeds, or take all prescribed tuberculosis drugs on time. And sometimes the actual product is simply a behavior with specified features: breastfeed exclusively for the first six months, live within your means, or engage in regular physical activity.

The *augmented product* offers additional tangible objects, features, and services. Sony, for example, offers buyers a warranty on parts, a website with detailed instructions on how to use the camcorder, quick repair services when needed, and a toll-free number to call if buyers have problems or questions. You could consider these additions optional on the part of the company. Sometimes, however, it adds just enough value to the bundle of benefits to tip the scale in favor of one brand over another. In social marketing, the augmented product typically is a tangible object or service that helps the person adopt the new behavior. Sometimes these augmented products are ones produced and distributed by the social marketing campaign sponsor (such as wallet-sized immunization cards to keep track of immunizations). Other times they are produced and distributed by a separate organization that the social marketer just supports and promotes (such as mosquito nets).

To illustrate a strong product strategy, we turn our attention from Africa to Sri Lanka, a country that has a long history of being plagued by malaria epidemics, reaching a peak of 687,599 confirmed cases in 1987.[16] And yet, in 2003, there were only 10,510, and in 2007 there were only 196—and no deaths.[17] What happened? Let's review their product evolution:

- *Extensive indoor residual spraying* began in the late 1950s. It was carried out at regular intervals throughout the year on a blanket coverage basis, resulting in a considerable degree of community resistance. In addition, inevitable leakage of residual insecticides used by the program into the hands of farmers accelerated fears.

- *Selective spraying* was then introduced, based on relevant factors predicting the need for spraying. In addition, more sophisticated assessments were able to determine whether what was needed was year-round coverage, seasonal coverage, or coverage only when evidence of transmission was observed. Community acceptance increased.

- *Mosquito nets* were used in very high malaria risk areas, reducing the number of villages in which the indoor residual spraying needed to take place.

- *Outreach mobile malaria clinics* were introduced to increase early detection and prompt treatment, reducing the time between the appearance of fever and treatment seeking.

- *Rapid diagnostic kits* were given to medical practitioners, helping to identify and treat malaria patients without access to laboratory facilities.

Clearly, additional marketing mix strategies also contributed to this success (pricing of the products, access to them, and communications about them), as well as the political will and funding to support them.

Practical Steps to Developing a Product Platform

1. Determine the *core product*. Review your research on the benefits your target audience says they want or expect in return for performing the desired behavior. If several were identified, conduct informal interviews to help you prioritize them, ideally ending with the top one or two.

2. Clarify specific features of the *actual product* you will be promoting, including a name or brand. If you will be promoting testing for HIV/AIDS, for example, get agreement on how often your target market should get tested and how soon after having unprotected sex. If you are promoting mosquito nets, be clear about what type of net should be purchased, how many are needed, and how they should be installed. If you are promoting handwashing, decide on specific recommendations, including water temperature, type of soap, and length of time hands should be scrubbed.

3. Consider what possible *augmented products and services* you could include in your offer—ones that will assist your customer in performing the desired behavior. Remember that even though these are optional components, sometimes they are the very thing the customer needs in order to quit smoking (a quit line), apply for a job (counseling), or take tuberculosis medicines on time (someone watching).

The Second P: Price

Price is the amount of money that the customer pays for a product or service, or the sum of the values that they "give" for the benefits of having or using the product or service.[18]

Strategic thinking relative to pricing begins with careful consideration of what the customer will "pay" to adopt the behavior you have in mind. Sometimes there are monetary costs such as those for tangible goods and services (such as mosquito nets). But most of the time, social marketers are selling behaviors that require something else in exchange:

- *Fees* for an ITN
- *Time* to walk an hour to the nearest location to get the mosquito net
- *Effort* to install the net properly over the beds
- *Energy* to help my child get up in the middle of the night

- *Psychological cost* from feeling closed in, almost claustrophobic
- *Physical discomfort*, because sleeping under a net is hotter

Some of these costs can be reduced using the pricing tool. It should be noted, however, that the other three Ps will be needed as well. A place strategy could reduce travel time, bringing nets closer to a village. A product strategy to design nets that are more easily installed should be seriously considered. And the promotional strategy will be needed to make perceived benefits outweigh the costs of feeling closed in and warmer.

The opportunity and objective with the price tool is to set fees, when applicable, and to consider and possibly provide incentives that will increase benefits or decrease costs. These incentives may be monetary or nonmonetary in nature.

Prices set for any tangible objects and services will vary depending on your organization's objectives for the program. Typically they will fall into one of five potential categories:

- *Maximizing retained earnings*, with moneymaking the primary consideration
- *Recovering costs*, where revenue is expected to offset a portion or all of the direct costs, perhaps even indirect ones as well
- *Maximizing the number of customers*, where the primary purpose is just to get people to use the service and/or buy the product
- *Social equity*, where reaching underprivileged or high-risk segments is the priority
- *Demarketing*, where pricing strategies are used to discourage people from purchasing a competing product or service[19]

Four pricing tactics can be used to decrease costs and/or increase benefits:

- *Monetary incentives* reward customers for adopting the behavior. They can take many forms, including discounts, fees based on ability to pay, rebates, allowances, and cash incentives.

- *Monetary disincentives* are used to discourage people from engaging in a competing or undesirable behavior. Fines, increased taxes, and decreased funding are the most common.

- *Nonmonetary incentives* encourage changes in behavior that don't involve money, most often by offering some form of valued recognition, appreciation, or experiences (such as a chance to meet a celebrity).

- *Nonmonetary disincentives* are used to decrease the actual or perceived value of alternative, competing behaviors, using public embarrassment (such as having to register as a sex offender) or mandatory community service (such as picking up litter on the side of the road).

Let's return to Africa to illustrate the challenges of pricing. Tanzania is considered by many the epicenter of malaria because of the high incidence of disease there. For years, the government has subsidized sales of nets for the most vulnerable populations at prices typically between $1.50 and $3.50 each. Proponents of keeping this fee, versus widely distributing nets for free, argue three points. First, they worry about creating a sustainable system for disseminating nets after the topic has fallen off the front page or the top of donors' priority lists. Second, the nets provide jobs and earnings for locals involved in the supply chain. Free nets would undermine the business ecosystems that have sprung up to manufacture and distribute the nets. Finally, they believe that people who buy nets tend to use them more regularly and take better care of them (such as respraying when needed) than those who don't pay.

But even with subsidies, more than two-thirds of the adults and children do not have nets to protect themselves against mosquitoes when they sleep. Some poverty spokespeople advocate distributing free nets to everyone to abate the problem. Others propose stimulating private distribution channels who will charge a few dollars per net while agreeing to give them free to those who cannot pay.

We suggest that this dilemma would be best resolved by committing (or recommitting, in some cases) to a "sales" goal. Is it 100% coverage or 50% coverage, and by when? What goals will be sustained in years 1, 2, and 3? Then assess what price and distribution channels will get the job done, revisiting progress relative to goals on a regular basis.

Practical Steps to Developing a Pricing Strategy

1. Identify all costs your target market will associate with performing the behavior. Highlight those that are monetary in nature, because these are ones the pricing tool will address.

2. If fees are involved for products, first reach an agreement on your organization's pricing objective for these fees. Do you need to recover your costs? Will you be subsidizing any target segments? Are you interested in stimulating demand by setting a low price (for mosquito nets) or in reducing demand by establishing a higher price (for tobacco products)?

3. Consider whether you will need to introduce any monetary or nonmonetary incentives to reach behavior change goals. To decide, you may want to informally test a few ideas with your target audience. If a more rigorous test is needed to decide, you may want to conduct a pilot where one group is offered an incentive (free food at the immunization event) and another (control) group is not. Then compare the results to determine whether the additional costs are justified in order to reach program goals when rolled out.

4. You might also consider disincentives—tactics that will discourage your target audience from engaging in competing/undesirable behaviors. As noted earlier, these might be in the form of increased taxes, fines, public embarrassment, or community service. This strategy may be warranted when the target market is far from "ready to buy" and/or has not responded to more positive tactics in the past.

The Third P: Place

Place is where and when the target market will be encouraged to engage in the targeted behavior and/or access any tangible objects or services associated with the campaign.[20]

In commercial marketing, place is often called the distribution channel, with options "to buy" beyond that of a physical location such as a store. The following list includes the range of potential distribution channels, with examples related to social marketing:

- *Physical location.* A community clinic for a malaria screening
- *Phone.* A domestic violence hotline
- *Fax.* A physician faxes a patient request for a call to a tobacco quit line
- *Mail.* An immunization schedule on a wallet-sized card
- *Mobile units.* To deliver high-yield seeds and fertilizers
- *Drive-thrus.* For flu shots
- *Home delivery/house calls.* To observe patients taking tuberculosis drugs
- *Where customers shop, dine, and hang out.* HIV tests at gay bathhouses
- *Kiosks/vending machines.* Condoms available in vending machines at bars

Your objective with this place tool is to make it as convenient and pleasant as possible for your market to engage in the targeted behavior and access any products and services. Walking for an hour one way to get a mosquito net, or waiting two weeks for the results of an HIV/AIDS test, or leaving it up to the patient to remember to take his or her tuberculosis drug, can "make or break" the deal. Your decisions will also include hours of the day and days of the week that you are "open." Your keys to success will include providing a location that is as close as possible and the hours as long as warranted, making the location appealing, overcoming psychological barriers (such as by offering a mobile unit for a needle-exchange program versus needing to go to a health clinic), looking for opportunities to be where your target audience hangs out, and working with existing distribution channels.[21]

When tangible objects are included in your campaign or program, a network of intermediaries may be needed to reach your market. Kotler and Roberto identify three "players" in the distribution channel, in addition to the *change agent* (you) and the target *adopter* (your customer): *distributors, wholesalers,* and *retailers.* As it would seem, the distributors, when involved, provide products to a wholesaler or retailer; the wholesaler interfaces with the retailer; and the retailer interfaces with the customer.[22]

Returning to our malaria discussions, decisions about distribution channels and a network of intermediaries have been shown to be crucial, as well as controversial. A range of delivery systems have been utilized over the last two decades to deliver ITNs. In an article in the Oxford University Press in June 2007, authors Webster, Hill, Lines, and Hanson proposed a categorization of net delivery systems in Africa. Table 8.1 summarizes their approach. They assume that the channel through which the nets are delivered and the cost to the end user are the major factors affecting outcomes. They hope that a framework such as this one can be used on a consistent basis to report outcomes based on large-scale evaluations, which will help settle debates about the most effective delivery systems.

TABLE 8.1 Matrix of Net Delivery Systems by Category and Cost to the End User, with a Partial Listing of Countries in Africa Where Strategy Exists[23]

Delivery System			Cost to the End User		
Sector	Delivery Channel	Timing/Event/Location	Free	Partially Subsidized	Unsubsidized
Public sector	Routine services	Child clinics, antenatal care, immunization programs, maternal and child health	Kenya, Eritrea	Ghana	
		Intervention packages: mixed delivery	Mali	Benin, Ghana, Senegal	
	Enhanced routine	Child health week/days	Ghana, Senegal		
	Campaigns	Measles	Ghana, Niger, Togo, Zambia		
		Polio national immunization days		Ghana	
Mixed public-private sectors	Assisted routine services	Antenatal care, immunization programs		Kenya, Malawi	
	Voucher scheme	Routine service: retail		Ghana, Senegal, Tanzania, Uganda	
		Campaign: retail	Zambia		

Private sector	Employer-based	Workplace	Kenya	
	Nonprofit organizations	Retail outlets	Ghana, Kenya, Malawi, Tanzania	
	Retail sector	Formal/informal		Tanzania and Cameroon, Ethiopia, Kenya, and others
		Formal		Burkina Faso
		Informal		Gambia
Community-based (a mix of systems with a philanthropic aim)	Community-based	Community-based organizations, NGOs, women's groups	Kenya, Tanzania	Mali, Zambia

Practical Steps to Developing a Place Strategy

1. Decide where and how your market will access any tangible objects or services. Consider ways to make this as convenient as possible, focusing on strategies that will reduce time spent, either traveling or waiting. Are there opportunities for your products and services to be offered in locations where your target market already works, shops, visits, or travels?

2. Are there options to partner with others in the distribution channel who might be influential and/or more convenient? You read in an earlier chapter, for example, how New York City partners with multiple retail outlets to distribute free condoms.

3. Determine hours and days of the week that you will be "open for business," keeping in mind the lifestyles and preferences of the target market.

The Fourth P: Promotion

> Promotions are persuasive communications designed and delivered to inspire your target audience to action. In social marketing, the key word here is action.[24]

Developing these communications is a process that begins with determining key messages. It moves on to selecting messengers and creative elements, and then ends with a selection of media channels. Of course, this step considers prior decisions regarding your target market, behavior objective, audience barriers, and benefits. This process is needed to support the desired positioning for this behavior. It also is the tool you count on to highlight your product, price, and place strategies. Each step in developing this communications strategy involves important decisions, as discussed next.

Message Decisions: What Do You Want to Communicate?

Those developing specific key messages for your campaign or program should be inspired first and foremost by a clear response to the question "What do you want your target audience *to do?*" Hopefully this has been articulated in your behavior objective and product platform, and you merely need to reference it. There may also be things you need your audience *to know*, in order for them to be inspired to act (where to get a mosquito net) or have the skills to perform (how to install the net). These knowledge-based messages are informative in nature, providing key facts about the benefits of the behavior, where and when a product can be accessed, and how to perform the behavior. Often there will be something they need *to believe*—something that, if not altered, could get in the way (such as a concern that the chemicals in the treated net might be harmful to a newborn). Your inspiration for these points will be the research conducted on barriers, pointing to real or perceived concerns with behavior adoption. Your messages will seek to assuage these concerns.

For example, in Zambia, the nation's malaria-control budget has grown from US$30,000 in 1985 to more than $40 million in 2007. Messages inform people of malaria's causes and symptoms and stress the importance of seeking help. Boy Scout merit badges are even awarded for knowledge about malaria. Some messages are designed to help correct widespread traditional beliefs that malaria is transmitted by witchcraft, drinking dirty water, getting soaked in the rain, or chewing immature sugarcane. Others emphasize the proper use of bed nets, correcting misperceptions that they can or should be used for fishing instead.[25]

Messenger Decisions: Who Will Deliver Your Messages or Be Perceived to Be the Campaign's Sponsor?

Who your target audience perceives to be delivering your messages and what they think of this particular messenger can be critical to whether your target audience "buys it." Most often, the messenger is the sponsoring organization and any partners in the effort. It may also include any spokespeople, actors, endorsements, or mascots used to deliver or reinforce messages. In the end, particularly in social marketing efforts, you want your target audience to see the messenger, or messengers, as a *credible source* for the message. Three major factors have been identified as key to source credibility: perceived expertise, trustworthiness, and likeability.[26] An expert source is perceived as having the knowledge and experience to back the claim. A trusted source is perceived as objective and honest. A likable source is attractive, with qualities such as humor, candor, and naturalness.[27]

For example, in Tanzania, managers of the Bagamoyo Bednet Project found that posters and meetings had a limited impact in persuading the predominantly Muslim population to use bed nets. A different approach was needed. When a sheik in each village was recruited to teach during Friday religious services about the merits of regular bed net usage, regular usage levels rose to 53% and, in some areas, 98%. And traditional healers who were being consulted for treating convulsions and fever were incorporated into local project activities.[28]

Creative Strategy/Execution: What Words, Graphics, and Images Will You Use?

A creative strategy translates the content of your intended, desired messages to specific communications. Traditional elements include copy elements such as taglines, headlines, and any scripts; design elements such as logos, colors, graphic images, and typeface; and any actors, scenes, and sounds when using broadcast media. Factors that are considered when making these creative decisions include the brand image of the sponsoring organization, the desired positioning of the offer, and budget realities (such as whether materials will be in black and white or color).

In their book *Made to Stick*, the Heath brothers present six key qualities to consider when developing ideas and creative strategies: Simplicity, Unexpectedness, Concreteness, Credibility, Emotion, and Stories. (And they make it easy to remember these, because they almost spell SUCCESs.)[29]

Media Channels: Where Will Your Messages Appear?

Media channels, also called communication channels, include traditional ones that you are probably most familiar with and exposed to. Media channels also include nontraditional and new-media options—ones that may be more successful in "catching your audience by surprise" and establishing source credibility.

Traditional methods include the following:

- *Advertising* on radio, television, billboards, newspapers, magazines
- *Public service announcements*, which are unpaid advertising
- *Public relations*—working with the media for "free" coverage of events and issues
- *Special events* such as health fairs, demonstrations, and public meetings
- *Printed materials* including brochures, newsletters, posters, and bumper stickers
- *Special promotional items* with messages on clothing, functional items such as water bottles, and temporary items such as balloons
- *Signage and displays* including posters, retail displays, and public signage
- *Personal selling* either face to face, by phone, or through electronic media

Nontraditional and new-media options include the following:

- *Social media* such as YouTube, Facebook, Twitter, blogs, and social networking groups
- *Public art* including exhibits and street theater
- *Other electronic media* including websites and emails
- *Popular entertainment media* such as songs, movie scripts, television shows, and video games

Decisions on channels will be impacted by your campaign goals, desired exposure (reach and frequency), target audience media habits, achieving a desired integrated approach utilizing a variety of media options, and, of course, the budget.

For a malaria media channel example, in Assam, India, a few weeks before the heavy rains of the monsoon, a three-day health fair was held to raise awareness and usage of bed nets among tribes. The fair was attended by over 30 doctors, nurses, and lab technicians with provisions for undergoing blood tests sponsored by the health department. And theater troupes appeared in the Zambian countryside, emphasizing the proper use of bed nets through stage productions in settlements large and small.

Practical Steps to Developing a Promotional Strategy

1. Determine your key *messages*. These are not your slogans. They are simple sentences describing what you want your target audience to know, believe, and do.

2. Decide on *messengers* who will deliver these messages. What organization or organizations' names will be associated with the campaign? Will you use any spokespersons, endorsements, actors, or mascots?

3. Develop a *creative strategy*. This includes graphics, slogans, copy, and visual elements. For those with minimal or tight budgets, try involving your target audience in at least brain-storming ideas and concepts, and then use professionals to refine them.

4. Select *media channels*—where your messages will appear and be delivered. This selection will be based on the lifestyles and preferences of your target audience. Sometimes you can deter-mine these informally by asking "What would be the best way to let you know about the availability of these new mosquito nets?"

Summary

This chapter began by discussing how to determine a desired positioning for your offer. This was defined as the act of designing the organization's actual and perceived offering so that it lands on and occupies a distinctive place in the mind of the target market—where you want it to be.[30]

We then opened the marketing toolbox and defined and described the four traditional Ps inside: product, price, place, and promotion. As stressed, our experience is that you need all of them to create and deliver the value your target market expects in exchange for a new behavior.

- A *product* is anything that can be offered to a market to satisfy a want or need. It isn't, as many typically think, just a tangible offering like soap, tires, or hamburgers. It can be one of several types: a physical good, a service, an experience, an event, a person, a place, a property, an organization, information, or an idea.[31]

- *Price* is how much the customer pays for a product or service, or the sum of the values that the customer "gives" for the benefits of having or using the product or service.[32] The opportunity and objective with the price tool is to set fees, when applicable, and to consider and provide incentives that will increase benefits or decrease costs. These incentives may be monetary or nonmonetary in nature.

- *Place* is where and when the target market will be encouraged to engage in the targeted behavior and/or access any tangible objects or services associated with the campaign.[33] Your objective with the place tool is to make it as convenient and pleasant as possible for your market to engage in the targeted behavior and access any products and services.

- *Promotions* are persuasive communications designed and delivered to inspire your target audience to action. In social marketing, the key word here is action.[34] Developing these communications is a process that begins with determining key *messages*, moves on to selecting *messengers* and *creative elements*, and ends with a selection of *media channels*.

Endnotes

[1] P. Kotler and N. R. Lee, *Social Marketing: Influencing Behaviors for Good* (3rd edition) (Thousand Oaks, CA: Sage Publications, 2008), p. 3.

[2] CDC. "The Impact of Malaria, a Leading Cause of Death Worldwide." Retrieved August 4, 2008 from http://www.cdc.gov/malaria/impact/index.htm.

[3] NetMark Communications. Retrieved August 4, 2008 from http://www. netmarkafrica.org/Communications/.

[4] Ibid.

[5] Ibid.

[6] NetMark Baseline Survey on Insecticide Treated Materials in Nigeria, May 2001. Retrieved August 4, 2008 from http://www.netmarkafrica.org/research/index.html.

[7] AED NetMark: A Case Study in Sustainable Malaria Prevention Through Partnership with Business.

[8] Adapted from P. Kotler and G. Armstrong, *Principles of Marketing* (9th edition) (Upper Saddle River, NJ: Prentice Hall, 2001), p. 269.

[9] A. Ries and J. Trout, *Positioning: The Battle for Your Mind* (New York: Warner Books, 1982), p. 3.

[10] P. Kotler and G. Armstrong, op. cit., p. 269.

[11] Adapted from P. Kotler and N. R. Lee, op. cit., p. 187–188.

[12] Adapted from P. Kotler and N. R. Lee, op. cit., p. 188.

[13] P. Kotler and G. Armstrong, op. cit., p. 294.

[14] Ibid.

[15] Ibid.

[16] WHO. "Malaria—Success Stories in Malaria Control from the SEA Region." Retrieved August 6, 2008 from http://www.searo.who.int/LinkFiles/Malaria_Srilanka_Mal_Story.pdf.

[17] UN Office of the Coordination of Humanitarian Affairs. "Sri Lanka: On Track to Eliminate Malaria." Retrieved August 6, 2008 from http://www.irinnews.org/report.aspx?ReportID=77899.

[18] P. Kotler and G. Armstrong, op. cit., p. 371.

[19] P. Kotler and N. R. Lee, op. cit., p. 237.

[20] P. Kotler and N. R. Lee, op. cit., p. 247.

[21] P. Kotler and N. R. Lee, op. cit., p. 262.

[22] P. Kotler and N. R. Lee, op. cit., p. 258.

[23] Adapted from "Delivery systems for insecticide treated and untreated mosquito nets in Africa: categorization and outcomes achieved" by Jayne Webster, June 28, 2007. http://heapol.oxfordjournals.org/cgi/content/full/czm021v1.

[24] P. Kotler and N. R. Lee, op. cit., p. 268.

[25] Michael Finkel, "Raging Malaria," *National Geographic*, July 2007, p. 32–67.

[26] H. C. Kelman and C. I. Hovland (1953). "Reinstatement of the Communication in Delayed Measurement of Opinion Change," *Journal of Abnormal and Social Psychology*, 48, 327–335. As cited in Kotler and Keller, *Marketing Management* (12th edition), p. 546.

[27] P. Kotler and N. R. Lee, op. cit., p. 275.

[28] "Participatory communication in malaria control: why does it matter?" *Findings*, Number 4, October 2005.

[29] C. Heath and D. Heath, *Made to Stick: Why Some Ideas Survive and Others Die* (New York: Random House, 2007).

[30] Adapted from P. Kotler and G. Armstrong, op. cit., p. 269.

[31] P. Kotler G. Armstrong, op. cit., p. 294.

[32] P. Kotler and G. Armstrong, op. cit., p. 371.

[33] P. Kotler and N. R. Lee, op. cit., p. 247.

[34] P. Kotler and N. R. Lee, op. cit., p. 268.

Part III

Ensuring an Integrated Approach

9

Developing a Social Marketing Plan

Vision without action is a daydream.
Action without vision is a nightmare.

—Japanese proverb

The traditional marketing planning framework presented in this chapter is a simple and effective mechanism for creating a strategic action plan. We hope it helps ensure that visions for moving people up and out of poverty are more than a daydream. The plan outline will make clear where the five tools presented in Part II, "Applying Marketing Perspectives and Solutions," of this book fit in the marketing planning process (segmenting the market; choosing target priorities; determining desired behaviors; understanding barriers, benefits, and the competition; and developing a strategic marking mix).

The following sidebar describes a 10-step model for developing a social marketing plan that reflects a systematic process. It begins with providing background on the purpose of the project and analyzing the current situation and environment. It moves on to identifying target audiences, determining desired behaviors, and designing a strategic marketing mix (the Four Ps). It wraps up with developing evaluation, budget, and implementation plans. You will also see a note at the end of the chapter summary on how to obtain an electronic copy of worksheets that walk you through this 10-step model—one that you can download for free.

To illustrate each step in the model, we use highlights from a case story featuring Peru's social marketing efforts to decrease tuberculosis (TB). These efforts contributed to the country's success in reducing the incidence of TB by an estimated 7% per year between 1990 and 2000, from about 190 per 100,000 to 140 per 100,000.[1] Nearly 2 billion people around the world are infected with the rod-shaped bacterium that causes TB. This is almost one out three human beings. If TB is detected early and fully treated, people with the disease quickly become noninfectious and eventually are cured.[2] Their story should inspire those working to achieve 2015 Millennium Development Goal #6 to reduce TB prevalence and death rates by 50% relative to 1990.[3] Peru's story also confirms points made throughout Part III, "Ensuring an Integrated Approach," that this kind of success is rarely possible without the public, private, and nonprofit sectors working with an integrated approach to "get the job done."[4]

Social Marketing Planning: A One-Page Outline

1.0 Background, Purpose, and Focus

Who's the sponsor? Why are they doing this? What social issue and population will the plan focus on, and why?

2.0 Situation Analysis

2.1 SWOT: Organizational Strengths and Weaknesses, and Environmental Opportunities and Threats

2.2 Literature review and environmental scan of programs focusing on similar efforts: activities and lessons learned

3.0 Segment the Market, and Choose and Describe Target Audiences

3.1 Demographics, geographics, relevant behaviors (including risk), psychographics, social networks, community assets, and stage of change (readiness to buy)

3.2 Size of the target audience

4.0 Marketing Objectives and Goals

    4.1 Campaign objectives: specifying targeted behaviors and attitudes (knowledge and beliefs)

    4.2 SMART goals: Specific, Measurable, Achievable, Relevant, Time-bound changes in behaviors and attitudes

5.0 Factors Influencing Adoption of the Behavior

    5.1 Perceived barriers to the targeted behavior

    5.2 Potential benefits of the targeted behavior

    5.3 Competing behaviors/forces

    5.4 Influence of important others

6.0 Positioning Statement

How do we want the target audience to see the targeted behavior and its benefits relative to alternative/preferred ones?

7.0 Marketing Mix Strategies (Using the Four Ps to Create, Communicate, and Deliver Value for the Behavior)

    7.1 Product: Benefits from performing behaviors and any objects or services offered to assist adoption

    7.2 Price: Costs that will be associated with adopting the behavior and any monetary and nonmonetary incentives and disincentives

    7.3 Place: Making access convenient

    7.4 Promotion: Persuasive communications highlighting product benefits, features, fair price, and ease of access

8.0 Plan for Monitoring and Evaluation

9.0 Budget

10.0 Plan for Implementation and Campaign Management

Developed September 2008 by Philip Kotler, Nancy Lee, Alan Andreasen, Carol Bryant, Craig Lefebvre, Bob Marshall, Mike Newton-Ward, Michael Rothschild, and Bill Smith.

Step 1: Background, Purpose, and Focus

This first section of the plan identifies the plan's sponsor and summarizes factors leading to its development. Why are you doing this? It also includes a clear statement of purpose and focus for the plan. What social issue (problem) is the plan intended to impact? What population and broad solution will the plan focus on, and why?

Example: Reducing Tuberculosis in Peru

In 1991, Peru accounted for about 15% of TB cases in the Americas even though it had only 3% of the population. It had approximately 190 TB cases per 100,000 adults; the abandonment rate of drug therapy was 12.1%;[5] and only 50% of people diagnosed with TB were getting treated and, of those, only half were cured.[6]

In response, increased resources were allocated for the country's National Tuberculosis Control Program (NTCP), recognizing the impact that the disease was having on its citizens, as well as the country's economy, with TB affecting primarily the most economically productive age groups. The *purpose* of this bolstered effort was to decrease the incidence of TB with two areas of *focus*. The first was an internationally recommended approach for TB control programs in which a trained healthcare worker monitors the patient taking each dose of antituberculosis medication. A second effort focused on identifying patients who were currently infected, but not diagnosed or receiving treatment.

Step 2: Situation Analysis

In Step 2, you conduct a SWOT analysis (*organizational* strengths and weaknesses and *environmental* opportunities and threats). Organizational strengths to maximize and weaknesses to minimize include factors such as levels of funding, management support, current partners, delivery system capabilities, and the sponsor's reputation. Environmental opportunities to take advantage of and threats to prepare for include major trends and events typically outside your influence—ones associated with cultural, technological, demographic, economic, political, and legal forces.

At this step you will also conduct a literature review and environmental scan of current and past programs, focusing on those with similar efforts, and summarizing major activities and lessons learned.

Example Continued:
Reducing Tuberculosis in Peru

The greatest strength the NTCP had was the increase in its annual budget from US$600,000 to US$5 million. This funding represented a renewed political will and would help address current system weaknesses, including short supplies of drugs, poor record-keeping systems, and overworked healthcare workers.[7] In terms of environmental forces, nutrition and sanitation tended to be the main causes of chronic health problems. Health concerns were being compounded by a lack of basic health education among a majority of the rural population, as well as a lack of convenient and affordable medical care.

Other programs around the world combating tuberculosis were reporting success with the Directly Observed Treatment—Short Course (DOTS) program. Experience of others had shown that this intervention was critical to persuading patients to take their medication in a timely manner and to complete their regime.

Step 3: Target Audience Profile

As elaborated upon in Chapters 4, "Segmenting the Poverty Marketplace," and 5, "Evaluating and Choosing Target Market Priorities," you select target audiences by segmenting the market into homogeneous segments, evaluating each one, and then choosing one or more as the focus point for the plan. You want to provide an estimated size and rich description of that target audience in this section of the marketing plan. You should highlight key demographics, geographics, relevant behaviors (including risk), psychographics, social networks, community assets, and stage of change (readiness to buy). An ideal description is one that makes you believe you'd know your target audience if they walked into the room.

Example Continued:
Reducing Tuberculosis in Peru

Getting more people identified who are currently infected and then getting those diagnosed to accept and complete recommended drug therapies required a plan to inspire three target audiences:

- Downstream, high-risk groups were a top priority, especially the urban poor living in crowded, urban areas known as "TB pockets" or "hot spots." An example was the capital city of Lima, with 60% of all cases in the country, but only 29% of the population.[8] Most were between the ages of 15 and 54,[9] and many were considered "closed populations" because they required special outreach (such as prisoners, patients in mental institutions, and homeless people sleeping in shelters).

- Midstream target audiences are important influential others in the target markets' community. They include individuals and groups such as family members, neighbors, religious leaders, coworkers, and friends of those at risk.

- Upstream target audiences included the following:

  - Policy makers, seen as critical for funding

  - Healthcare providers and their staff, essential for increasing the identification of those infected, as well as getting those identified into programs that would help treat and cure the disease

  - The media, for creating high visibility for major events and to stimulate public and political will

  - Pharmaceutical drug representatives, seen as an important potential distribution channel for communications, as well as potential price reductions or free drugs

As we continue with our TB case as an illustration, we will present only strategies developed for the TB patient market. Separate marketing plans would be needed for the other two distinct markets midstream and upstream.

Step 4: Marketing Objectives and Goals

Marketing objectives specify desired behaviors and changes in attitudes (knowledge and beliefs). Social marketing plans will always have behavior objectives, specifying desired behaviors the plan is intended to influence. Often, you will also find there are facts and information that the target audience needs to know in order to act (knowledge objectives), and things they need to believe in order to "change their mind" (belief objectives).

Goals are quantifiable and measurable expressions of marketing objectives. We recommend ones that are SMART:[10] Specific, Measurable, Achievable, Relevant, Time-bound changes in behaviors and attitudes.

Example Continued: Reducing Tuberculosis in Peru

The NTCP established bold and clear *marketing objectives and goals.*

Behavior objectives:

- Influence those with symptoms to get diagnosed.
- Influence those who have been diagnosed to accept treatment.
- Influence those receiving treatment to complete the regime.
- Influence those successfully treated to become advocates.

Knowledge objectives:

- Know what symptoms to watch for.
- Know how the disease is spread (and is not spread).
- Know the effectiveness of treatment.
- Know that treatment is free.
- Know that fully completing treatment is necessary in order to be cured.

Belief objectives:

- Reduce stigma for those with TB.

- Correct misconceptions about the disease.

Marketing goals:

- Diagnose 70% of pulmonary TB cases.

- Cure at least 85% of cases. (At the time, they were curing only 50%, representing a 70% increase.)

- Decrease treatment abandonment. (At the time, 12.1% of those being treated were abandoning their treatment.)[11]

Step 5: Factors Influencing Adoption of the Behavior

Elaborate here on key factors that will influence your audience's decision making, including a list of barriers, benefits, the competition, and the influence of others that are important to the target audience. Barriers are reasons your target audience does not want, or might not want, or doesn't think they can adopt the behavior. They may be real, or just perceived. Benefits are what they see in it for them to adopt the behavior, or what you might promise that would make it more likely that they would be motivated. Competitors are related behaviors (or organizations promoting them) that your target audience is currently engaged in, or prefers to do, instead of the ones you have in mind. This is also a good time to note any "important others" who could influence your target audience—people such as family members, social networks, the entertainment industry, and religious leaders.

Example Continued:
Reducing Tuberculosis in Peru

Research conducted by the NTCP confirmed suspicions of widespread stigma, misconceptions, and lack of facts about the disease. It also highlighted concerns about access to diagnosis, drugs, and coordinated care. Specific barriers included the following:

- Not knowing that a persistent cough was a signal they should get tested

- Not knowing where to go for diagnosis

- Believing they could not afford treatment

- For those being treated, believing that because they felt better, they were cured

- Seeing the burden of traveling on foot to a clinic several times a week as too exhausting

Step 6: Positioning Statement

A positioning statement describes what you want your target market to think and feel when they hear about the targeted behavior. Emphasize findings from your research on perceived barriers and benefits of the behaviors. How do we want the target audience to see the desired behavior and its benefits relative to alternative/preferred ones? Our desired positioning will guide the development of a marketing mix strategy, one that helps ensure that our offer lands on and occupies a distinctive place in the minds of the target market.

> ### Example Continued:
> ### Reducing Tuberculosis in Peru
>
> Planners wanted those with TB symptoms to have a sense of urgency about getting tested and, at the same time, to be hopeful, because cures are available, as well as convenient resources for free diagnoses. Planners wanted those who had been diagnosed with TB to see completing the drug treatment regime on time as the only way to ensure that they would get well.

Step 7: Marketing Mix Strategies

The traditional marketing toolbox contains four major tools, as described in Chapter 8, "Developing a Desired Positioning and Strategic Marketing Mix." We count on them to create, communicate, and deliver value for the behavior. They are highlighted here again, and are illustrated using the tuberculosis case story from Peru.

Product Strategy

In social marketing, the core product is the benefit that the target market wants and expects in exchange for performing the behavior. The actual product describes features of the basic product (such as a TB test). And the augmented product includes any additional objects and services to help perform the behavior or increase the appeal (such as counseling for those with positive test results).

Actual product strategies focused on testing and DOTS. The core product for getting tested was "peace of mind" and, for taking the full regime of medications, was "getting well." Mentioned earlier, DOTS involves a health case worker who directly administers, observes, and then documents the patient's ingestion or injection of the tuberculosis medication. Product quality efforts (also considered a component of augmented product) were to ensure that when people arrived for testing, and patients arrived for drugs, ample supplies and assistance would be available. It was fully recognized that clinical services would need to be in place to serve the demand that communications were anticipated to create. If patients or potential patients were unable to receive high-quality services and drugs, as promised, they might not return or complete treatment.

And to the point regarding sector partnerships, collaboration with international and national pharmaceutical companies helped ensure a sufficient drug supply, and a centralized procurement system increased efficiencies and cost-effectiveness of their distribution. Funding from the government and international donors increased the number of microscopes and other supplies for laboratories. TB services were integrated into the primary healthcare system. Also, upgrades were made to hospitals and clinics to provide more effective diagnostic services, counseling, and treatment.

Price Strategy

Price becomes the sum of the costs that the target market will "pay" to adopt the desired behavior in exchange for the benefits promised. Sometimes these costs are monetary in nature, such as those for tangible goods and services. But most of the time social marketers sell behaviors that require something else in exchange: time, effort, energy, psychological costs, and/or physical discomfort. The price tool is used to reduce some of these costs, offering monetary or nonmonetary incentives to reward behaviors, or monetary or nonmonetary disincentives to discourage competing, or undesirable, behaviors. (As a reminder, the other three P tools are needed to reduce these costs as well.)

Example Continued:
Reducing Tuberculosis in Peru

Several options were available for reducing monetary costs, including free testing, free drugs for those who could not afford them, reimbursement for travel, and, for some, free lodging. One of the largest nonprofit organizations in Peru, Socios En Salud, provided food baskets and other social support for impoverished patients whose needs had been confirmed by an extensive interview and evaluation. The organization also helped women in the community earn an income to help support their families through a cooperative workshop that participated in craft fairs in Peru, selling handicrafts as far away as the United States, Japan, and Switzerland (see Figure 9.1).

FIGURE 9.1   Microloans supported small craft businesses.
Source: Terry Lee

Place Strategy

Think of "place" as where and when the target market will be encouraged to engage in the behavior and/or to access any tangible objects or services associated with the effort. Your objective with this tool is to make it as convenient and pleasant as possible for the customer to engage in the targeted behavior and access any products and services.

Example Continued:
Reducing Tuberculosis in Peru

Access to diagnosis and treatment was significantly enhanced when the Ministry of Health integrated TB services into the primary healthcare system. In addition, clinic hours were extended into the evenings, healthcare workers visited patients in their homes, and the DOTS program was expanded to remote areas of the country.

Promotion Strategy

Promotions are persuasive communications to highlight product benefits, features, fair price, and ease of access. They are intended to inspire your target audience to action. Developing these communications is a process that begins with determining key messages, moves on to selecting messengers and creative elements, and ends with selecting media channels.

Several components of your plan will help you decide on key *messages*, beginning with your marketing objectives, which reflect what you want your target market to do, know, and believe. Barriers, benefits, the competition, and details of your offer will also inspire your choices. *Messengers* are those delivering the messages. Audiences will decide how credible they think a messenger is and will form this judgment based on perceived expertise, trustworthiness, and likeability. *Creative elements* translate the content of intended, desired messages into specific communication elements including copy, graphic images, typeface, interactive features of electronic media, and any actors, scenes, and sound used in broadcast media. Messages are delivered through *media channels*, also called communication channels. They include traditional ones such as advertising, printed materials, and signage, and nontraditional ones such as blogs, podcasts, forums, and public art and entertainment.

Example Continued: Reducing Tuberculosis in Peru

Key messages for the campaign clearly reflected behavior, knowledge, and belief objectives: "If you cough for more than 15 days, you should go to the health center." "All TB services are free." "Treatment for one is prevention for all."

Key messengers delivering the messages in person included healthcare workers, family members, and community organization volunteers.

> Key media channels included mass media (television, radio,
> billboards, print media), print materials (posters, letters, fact
> sheets), special events (World TB Day, street theater), videos
> (at healthcare facility waiting areas), personal communications
> (health workers), community mobilization (surveillance
> groups), and advocacy (local groups targeting families and
> political leaders).

Step 8: Plan for Monitoring and Evaluation

You will develop your plan for monitoring and evaluation before
the final budget and implementation plans. One distinction is important up front—the difference between "monitoring" and "evaluation." *Monitoring* generally refers to a measurement conducted
sometime after a new program or campaign has been launched, but
before it is completed. This is often executed to determine whether
mid-course corrections are needed to ensure that ultimate marketing
goals will be reached. An *evaluation* is a measurement and final
report on what happened, answering questions on everyone's mind:
Were goals reached? What components of the campaign can be
linked with outcomes? Was the program on time and on budget?
What worked well? What didn't? What should be done differently
next time?

To develop this plan, your answers to five basic questions will
help:

- Why are you conducting this measurement, and for whom?
- What inputs, processes, outputs, outcomes, and impacts will be
  measured?
- What methodologies will be used to conduct these measurements?

- When will these measurements be taken?
- How much will it cost?

At the heart of this program's evaluation would be outcomes relative to goals. Did 70% of TB cases get diagnosed? Did 85% get cured? Did the treatment abandonment rate of 12.1% decrease? (By 1998, in fact, an estimated 94% of TB cases were being detected, and 90% of patients were being cured, preventing close to 70,000 cases and deaths.)[12]

Step 9: Budget

Your budget for the program or campaign reflects costs for implementing the marketing plan, including those associated with the marketing mix strategy (product, price, place, and promotion), as well as any additional costs anticipated for monitoring and evaluation. In the ideal objective-and-task method of budgeting, these anticipated costs become a preliminary budget, one that is based on what is needed to achieve established goals. When this preliminary budget exceeds available funds, consider options for additional funding, as well as the potential for creating campaign phases (spreading out costs over a longer period of time), revising strategies, and/or reducing behavior change goals. Sources of additional funding include government grants and appropriations, nonprofit organizations and foundations, advertising and media partners, coalitions, and corporations.

As mentioned earlier, the country's government increased the budget for the National Tuberculosis Control Program from US$600,000 to US$5 million. To bolster the program even further, partnerships were created with private and nonprofit organizations as well. Important international partners included the Pan American Health Organization, which provided technical support and training, and USAID, which supported the communication strategy development and collaboration with international pharmaceutical companies to help ensure a sufficient drug supply.

Step 10: Plan for Implementation and Campaign Management

For some, this implementation plan *is* the marketing plan, because it outlines who will do what, when, and for how much, including partners and their roles. It functions as a concise working document to share and track planned efforts. It provides a mechanism to ensure that all involved do what is intended, on time, and within budgets. Most commonly, these plans represent a minimum of one-year activities and, ideally, two or three years.

Summary

Marketing planning is a systematic process, and the 10-step model presented in this chapter is the recommended framework for developing a strategic social marketing plan. It begins with clarifying the plan's purpose and focus. It moves on to analyzing the current situation and environment, identifying target audiences, establishing marketing objectives and goals, and understanding your target audience's position. It then determines a desired positioning for the offer; designs a strategic marketing mix (the Four Ps); and develops evaluation, budget, and implementation plans. Although the process appears sequential, it is more accurately described as iterative in nature, with components drafted, and then adjusted, based on findings or decisions in subsequent steps.

> **NOTE**: To download a free electronic version of a planning document that walks you through each of these 10 steps in more detail, go to www.socialmarketingservice.com and click on Planning Worksheets.

Endnotes

[1] The Global Fund. "Stopping Tuberculosis in Peru." Retrieved April 28, 2008 from http://www.theglobalfund.org/en/in_action/peru/tb1/; F. Llanos-Zavalaga, P. Poppe, Y. Tawfik, and C. Church-Balin, "The Role of Communication in Peru's Fight Against Tuberculosis," Health Communication Partnership, September 2004, p. 13.

[2] WHO. "Worldwide Efforts to Confront Tuberculosis Are Making Progress But Too Slowly." Press release March 17, 2008, Geneva. Retrieved April 18, 2008 from http://www.who.int/tb/en/.

[3] WHO. Tuberculosis Fact Sheet. Retrieved April 18, 2008 from http://www.who.int/mediacentre/factsheets/fs104/en/print.html.

[4] A more detailed version of this case is scheduled to be published in 2009 in a book with the working title *Social Marketing for Public Health: Global Trends and Success Stories* by Cheng, Kotler, and Lee. Jones and Bartlett Publishers.

[5] F. Llanos-Zavalaga, et al., op. cit., p. 13.

[6] Health a Key to Prosperity: Success Stories in Developing Countries. "Peru set to halve new TB cases every 10 years." Retrieved April 11, 2008 from http://www.who.int/inf-new-tuber1.htm.

[7] F. Llanos-Zavalaga, et al., op. cit., p. 2 ; WHO. "Peru set to halve new TB cases every 10 years."

[8] F. Llanos-Zavalaga, et al., ibid.

[9] F. Llanos-Zavalaga, et al., ibid.

[10] Project Smart. (n.d.). Smart Goals. Retrieved August 11, 2007 from http://www.projectsmart.co.uk/smart-goals.html.

[11] F. Llanos-Zavalaga, et al., ibid, p. 7.

[12] WHO. "Peru set to halve new TB cases every 10 years."

10

The Public Sector's Role in Poverty Reduction

"If we're willing to apply the critical lessons we've learned in fighting poverty—beginning with the need to discard ideology in favor of innovation and experimentation—then I believe we can build on the progress we've made over the past ten years and drop poverty to historic lows over the next ten years."

—Michael R. Bloomberg
New York City Mayor
Speech to the Brookings Institution, August 28, 2007

In every country, the poverty problem is a national problem as well as a local problem. The resources needed to reduce poverty are in the hands of the public sector (government agencies), the nonprofit sector (NGOs and other civil organizations), and the private (business) sector. The institutions in each sector have to define their respective roles as potential poverty-fighting agencies. The three sectors must partner and integrate their separate efforts to get more synergy in the outcomes. It is in the partnership work of these sectors where the true key to poverty reduction is to be found.

In the 1960s, countries relied mainly on governments to reduce poverty. In most countries, this did little to help. In the 1970s to mid-1990s, nonprofit organizations began to engage in the task. This too did not lead to significant poverty reduction. Then, in the '90s and into the first decade of the 21st century, the private sector—especially multinational corporations—came to occupy a prominent center of power in the economic, financial, and political world. Some businesses became engaged in poverty reduction and saw some encouraging results. But the contributions of the three sectors working independently did not greatly reduce poverty.

In this chapter, we take a closer look at the role that government can play in addressing the poverty problem. We examine the role played by three different governments—the United States, China, and Bangladesh—and discuss their successes and challenges. We begin with this chapter's case story, featuring poverty reduction in New York City. Note as you read the application of marketing principles and techniques discussed in earlier chapters, especially those of segmentation and prioritization of target populations, and the development of strategies addressing their unique barriers and motivators.

New York City: Center for Economic Opportunity

In 2006, over 350,000 *working New Yorkers* were living in poverty. Over 25% of *young adults* (ages 16 to 24) were living below the federal poverty line. And over 185,000 *young children* (ages 0 to 5) in New York City were poor, representing one out of three young children.[1]

In December 2006, Mayor Michael Bloomberg created the Center for Economic Opportunity (CEO), whose mission it is to reduce these numbers through the implementation of results-driven and innovative initiatives. Earlier that year, the mayor appointed 32 civic leaders to The New York City Commission for Economic Opportunity, charging them with devising strategies to pinpoint concrete ways in which the city could act to ensure that poor New Yorkers have the resources they need to help themselves move up and out of poverty.

By September, the commission had undertaken extensive research and presented 31 recommendations. These then inspired the development of 41 initiatives that would turn recommendations into policy and practice, coordinated by the newly formed center. The commission believed that by rewarding personal initiative and building hope for the poor, they would create a future benefiting every New Yorker.

Programs and Services

The selection process for the 41 initiatives was guided by the need for strategies that could achieve quick results and bring long-term gains. They needed to be based on best practices, new ideas, and/or expansions of existing model programs that would build human capital and improve access to and utilization of public services. This section describes a sample of initiatives that were implemented for each of the major targeted populations. As marketers, we think of these as the product offerings we want our target audiences to "buy."

For the Working Poor

The 350,000 working New Yorkers living in poverty in 2006 represented approximately 46% of poor households in New York City. Due to a lack of job skills and, for many, English-speaking skills, many working poor were not securing adequate paid jobs with growth potential. Several programs are helping to reduce these barriers:

- The *Earn More* program is available to city residents who have worked consistently for the past six months in full-time or part-time jobs paying $14 or less an hour. The program provides free personalized services to help working individuals obtain and retain higher-paying jobs and then advance in their careers (see Figure 10.1). The program provides services including a career advancement coach, English as a Second Language (ESL) classes, tutoring and assistance with obtaining a GED and associate's degree, financial counseling, and assistance with child care. There are even financial incentives for completing a qualifying training program and reaching career advancement milestones.[2]

FIGURE 10.1   A city resident, on the job, benefits through the Earn More program.

- The *NYC Training Guide* enables customers to access job training options. It lists nearly 400 training providers and

4,000 vocational training offerings, as well as prior students' course completion and job placement rates for courses that already received vouchers. In March 2009, the Training Guide will feature an innovative ratings system that provides more funding for training for jobs that require less education but offer the greatest employment prospects and wage increases. You can see the guide at www.nyc.gov/trainingguide.

For Young Adults (16 to 24 Years of Age)

Many of the young adults in New York City living below the federal poverty line are disconnected from school or work and face an uncertain future. The center supports initiatives to reduce teen pregnancy rates, engage young people in school, provide alternative education models, and increase the number of internship and job placement opportunities for these young adults:

- The *Young Adult Internship Program (YAIP)* offers participants the chance to develop essential skills for today's workforce through a combination of educational workshops, counseling, and short-term paid internships. Participants range in age from 16 to 24 and are provided an opportunity to develop important social and professional skills. YAIP operates three 14-week cycles each year and serves approximately 1,360 young adults annually who are out of school and not working. The goal of the program is to reconnect youth to one or more of three outcomes: work, advanced training, or education.

- The *Office of Multiple Pathways to Graduation* initiative targets the approximately half (48%) of all incoming freshmen who are likely to become overage and under-credited during high school. These students fall behind early, and once they get off track, they leave the system rapidly. This initiative has four main components:

- Learning to Work engages students in intensive employability skills development workshops.

- Transfer High Schools are small schools for overage and undercredited 16- and 17-year-olds working toward a high school diploma.

- Access GED Programs include age and culturally appropriate curricula and pathways to postsecondary training and employment.

- Young Adults Borough Centers are full-time evening academic programs that operate in existing schools.[3]

For Young Children (0 to 5 Years of Age)

Children born into poverty are more likely to have had late or inadequate prenatal care, and they face a higher risk of low birth weight and infant mortality. Such risk factors are strongly correlated with poverty. They make children susceptible to a host of problems that, if not addressed early on, will have negative consequences in later years. Two programs coordinated by the center address this:

- The *Nurse-Family Partnership* seeks to improve the health, well-being, and self-sufficiency of low-income first-time parents and their children through regular home visits. The objective is to have 60% of clients enrolled by the sixteenth week of pregnancy and the remainder enrolled by the twenty-eighth week. Registered nurses make an average of two visits per month during the pregnancy, and until the infant's second birthday[4] (see Figure 10.2).

FIGURE 10.2   An NFP Nurse Home Visitor completes her visit checklist with her client.

- The *Child Care Tax Credit*, signed into law in 2007, assists low-income families (earning $30,000 annually or less) with the cost of child care for children under the age of 4. Campaign posters in both Spanish and English appear in bus shelters and phone kiosks in low-income communities. The approach is evidence-based, showing that former welfare recipients with young children are 60% more likely to remain employed after two years if they receive help paying for child care.[5]

> **Evaluation: Holding Programs Accountable**
>
> As of December 2007, approximately 100,000 New Yorkers were benefiting from the Center's programs, with 31 of the 41 initiatives implemented. As recommended by the Commission, the Center and partner agencies have identified target outcomes and performance measurement strategies. Agencies and their contractors are required to document robust client outcomes to maintain funding. Successful programs are then positioned to receive ongoing or increased public funding to serve additional participants.[6]

What Distinct and Critical Role Do Government Agencies Play in Reducing Poverty?

Governments, for the most part, are in the lead position to provide essential services that not only help people move out of poverty, but keep them from this condition in the first place. Governments at all levels—national, regional, and local—need to be counted on to contribute to vital functions:

- *Build a robust economy.* You'll read in this chapter about China's economic growth success, cutting in half the proportion of people living on less than $1 a day, down from 33% in 1990 to 16% in 2000. Policies contributing to this decrease included privatizing agriculture, locating new industries in rural areas, and inviting foreign companies to come to the country for joint ventures.

- *Protect and enhance public health and safety.* You read in Chapter 4, "Segmenting the Poverty Marketplace," that in 2005, New York City had 18% of the HIV/AIDS cases, but only 3% of the country's population. Certainly their efforts in 2007 to go from distributing 2.5 million free "Get Some" condoms per year to 39 million will help reduce the spread of this disease.

- *Provide basic infrastructures.* You've read in several chapters about how transportation-related factors can be "deal breakers" when trying to influence poverty-reduction and prevention behaviors, including taking tuberculosis medicine; getting a mosquito net; talking with someone about contraceptives at a family planning clinic; and getting new, improved seed to rural farmers in remote villages.

- *Educate children and youth.* We will certainly be counting on governments in all countries around the world if we are to reach the Millennium Development Goals presented in Chapter 2, "Examining a Barrel of Current Solutions." Recall Goal 2, achieving universal primary education, ensuring that by 2015, children everywhere, boys and girls alike, will be able to complete a full course of primary schooling. Goal 3 is to eliminate gender disparity at all levels of education by 2015.

- *Provide public assistance to those in need.* You learned in Chapter 8, "Developing a Desired Positioning and Strategic Marketing Mix," about NetMark's success story in malaria prevention. Discounted or free mosquito nets made possible by government subsidies for those who could not afford nets were an essential part of a strategy to protect nearly 15 million more people from malaria. Impressively, among the 350,000 pregnant women and children younger than 5 who received discount vouchers for insecticide-treated bed nets, more than 243,000 were redeemed.

- *Protect the environment.* Perhaps the fishermen in the Philippines you read about in Chapter 5, "Evaluating and Choosing Target Market Priorities," who are among the poorest in their society, would be thriving if the government had done more to regulate overfishing, destructive fishing, and pollution caused by commercial manufacturing establishments.

- *Offer grants and subsidies.* It is doubtful that Malawi would be the "shining needle within a haystack of gloom" you read about in Chapter 7, "Understanding Barriers, Benefits, and the Competition for Change," without the government-led fertilizer

subsidies program that produced record-breaking corn harvests and an 80% drop in child malnutrition. Malawi's success,
most believe, was the result of helping the poorest of the poor
grow more food, not relying on food supplies provided by other
countries.

The U.S. Government's Role in Poverty Reduction

When the Founding Fathers of the United States signed the Declaration of Independence, the document said that all men are created
equal and endowed with rights, and that to secure these rights, the
government is created. So it is the citizens who created the government. They created the government to serve them, to serve the common good.[7] They want government to be effective as well as efficient
in serving the public. Government employees are to be viewed as
"public servants." They are to fulfill the wishes and will of the people.
They are to be customer- (that is, citizen-) oriented. It is expected
that the servants will place the common good above self-interest.[8]

The U.S. federal government operates on a model of checks and
balances between three groups: the executive branch, the legislature,
and the judiciary. Each substructure exercises power and authority
but is checked by and in balance with the others. Each substructure
also functions in several layers, from a national level down to regional
offices, to states, and then down to city offices, towns, and villages.

In practice, government officials and citizens typically act more
out of self-interest than public interest. Government officials respond
to all kinds of pressures to serve special-interest groups. Citizen
groups and businesses groups continually influence government
bureaucrats and officials to gain special favors. Because the poor are
not organized, their needs are largely neglected until some major figure or president takes up their cause.

In the case of the federal government, power shifts take place over time between the executive, legislative, and judicial branches. A strong president such as Franklin D. Roosevelt, Lyndon B. Johnson, or Ronald Reagan can assert and push new ideas into public thinking and acceptance. Congress and the Supreme Court largely go along with this leadership. At other times, Congress dominates, either in pushing new legislation or preventing any new legislation from occurring. At still other times, the Supreme Court takes a stand on a landmark issue such as discrimination or abortion and changes the temper of the times.

With regard to the poverty issue, President Johnson took the strongest stand of all recent presidents. He declared a "War on Poverty" in his first State of the Union address on January 8, 1964 as part of his Great Society program. The U.S. national poverty rate was around 19%. The U.S. Congress obliged by passing the Economic Opportunity Act, which established the Office of Economic Opportunity (OEO) to administer federal funds locally to targeted poverty areas. The following organizations were started:

- VISTA (Volunteers in Service to America) provided employment opportunities for conscientious persons who felt they could contribute to reducing poverty. Volunteers focused on enriching educational and vocational programs for the underprivileged classes.
- Job Corps served low-income U.S. citizens between the ages of 16 and 24. They received academic, vocational, and social skills training so that they could find quality jobs and career paths and attain a degree of independence.
- Head Start was designed to reduce poverty by providing preschool children from low-income families with ways to meet their social, emotional, health, nutritional, and psychological needs.
- Legal Services set up 269 local legal-services programs to secure equal access to justice by providing civil legal assistance to those who might not be able to afford it.

- Community Action Programs were established in different communities to provide a variety of services to help low-income people.

The poverty rate, which was 19% when the War on Poverty was launched in 1964, fell to around 11% in the following decade. Yet poverty fell out of favor as a concern in subsequent administrations. In the last few years it has hovered at 12 to 13% and is now trending clearly upward.

The fact is that the poverty rate varies considerably between urban and rural areas, between different regions of the country, and between different age, racial, ethnic, and gender groups. For example, 30% of African-American minors are living below the poverty threshold. The United States in 2006 had the highest child poverty rate (22%) of any country in the developed world. The United States ranks 16th on the Human Poverty Index, surpassed only by Ireland and Italy. Clearly, the richest nation in the world is not serving all its people.

Each state and city in the United States has set up its own poverty-reduction programs. Wide experimentation has gone on, with different approaches and solutions resulting, as illustrated in the case story about New York City's efforts to determine priority poverty segments. Each U.S. community should consider doing this and choose where its poverty-fighting resources will do the most good.

The Chinese Government's Role

Consider the case of China, whose government The World Bank has acknowledged as the world's most successful poverty-reducing institution. In contrast to the United States, whose government has waged a War on Poverty on only a few occasions, China's government has made the War on Poverty a priority. Within just a decade, it cut in half the proportion of its people living on less than $1 a day: 33% in

1990, and down to 16% in 2000.[9] In population size, that is equal to about 150 million people brought out of extreme poverty.

China's success becomes even more impressive when contrasted with Russia's failure. One such contrast compared China's average economic growth rate of over 10% during the 1990s with Russia's average annual rate of decline of 5.6%.[10] At the end of the 1990s, the two opposing slopes made the real income of the Chinese equal to that of the Russians.

The Chinese government believed that its record-breaking economic growth was mainly responsible for its historic poverty-reduction accomplishment. The World Bank says that it was Russia's continuous economic decline that led to just as historic a poverty increase, said to be the largest in the history of world poverty during normal times.

In analyzing China's economic miracle, it is instructive to look at its segmentation of the sources of its economic development. There were four significant segments. The first was the *agricultural* segment. The reform that the government central authority introduced in this segment was the movement away from its "commune or collective system" of agricultural production and into what it called the "individual responsibility system" of production. This was effectively a privatization strategy, although only partially, because land ownership by an individual farmer was still not allowed. The government did eliminate the agricultural land tax. The economic gains from increased production went to individual farmers. Hundreds of millions of farmers and their families enjoyed the bonanza, and the new system gained immediate widespread support.

The second significant segment was *industrial enterprises*. The Chinese government opted to locate new industries more in rural areas and less in urban locations. This was done partly to discourage the vast migration of rural people to the urban areas. This was also done to locate industry closer to many of the natural resources, such as iron ore, coal, and bauxite. The central leadership believed that this strategy would help "reduce the social upheaval that inevitably accompanies industrialization."[11] Today, China is moving some of its urban-based industries back to rural areas to take advantage of lower labor costs.

Millions of new enterprises were allowed to start business in rural townships and villages. Because townships and villages were small markets, it was relatively easy to stimulate competition. Within a short period, strong competition for success prevailed. Accountability and transparency, two governance criteria, were also easier to obtain. In the townships and villages, practically everyone knew one another and knew what was going on. People knew if jobs were being created and if incomes were increasing. They also knew about and were ready to correct wrongdoings.

The third critical segment was *joint-venture businesses*. This required attracting foreign investors. The Chinese government wasted no time in inviting foreign companies to come to the country for joint ventures. It set up the necessary credible financial and legal infrastructures to get foreign investors interested. China put into place an effective securities and exchange commission, bank regulations, investment incentive laws, and other safety nets.

The central government continues to aggressively promote the country to foreign investors by progressively liberalizing and even scrapping restrictions. For example, in December 2004, China opened its retail doors to foreign retailers without the need for them to first look around for a joint-venture partner.[12] As a consequence, a record number of foreign companies came. Among the emerging economies, China quickly became the recipient of the largest foreign direct investments in the world.[13]

Fourth, China segmented its poverty marketplace by *geographic* areas to tackle the poverty problem. The coastal areas showed the fastest economic growth. The highest poverty reduction took place in this area of China. At the other extreme were the poor in northwestern regions. The poverty problem here was twofold. This area had the highest human and income poverty index, and it also had the provinces where the highest inequality existed. China's model of poverty reduction via economic growth had not worked as well here. This led to the "out migration" from the poor regions into the coastal areas, especially into China's three richest urban centers: Shanghai, Beijing, and Tianjin. To discourage this flight to the coastal cities, China is laying plans to build at least four new cities.

In addition to these four segmentation approaches, another strategy is noteworthy. The central government also removed the Communist-based system of social security. Data from the Ministry of Labor and Social Security indicated that today health insurance covers only 14% of the population, only 8% has unemployment insurance, and only 16% gets pensions.[14] A *Wall Street Journal* article reported that in the cities, a beggar can earn 10 times the amount that a northwestern rural farmer earns.[15] Clearly China still has a long way to go in building in safety nets for its still large-in-numbers poor population.

The Bangladesh Government's Role

Bangladesh, an evolved democracy of 133 million people, achieved an impressive record of moving its poor population out of extreme poverty after its independence in 1971 and over the next two decades.

Near the start of the new millennium, the Bangladesh government decided to get actively involved with its poverty problem.[16] It requested the assistance of the World Bank to craft its poverty reduction program. The government antipoverty program decided to give special focus to four "vulnerable" segments:

- Rural poor women, especially those who are victims of different kinds of oppression, including rape and other sexual abuse, acid throwing, dowry, and illegal trafficking.

- Children of impoverished families, especially street children, and children in high-risk work. Examples are male children working as bus helpers, porters, rickshaw-van pullers, tannery workers, construction workers, lathe machine workers, and battery factory workers, and female children working as maidservants, brickfield laborers, bangle factory workers, and child sex workers.
- Poor people with disabilities and physical handicaps.
- Impoverished ethnic, indigenous and cultural minority, and religious groups.

Aside from the vulnerable segments, the government's poverty-reduction program specified the rest of the poverty market in spatial terms. There were seven of these: the rural poor, the urban poor, the poor in wetland areas, the poor in areas surrounded by water, the poor in hilly areas, the poor in coastal areas and islands, and boat and "floating" migrant poor.

The segments were "naturally occurring." There is a distinct practical advantage to segmenting the poverty marketplace in this way. First, the segments are readily identifiable and physically accessible. It is relatively easy to locate them in the country's map. Second, it takes no great effort to communicate with them. Their communication media habits are known or not difficult to understand.

The Bangladesh government's antipoverty program remains a work in progress. The country at times is hit by major floods and other disasters, requiring emergency aid from other countries. But it is trying to lift as many people out of poverty as its meager resources permit.

Overall View of the Government's Role in Poverty Reduction

Clearly governments play a different role in different countries with respect to active involvement in trying to reduce poverty. Most governments pin their ultimate hope on building a *growing economy*. China well illustrates how economic growth helps decrease the number of people living in poverty. But economic growth does not deliver its benefits equally to all inhabitants of a country. The rich tend to get richer, and the middle class grows a little, and the working poor and the very poor get less benefit from the growth. Government must compensate for the failure of economic growth to distribute the benefits in the best possible way. Governments use taxes and regulations to force the flow of some benefits to the poor.

In addition to economic growth, less-developed countries depend on *foreign aid, public and private charity*, and *emergency relief* to help their poor. Their governments must play an active role in courting foreign aid from international agencies such as the World Bank and the International Monetary Fund (IMF), as well as from individual countries such as the United States, China, and Russia.

The United Nations has developed a Human Poverty Index for measuring poverty in developing countries. This index uses three measures:

- Probability at birth of not surviving to age 40
- Adult illiteracy rate
- Unweighted average of the population who lack sustainable access to an improved water source and children who are underweight for their age

Among the developing countries, the ones with the most poverty on these measures included Chad, Zimbabwe, and Ethiopia.

Governments in developed countries have largely introduced safety net systems and "welfare state" legislation to make sure that the poor are supported in some way. They also have offered training and financial assistance to increase the poor's chances of escaping from poverty. The United Nations recently started publishing the Human Poverty Index for industrial countries. It focuses on economic deprivation in four dimensions:

- The percentage of people likely to die before age 60
- The percentage of people whose ability to read and write is far from adequate
- The proportion of the population with a disposable income of less than 50% of the median
- The proportion of long-term unemployed (12 months or more)

Sweden has the lowest overall incidence of *human poverty*, followed by Norway, the Netherlands, Finland, and Denmark, with a 6 to 8% index. Of the top 19 developed countries, the United States ranks 17th, Ireland ranks 18th, and Italy ranks 19th.[17]

Social Marketing in the Public Sector

How Does the Social Marketing Approach Differ from Current Traditional Approaches?

The premise of this book is that the social marketing approach to reducing the number of people living in poverty has been missing from the mix of traditional solutions—and that this is true in all three sectors. Table 10.1 describes typical solutions for the public sector and contrasts them with potential social marketing solutions. In some cases, the social marketing solution should be added to the mix of current strategies. In others, program administrators should consider replacing the current strategy to create a greater impact.

TABLE 10.1   Adding the Social Marketing Solution to the Mix for Public-Sector Agencies

Poverty-Related Issue	Traditional Solution	Social Marketing Solution
Hunger	Provide food stamp programs that subsidize food for low- and no-income people, with benefits distributed by individual states.	Offer food stamp recipients menus, recipes, and classes on cooking with fruits and vegetables from the local farmers' market.

Poverty-Related Issue	Traditional Solution	Social Marketing Solution
HIV/AIDS	Provide testing for HIV/AIDS at community health centers, during regular business hours, five days a week, with clients required to return for results in two weeks.	Offer free rapid HIV/AIDS testing in gay bathhouses Friday and Saturday nights, where public health staff provide results in 30 minutes. Also provide counseling.
Agricultural productivity	Provide cash subsidies to farmers who can't produce enough crops to make ends meet.	Provide new and improved seeds and hold workshops on ways to increase agricultural productivity.
Tuberculosis	Provide tuberculosis testing and drug treatments only at special clinics, often not located in the same village as the patient.	Integrate tuberculosis testing and drug dispensing into existing, conveniently located primary healthcare networks. Offer house calls to those who can't travel.

What Does It Take to Adopt a Social Marketing Approach?

Several attitudes and commitments are essential to adopting a social marketing approach. Thankfully, most are more a matter of will than ability:

- *A willingness to prioritize market segments.* People working in public-service agencies often find it difficult, if not painful, to target resources to one or only a few market segments. They feel responsible for serving all citizens equally. But different market segments need different interventions. Developing and successfully disseminating a variety of unique programs is necessary and possible.

- *A willingness to focus on single, simple, doable behaviors.* It is also difficult for program managers to pick only a few behaviors to promote at a time. The inclination and desire is to present "all the helpful" behaviors that the target market should do. The problem is that costs are associated with adopting these behaviors, and the more behaviors you sell, the higher the adoption price.

- A *willingness to spend time and resources on market research.* Often when an agency knows what citizens it wants to influence and what behaviors it wants them to adopt, the agency just wants to "get going." Making the effort to find out what the adopters think about the behavior might seem like a luxury you can't afford. However, we encourage you to consider the greater costs of implementing a program that will likely fail or have disappointing results if it does not offer the value the market wants in exchange for the price of adoption. Only the adopters can tell you if it will.

- A *willingness to develop products, enhance services, and improve distribution channels.* Social marketing is more than a communication strategy. We believe that if you develop a great product, price it fairly, and make it available at convenient locations, you will spend less time and money communicating about it. Free word of mouth and positive publicity will do some of the heavy lifting for you.

- A *willingness to establish quantifiable goals and measure performance.* One of the benefits of a social marketing approach is that you will be working to influence increases in a specified behavior—one that is measurable. The good news is that you should be able to determine levels of behavior change and then compare these with targeted goals. The bad news for some is that this increases performance accountability.

Summary

Every government needs to craft an antipoverty program, fund it adequately, and revise it when new factors come into play. The program should be done in partnership with key civil organizations and with representatives from the business sector. Getting a commitment from all three parties is a necessary and desirable step if the poverty problem is to be actively addressed. We have seen how New York

City discerned three poverty groups and created and aligned different organizations to assist these groups. We also reviewed the impressive efforts of China and Bangladesh to help reduce poverty in their
respective countries. We concluded by contrasting traditional
poverty-reduction solutions in the public sector and social marketing
solutions. We described solutions that should be included in the mix.
These might even replace current solutions.

Endnotes

[1] Center for Economic Opportunity: Strategy and Implementation Report.
Michael R. Bloomberg, Mayor. December 2007. Statistics for the young adults
is based on 2000 census.

[2] Center for Economic Opportunity, Earn More Program. Retrieved May 15,
2008 from http://www.nyc.gov/html/ceo/html/programs/earnmore.shtml.

[3] Ibid.

[4] Ibid.

[5] Ibid.

[6] Center for Economic Opportunity: Strategy and Implementation Report.
Michael R. Bloomberg, Mayor. December 2007.

[7] See, for example, Willa Marie Bruce, "Administrative Morality," in Jay Shafritz
(editor), *Defining Public Administration* (Boulder, CO: Westview Press, 2000),
pp. 407–415.

[8] This philosophy is elaborated on in Philip Kotler and Nancy Lee, *Marketing in
the Public Sector: A Roadmap for Improved Performance* (Upper Saddle River,
NJ: Pearson, 2007).

[9] United Nations Development Programme (UNDP), *Human Development
Report 2003—Millennium Development Goals: A Compact Among Nations to
End Human Poverty* (New York: Oxford University Press, 2003), p. 73.

[10] Joseph Stiglitz, *Globalization and Its Discontents* (New York: W.W. Norton,
2002), Chapter 7.

[11] Ibid., p. 185. This strategy came from the consulting work of Stiglitz and Kenneth Arrow, who were hired as advisers by the Chinese government during this
period of the country's transition to a market economy.

[12] The *Wall Street Journal Asia*, December 14, 2004, p. A8.

[13] Stiglitz, op. cit. Stiglitz noted that in 1990, "China's net private capital inflows
were $80 billion. By 1999, its capital inflows had soared to $41 billion, more
than 10 times the amount of money attracted by Russia in that same year."

[14] The *Wall Street Journal Asia*, December 7, 2004, p. A1.

[15] Ibid.

[16] Government of the People's Republic of Bangladesh, *Poverty Reduction Strategy Paper: Status Report*. July 14, 2004. Sourced from http://poverty. worldbank.org/files/Bangladesh_PRSP_Prog_Rep.pdf. Viewed December 22, 2004.

[17] http://en.wikipedia.org/wiki/Human_Poverty_Index.

11

The Nonprofit Sector's Role in Poverty Reduction

"The nonprofits are ... dedicated to 'doing good.'

"But they also realize that good intentions are no substitute for organization and leadership, for accountability, performance, and results.

"Those require management, and that, in turn, begins with the organization's mission."

—Peter Drucker

We now turn our focus to the role played by the nonprofit sector, composed of civil organizations and philanthropists contributing to the public interest and reducing poverty. Discussions include the nature of nonprofit organizations (NPOs) and their role in poverty reduction, and a summary of the activities of major leading international organizations. We conclude with inspiring examples of some within-country nonprofit organizations dedicated to reducing poverty.

What Are Nonprofit Organizations, and Why Are They Necessary?

Nonprofit organizations (also called civil organizations or non-government organizations [NGOs]) stand in the middle between for-profit organizations and government organizations, performing functions that the other two major sectors do not provide or do not provide adequately. The collection of NPOs is sometimes called the Civil Society. The Centre for Civil Society of the London School of Economics provides this definition:

> "Civil society refers to the arena of uncoerced collective action around shared interests, purposes and values. In theory, its institutional forms are distinct from those of the state, family and market... Civil society commonly embraces a diversity of spaces, actors and institutional forms, varying in their degree of formality, autonomy and power. Civil societies are often populated by organizations such as registered charities, development nongovernment organizations, community groups, women's organizations, faith-based organizations, professional associations, trades unions, self-help groups, social movements, business associations, coalitions and advocacy groups."[1]

Usually, a society has many pressing issues that neither the government nor private for-profit organizations are handling. The vacuum is often best filled by NPOs, frequently providing the most effective voices for the concerns of ordinary people, as well as needed resources. NPOs claim that when governments finally pay attention to a social problem, it is often because civil organizations have led the way and put pressure on government. NPO pressure groups play a role as "trustees for the poor."[2] They prod government to act and be accountable. And they spread their passion and expertise, as you will read in the following case story.

Community Emergency Response and Disaster
Mitigation in Central America:
A Case Story from World Vision[3]

World Vision is one of the largest international Christian relief and development organizations in the world, with a budget in 2007 of $2.6 billion. Its stated goal is "working for the well-being of all people, especially children." It was founded in 1950 by Dr. Bob Pierce, who later founded the evangelical organization Samaritan's Purse. World Vision began by caring for orphans and other needy children in South Korea. Then it expanded throughout Asia and, eventually, into more than 90 countries. It added larger issues of community development and advocacy for the poor as part of its basic mission to help children and their families build a sustainable future. World Vision contributes to people's needs in five major areas: emergency relief, education, health care, economic development, and promotion of justice. It helps communities recognize the resources within themselves and carry out their own development projects in healthcare, agriculture production, water projects, education, microenterprise development, advocacy, and other community programs.

Hurricane Mitch, which hit Central America in 1998, was so devastating that within a few days Central America's economic development was set back by about 20 years. Gross Domestic Product (GDP) was reduced by an estimated 60% in countries with already fragile economies. The impact of natural disasters such as this is the greatest on the poor because it increases already marginalized nutrition, reduces resistance to disease, interferes with children's school attendance, increases the workload of women and children, and damages infrastructures that then affect productivity and growth. Perhaps the most tragic aspect of the hurricane was that much of the damage would not have occurred if appropriate disaster mitigation efforts had taken place prior to the storm.

Although Hurricane Mitch was a massive disaster, it brought to light the issue of preparation. In 2001, USAID funded the World Vision Central America Mitigation Initiative to improve disaster preparedness, risk reduction, and response initiatives, beginning in Honduras.

The key premise of disaster mitigation is that disasters do not just happen; they result from failures of preparation and development, which increase vulnerability to hazards such as hurricanes. Although nothing can keep most natural disasters from occurring, several actions (desired behaviors, as we have been referring to them in this book) can minimize the impact of annual emergencies:

- Implement proper flood-control measures, including watershed protection and reforestation
- Ensure adherence to building codes
- Install early-warning systems
- Conduct risk assessments, and employ best practices for risk management
- Train communities in basic first aid, evacuation, and rescue techniques

Many communities are aware that these actions need to be taken to reduce disaster impact, but they do not always or often have the human and financial resources necessary to implement them.

World Vision's Community Emergency Response and Disaster Mitigation (CERDM) program was designed to strengthen capacity at the community level by providing training to key individuals in each of the essential areas of disaster management. Armed with the skills taught in this program, communities stand a better chance of reducing the effects of many disasters and possibly even preventing some. This means that rather than seeing all or part of their hard-earned personal and public capital destroyed, communities can use accumulated capital to build better lives for themselves and their children.

World Vision International (WVI) Honduras applied for and was granted funds from USAID to carry out the Central America Mitigation Initiative's (CAMI) activities. Working with communities within World Vision (WV) Area Development Programs (ADPs), local government, national emergency structure, and WVI resources, the Honduras National Office was able to establish a viable preparedness and mitigation program in 13 ADPs (224 communities). The needs in the Latin America and Caribbean (LAC) region, however, extend far beyond what is currently being carried out.

Following the Honduran program, in 2003 WVI extended the scheme to Ecuador, Nicaragua, Guatemala, and Colombia. Thirty communities were included in Ecuador, 37 in Nicaragua, 21 in Guatemala, and 18 in Columbia. Major activities emphasized capacity building for communities in risk management and planning. Eight main workshops were held on the following topics:

- Organization of local emergency committees and rapid-response teams
- Basic concepts of risk management

- Damage assessment and needs analysis

- Risk and resource mapping (see Figure 11.1)

- Basic first aid (see Figure 11.2)

- Evacuation and rescue

- Mitigation measures

- Early-warning systems

A school safety and disasters project also helped establish a culture of preparedness and mitigation among children and adolescent boys and girls attending 30 schools—10 each in Ecuador, Nicaragua, and Honduras.

The CERDM program has been formally evaluated at regular intervals to determine its efficacy. In 2007, a final report on the CERDM program presented encouraging results, with 291 communities in Ecuador, Nicaragua, and Honduras having created emergency response teams and disaster-mitigation processes that were self-sufficient at the grassroots level. Participants reported that the active and skill-based nature of the training workshops provided tangible evidence for them of what they were learning. They particularly appreciated the skills they gained that were concrete in nature, including first-aid and evacuation strategies. And the community-level nature of the project is helping to ensure the sustainability of inputs, with local volunteer committees trained as part of the community's development activities. For the first time in some areas, local government authorities saw community groups as legitimate partners in disaster response.

In Ecuador the impact of the CERDM activities and capacity building in the communities has been so positive that locals even decided to rename the program "Preparing Ourselves for Life."

FIGURE 11.1 Risk map training in Guatemala

Source: World Vision

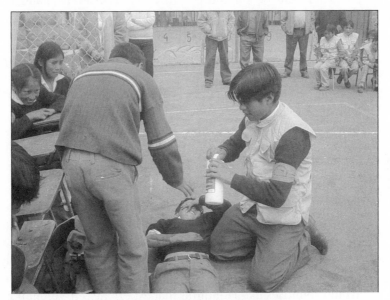

FIGURE 11.2 School first aid training in Ecuador

Source: World Vision

What Distinct and Critical Role Do NPOs Play in Reducing Poverty?

As defined by their mission statements, NPOs exist primarily to provide programs and services that have bottom-line benefit to others versus their shareholders. These programs and services might not be provided by local, state, or federal entities or might not be provided at levels that meet (all) citizen needs. Many think of their role as that of a safety net, catching citizens who fall through the cracks and ensuring the availability of programs and services not seen as mission-critical, even appropriate, for government agencies to offer. Their contributions to poverty alleviation and reduction take many forms:

- *Funding.* NPOs provide unique funding resources such as *microfinancing* for additional livestock; *grants* for medical research or for local agencies to carry out disease interventions, including ones for tuberculosis and malaria; and *cash* for medicines, vaccinations, or temporary food and shelter. How different would life be for those with HIV/AIDS in Thailand had they not received microloans for small-business ventures from the Population and Community Development Association?

- *Resources/supplies.* These contributions include a wide range of goods, such as mosquito nets, medicines for river blindness, clothing, food, fertilizers, improved seeds, and home birth delivery kits. How many more malaria cases would there be in Africa alone if the Academy for Educational Development (AED) had not been successful in forming partnerships that resulted in nearly 15 million more people being protected from malaria by insecticide-treated bed nets?

- *Direct services.* Many of these organizations' basic missions are to provide services such as alcohol and drug counseling, job training, tutoring, temporary shelters and meals for the homeless, group homes for orphans of HIV/AIDS, and free telephone counseling services for issues such as tobacco cessation. Would countries like Honduras that experiences frequent if not annual hurricanes be as prepared for next year's potential storms if World Vision had not provided training to reduce the effects of these inevitable disasters?

- *Expertise.* Often these organizations have developed strong areas of expertise in well-defined techniques such as emergency preparedness, agricultural and livestock productivity, disease prevention and intervention, water sanitizing systems, and family planning. Who would have helped women like Gulbibi in Pakistan if Population Services International (PSI) had not developed and launched the Green Star Network, which provided medical training, technical support for staff, and information for pharmacists when communicating with their customers?

- *Volunteers.* These organizations are "masters" at inspiring, recruiting, training, and organizing others to contribute their time and talents to efforts such as disaster relief, building homes, helping build check dams, and rescuing victims of a natural disaster. What would the incidence of polio be in the world today without volunteer Rotarians joining the teams of people who immunized more than 2 billion children around the world?

- *Advocacy.* With well-coordinated efforts, well-integrated messages, and considerable passion, NPOs have been successful at advocating for poverty-related issues ranging from subsidized housing to better systems for tracking children in foster care, to meeting the needs of special-needs students. How much progress would we have made on many poverty indicators if the UN had not developed and declared Millennium Development Goals, working to hold countries accountable to quantifiable, measurable goals, seen as key to poverty reduction?

- *Public awareness.* In some cases NPOs are the only ones that can provide the marketing expertise and garner the needed resources to ensure adequate visibility for poverty-related campaigns that need public attention. How effective would an advertising campaign for high school dropout prevention have been, and how much visibility would it have had, without the Ad Council garnering pro bono support from top advertising agencies and strong media partners?

What Important NPOs Are Operating in the Poverty Area?

Tens of thousands of NPOs around the world are dedicated to helping those in need. In developing countries, the rate of increase in the number of indigenous NPOs is said to exceed the rate in first-world countries.[4] The change is not only in numbers but also in the scope and character of civil society activities and projects. Many NPOs start as charity-based relief organizations. More in the developing world are now into educational reform programs, rural development, health and nutrition, environmental protection, human rights, and opposing corruption. The following sections describe several major NPOs.[5] Other sections have mentioned other key organizations, such as the UN, the World Bank, the World Health Organization, and World Vision.

CARE

CARE (Cooperative for Assistance and Relief Everywhere) is one of the world's largest international relief and humanitarian organizations, with a staff exceeding 12,000 persons, most of them coming from the nation in which they work. CARE was founded in 1945 to provide assistance to European survivors of World War II through CARE packages sent by friends and families. CARE's continues to provide emergency relief during and after disasters, but today CARE focuses more on addressing underlying causes of poverty as related to health, education, and economic development. CARE's antipoverty campaigns include the World Hunger Campaign, education, HIV/AIDS, Victories Over Poverty, and CARE for the Child. CARE is also an advocate for human-rights polices.

Bill & Melinda Gates Foundation

The Gates Foundation is the largest transparently operated charitable foundation in the world. Founded in 2000, it doubled in size as a result of Warren Buffett's promised gifts in 2006. It has an endowment of US$38.7 billion. The Foundation's primary aims are to enhance healthcare and reduce extreme poverty globally, and, in the United States, to expand educational opportunities and access to information technology. The Gates Foundation runs three programs. The Global Health Program supports eradicating polio, supports HIV/AIDS research, and promotes and distributes vaccines for children. The Global Development Program supports microlending, agricultural development and green revolution, global libraries, and aid to victims of disasters. The United States Program supports Internet access in U.S. libraries, computer science research, charter schools, predominantly black colleges, and scholarship programs for poor students.

Population Services International (PSI)

PSI is a Washington, D.C.-based nonprofit social marketing organization that works with the private sector to address the health problems of low-income and vulnerable populations in more than 60 developing countries. It runs programs in the areas of malaria, reproductive health, child survival, and HIV. PSI promotes products, services, and healthy behavior that enable low-income and vulnerable people to lead healthier lives. It encourages products and services to be sold at subsidized prices to motivate commercial sector involvement. PSI is the leading nonprofit social marketing organization in the world. It was founded in 1970 and spent its first 15 years promoting family planning. It started promoting oral rehydration therapy in 1985 and HIV prevention through abstinence, fidelity, and condoms in 1988. PSI added work on malaria and safe water in the 1990s. PSI estimates that its programs prevented 218,000 HIV infections, 6.7 million unintended pregnancies, more than 140,000 child deaths from malaria and diarrhea, and 34 million malaria episodes.

Plan International

Plan, founded over 70 years ago, is a nonreligious, nonpolitical, child-centered development charity with a staff of over 6,000 worldwide and over 50,000 volunteers. It works in 46 countries to provide programs to 1.3 million children and their families. It raised in excess of $540 million in 2006. Plan addresses health, education, shelter, and livelihood issues in the communities in which it operates. Plan's mission is to achieve lasting improvements for children living in poverty in developing countries. Plan encourages benefactors to sponsor individual children and correspond with them to create a personal bond. The sponsors can see what their money is going toward, and they know that it is properly spent. Donations are used to finance projects that benefit the entire community in which the child lives; they are not given directly to the child. This offers the opportunity to provide school and health services to the sponsor child, as well as his or her community.

Doctors Without Borders (Also Known by Its French Name, Médecins Sans Frontières)

MSF is a humanitarian-aid nongovernment organization known for its work in developing countries and war-torn regions facing endemic disease. People in a war-torn area often develop diseases and face epidemics due to malnutrition and/or unsanitary water. MSF personnel work to restore food supplies and sanitary water, among other things. They provide healthcare and medical training to populations in more than 70 countries. MSF was created in 1971 by French doctors. It has an international board of directors located in Geneva, Switzerland. MSF recruits annually about 3,000 doctors, nurses, midwives, and logisticians for projects. MSF's annual budget is about $400 million, with private donors providing about 80%; government and corporate donations provide the rest.

Habitat for Humanity International (HFHI)

Habitat is an international, ecumenical Christian, nonprofit organization devoted to building "simple, decent, and affordable" housing. Homes are built using volunteer labor and are sold at no profit. Millard and Linda Fuller founded Habitat in 1976. The international headquarters are located in Atlanta, Georgia. Habitat supports and promotes the activities of local, independent affiliate chapters, which initiate and manage all construction, mortgages, and homeowner selection. By 2004, Habitat had built 50,000 houses in the United States and over 175,100 abroad in over 100 countries, sheltering over 1 million people. Homeowner families are chosen according to their need; their ability to repay the nonprofit, affordable mortgage; and their willingness to work in partnership with Habitat. Habitat for Humanity does not discriminate according to race, religion, or ethnic group. Homeowners are usually expected to put approximately 500 hours of "sweat equity" into their own or other project homes. Former President Jimmy Carter has been a high-profile advocate of and participant in Habitat.

Save the Children

First established in 1919, Save the Children is a leading international organization helping children in need around the world. Its aim is to improve the lives of children through education, healthcare, and economic opportunities, as well as emergency aid in cases of natural disasters, war, and conflict. Members of the International Save the Children Alliance sponsor programs to bring quality education to 8 million children living in countries affected by conflict. Save the Children has also sponsored legislation on the rights of children to be protected from child labor and also has campaigned against the use of child soldiers.

Academy for Educational Development (AED)

AED is a nonprofit organization working globally to improve education, health, civil society, and economic development. AED operates more than 250 programs in the United States and 150 other countries around the world. Founded in 1961 to provide technical assistance to U.S. managers of higher education, AED subsequently added instructional technology, education reform, and civil society projects around the world. It promotes health in developing countries through environmental communication, social marketing, and other disciplines. Its projects in Africa include controlling malaria, educating girls, improving children's health literacy, and preventing HIV/AIDS.

Mercy Corps

Mercy Corps is a nongovernmental private voluntary organization. It was founded in 1979 as Save the Refugees Funds to help Cambodian refugees. In 1982, Mercy expanded to other countries and was renamed Mercy Corps. It adopted the broader mission of finding long-term solutions to hunger and poverty. Its income in 2006 was $205 million. It allocates more than 90% directly to programs.

NPOs Within a Country Battle the Poverty Problem

Several indigenous NPOs located within a country have had a major positive impact on poverty. This section describes two NPOs—one in Bangladesh and the other in India.

Bangladesh's BRAC (Bangladesh Rural Advancement Committee)

Preoccupied with serious post-independence problems of political and economic instability, the Bangladesh government initially handed over the bulk of the poverty alleviation job to civil society organizations. The civil society that made a name here was what became one of the world's largest NGOs—Bangladesh Rural Advancement Committee (BRAC).

BRAC was founded in 1972 by Fazle Hasan Abed after the Bangladesh Liberation War; it was set up as a relief organization assisting and resettling returning refugees from India. In nine months, BRAC rebuilt 14,000 homes and several hundred boats for fishermen. Medical centers were opened, and other essential services were ensured. At the end of 1972, BRAC turned toward long-term development needs. It reorganized itself as a multifaceted development organization focusing on the empowerment of the poor and landless, particularly women and children.

Until the mid-1970s, BRAC concentrated on community development through multisectoral village development programs. These included agriculture, fisheries, cooperatives, rural crafts, adult literacy, health and family planning, vocational training for women, and construction of community centers.

In 1974, BRAC started a microcredit program. The BRAC Bank makes a great number of microloans to the poor and has experienced a very high repayment rate. BRAC organized Village Organizations to serve the poorest of the poor—the landless, small farmers, artisans, and vulnerable women. Those who own less than half an acre of land and survive by selling manual labor were regarded as BRAC's target group. BRAC provides collateral-free credit using a solidarity lending methodology, as well as obligatory savings schemes through its Village Organizations. Reaching nearly 4 million borrowers, Village Organizations provide different levels of loans to different poverty groups. Through a recent initiative, BRAC has also reached out to those who, due to extreme poverty, cannot access microfinance. BRAC defines such people suffering from extreme poverty as the "ultra poor." It has customized a program for the ultra poor that combines subsidies with enterprise development training, healthcare, social development, and asset transfer, eventually pulling the ultra poor into its mainstream microfinance program. The BRAC Bank also actively finances small and medium-sized business enterprises.

In 1979, BRAC entered the health field in a major way. It established the nationwide Oral Therapy Extension Program (OTEP), a campaign to combat diarrhea, the leading cause of the high child mortality rate in Bangladesh. Over a 10-year period, 1,200 BRAC workers went door to door to teach 12 million mothers how to prepare homemade oral saline. Bangladesh today has one of the highest rates of usage of oral rehydration. BRAC's campaign decreased child and infant mortality from 285 per thousand to 75 per thousand.

In 1996, BRAC launched its Social Development, Human Rights, and Legal Services Program. The goal was to empower women with legal rights and help them become involved with community and ward-level organizations.

In 2001, Abed pushed forward BRAC's education program. As of June 2006, BRAC had established 31,877 primary schools and 16,025 pre-primary schools enrolling nearly 3 million children, 65% of whom are girls. The schools have a dropout rate of less than 5%. BRAC established a university called BRAC University with the aim to train future leaders.

BRAC's programs today fall into four groups: economic development, education, public health, and social development. Bill Gates had this to say about BRAC:

> "BRAC has done what few others have—they have achieved success on a massive scale, bringing lifesaving health programs to millions of the world's poorest people. They remind us that even the most intractable health problems are solvable, and inspire us to match their success throughout the developing world."

Today BRAC is present in all 64 districts of Bangladesh, with over 7 million microfinance group members, 34,000 nonformal primary schools, and more than 70,000 health volunteers. The organization is 76% self-funded through its commercial enterprises, which include a dairy and food project and a chain of retail handicraft stores. In recent years, BRAC has taken its range of development interventions to Afghanistan, Sri Lanka, and several countries in Africa. As a result, BRAC is one of the world's largest nongovernment development organizations.[6]

Besides Abed's great contributions to Bangladesh through BRAC, another Bangladesh contributor has been Muhammad Yunus. He was awarded the Nobel Peace Prize in 2007 for his work in his Grameen Bank to extend credit to the poor to empower them to start a business. Yunus calls his bank a "social business" because although it is run for profit, the profit isn't maximized so that it can help the poor. Microfinance today is a worldwide practice that has benefited millions of poor people.

Yunus recently added another social cause—helping beggars give up their life of begging. The Grameen Bank launched the Struggling (Beggar) Members Program. A beggar is given a loan of $9, collateral- and interest-free. The beggar can choose the repayment schedule. The repayment must not come from money earned from begging. Each beggar is given an identity badge as evidence of the bank's support. The goal is to boost the beggar's morale. Some local shops work with the Grameen Bank and allow beggars to pick up items such as bread, toys, and candy and sell them in the village. The bank pays for these items in case of defaults. The bank provides beggars with blankets, shawls, and umbrellas on credit to be repaid as interest-free loans. As a result, some beggars have given up begging, and others have become "part-time beggars."[7]

SEWA (Self-Employed Women's Association)[8]

Ela Bhatt organized SEWA in December 1971 in Ahmadabad, India. In April 1972, she registered it as a trade union. Then in 1974, she led 4,000 self-employed women to establish the SEWA Bank as a cooperative bank.

Bhatt saw SEWA Bank as freeing poor, self-employed women from their dependence on informal moneylenders and loan sharks who charged exorbitant interest rates of as much as 10% a day. This practice had trapped the striving self-employed woman starting a small enterprise into "a downward spiral of increasing indebtedness."

The *Washington Post* quoted Bhatt as saying that her motivation for organizing SEWA as a women's movement and trade union was to empower poor women in the "truest sense." According to Bhatt, when an oppressed Indian woman joins SEWA and starts earning, she undergoes a liberating change of self-image. "For the first time, she realizes she is not just someone's wife or daughter-in-law. She's a worker, an active producer."

Bhatt's first important victory came when she challenged an old but, at that time, still enforced British law that kept women from selling their wares in public. The law allowed the police to evict such women from the premises and arrest those who resisted. In the process, the produce that these women were selling got lost, and physical violence often accompanied the eviction or arrest. The Indian Supreme Court in a landmark ruling declared that it was "women merchants' right and a city's duty to provide a separate place for workers in the informal sector to ply their trades."[9] Then, in establishing SEWA Bank as a cooperative, Bhatt believed that SEWA was enabling the same woman "to nonviolently, in the most Gandhian way, eliminate the husband's total control" over her finances. Bhatt explained that most Indian bankers treated poor, self-employed Indian women "like dirt." At home and during those times when she had savings, she had "no place to hide her savings from her husband or son." At SEWA Bank, her money was safe. Her husband or son could not withdraw from her savings account.

SEWA has an all-Indian membership of close to a million women. It represents the interests of four types of female workers:

- Hawkers, vendors, and small businesswomen such as vegetable, fruit, fish, egg, and other vendors of food items, and household goods and clothes vendors.
- Home-based workers such as weavers, potters, ready-made garment workers, women who process agricultural products, and artisans.
- Manual laborers and service providers such as agricultural laborers, construction workers, contract laborers, handcart pullers, domestic workers, and laundry workers.
- Producers and services who invest their labor and capital in carrying out their businesses. This category includes agriculture, cattle rearers, salt workers, gum collectors, and cooking and vending workers.

Here is where a noteworthy difference between civil society and the government becomes clear. By its very definition, a civil society does not have to partition the entire poverty marketplace to arrive at a segment targeting decision. But the government must start its poverty-reduction planning by partitioning the total poverty marketplace. Then it has to understand the differing priority needs of the resulting segments before proceeding to segment targeting.

The case of SEWA also shines new light on market segmentation. Bhatt and her SEWA members segmented themselves as a group of vulnerable poor women with legitimate needs, calling for assistance. Because the required assistance was not forthcoming from the government because of legal and cultural circumstances, these women formed a self-help segment that sourced the assistance they sought from among themselves and from within their organized segment members.

Social Marketing in the Nonprofit Sector

How Does the Social Marketing Approach Differ from Current Traditional Approaches?

Nonprofit organizations offering social marketing solutions to reduce poverty are probably more likely to be thought of as social enterprises, with their leadership characterized more often as entrepreneurs than administrators. They are committed to wide-scale social change and recognize that this requires innovative new products and services, delivered through new sustainable networks, often in partnership with the public and private sectors. The change begins with a commitment to influencing the behaviors of the clients they serve, offering a "hand up" in addition to or instead of a handout— "teaching a man to fish and thus feeding him for a lifetime." Table 11.1 contrasts traditional poverty-related activities of a nonprofit, with those that are oriented toward social marketing. As with the public sector, these solutions may need to be added to the mix of offerings. In other cases, they should replace existing approaches to have the most impact.

TABLE 11.1   Adding the Social Marketing Solution to the Mix for Nonprofit Organizations

Poverty-Related Issue	Traditional Solution	Social Marketing Solution
Homelessness	Provide donated clothing, temporary shelter, and meals served by volunteers.	Provide programs to achieve self-sufficiency, including job training and placement services.
Disaster relief	Send food, clothing, and other basic necessities to communities hit by natural disasters.	Offer "train the trainer" programs on disaster preparedness in local communities.
Malaria	Provide funding to distribute free mosquito nets to pregnant women.	Provide information, often face to face, that will help persuade women that the treated nets will not harm their unborn child.

Poverty-Related Issue	Traditional Solution	Social Marketing Solution
Literacy	Develop and implement campaigns to increase awareness and concern about a country's literacy rate.	Recruit and train volunteers to conduct weekly study sessions and mentor high school students and young adults to help them achieve their full potential.

What Does It Take to Adopt a Social Marketing Approach?

As may be apparent, social marketing initiatives are likely to require new and different ways of doing business for the nonprofit. Although its mission and client focus might not change, several increased efforts and resources are often required. To illustrate, we describe what it took for a nonprofit called FareStart, founded more than 15 years ago in Seattle, Washington. Its mission is to "empower homeless and disadvantaged men, women, and families to achieve self-sufficiency through life skills, job training, and employment in the food services industry."[10] FareStart makes use of the following strategies:

- *Increased effort to identify and support specific behaviors.* FareStart's focus is working with homeless and disadvantaged people who are interested in a career in the food services industry. FareStart supports them in acquiring required job skills and then securing employment.

- *Increased direct contact with clients.* FareStart offers a 16-week program that includes on-the-job training in its downtown restaurants and kitchens. These locations offer weekday lunches; a Guest Chef Night once a week, where students work with volunteer premier regional chefs to prepare and serve a three-course gourmet meal; and catering for dinners, cocktail parties, and business lunches. These programs contribute over 40% of the organization's annual operating budget.

- *Increased partnering with the private and public sectors.*
  FareStart reaches out to potential employers in the food-
  service and espresso industries on behalf of its clients. Through
  its Contract Meals program, FareStart provides nutritious
  meals 365 days a year to homeless shelters and childcare centers, including public-sector programs such as Head Start.

- *Increased resources allocated for new-product development.* In
  2003, FareStart developed a new program, with a goal of
  addressing the estimated 800 homeless youth in Seattle. The
  eight-week Youth Barista Training and Education Program, in
  partnership with YouthCare, gives at-risk youth ages 16 to 21
  job training and placement, life-skills lessons, and employment
  counseling in a classroom setting. It also offers on-the-job
  training for the competitive espresso industry.

- *Increased attention to measuring results.* Graduates are prepared to step into and thrive at jobs in restaurants and other
  positions in the food-service industry. Over the past 16 years,
  FareStart has provided opportunities for over 2,400 people to
  transform their lives. More than 80% of FareStart graduates
  are employed within 90 days of program completion.

Summary

NPOs cover a great range and diversity of organizations that fill
the gap in people's needs that government and private enterprise fail
to address, or address inadequately. Several were mentioned in this
chapter, including funding, resources/supplies, expertise, direct services, advocacy, and public awareness. The activities of these organizations highlight problems and opportunities that often prompt a
positive, if delayed, response from government and private enterprise. Over time, government and private enterprise are becoming
more attuned to NPOs and are showing greater willingness to partner
with them in some of these activities. Chapter 13, "Getting the Three
Sectors to Work Together," describes examples of this partnering.

Endnotes

[1] The Centre for Civil Society, London School of Economics Web site, http://www.lse.ac.uk/collections/CCS/what_is_civil_society.htm. Retrieved March 9, 2009.

[2] Gerald Meier, *Emerging from Poverty: the Economics That Really Matters* (New York: Oxford University Press, 1985).

[3] World Vision, "Community Emergency Response and Disaster Mitigation E-Brochure," March 2007.

[4] See, for example, David Bornstein, *How to Change the World: Social Entrepreneurs and the Power of New Ideas* (New York: Oxford University Press, 2004). Bornstein reports a near-phenomenal growth of civil society and "citizen organizations" in just the past 20 years in all countries in the first world to the third world: "Today, Indonesia has more than 2,000 independent environmental organizations from only one 20 years ago. In Bangladesh, most of the country's development work is handled by 20,000 NGOs; almost all of them established in the past 25 years. India has well over a million citizen organizations. Slovakia, a tiny country, ... more than 12,000. Between 1988 and 1995, 100,000 citizen groups opened shop in the former countries of Central Europe. In France, during the 1990s, an average of 70,000 new citizen groups were established each year. ... In Canada, the number of registered citizen groups has grown ... to 200,000. In Brazil, this number has jumped ... to 400,000. In the United States, the number of public service groups registered with the IRS in 1998 is 734,000. ... Finally, during the 1990s, the number of registered international citizen organizations increased from 6,000 to 26,000."

[5] The information on these organizations is drawn from various articles in Wikipedia, where further annotations can be found.

[6] For more on BRAC, see BRAC online and in Wikipedia.

[7] See Muhammad Yunus's two books: *Banker to the Poor: Micro-Lending and the Battle Against World Poverty* (2003) and *Creating a World Without Poverty: Social Business and the Future of Capitalism* (2008).

[8] Kolima Rose, *Where Women Are Leaders: the SEWA Movement in India* (New York: St. Martin's Press, 1993).

[9] Sourced from http://www.gdrc.org/icon/sewa-1.html. Viewed December 14, 2004.

[10] FareStart information was retrieved from www.farestart.org on 12/17/08.

12

The Private Sector's Role in Poverty Reduction

"The one thing more tragic than an incurable disease is knowing effective treatment and withholding it or failing to ensure widespread use.... The challenge is to take what works and ensure its wider availability."

—Bill Shore[1]

Changes, both radical and evolutionary, have characterized the role of corporations. Businesses have long acted as the country's engine for economic growth and have managed the market economy and its resources. Businesses have performed this role well—in many instances, extraordinarily well.

Global corporations have grown so large and important that many have a GDP that exceeds that of many large nations.[2] Data on the world's 100 largest corporations shows that their combined sales are higher than the combined GDP of half the countries in the world. The top nine international and global corporations (ranked according to the value of their shares) are General Electric, Microsoft, Exxon, Coca-Cola, Intel, NTT, Toyota Motor, Royal Dutch Petroleum, and Merck. Their websites show that all of them now publicly present a written corporate social responsibility (CSR) commitment as well as ethics programs.

This chapter explores not only the unique role that corporations can play in reducing poverty, but also the passion that many corporate leaders have for the contributions they make. We make the case that corporations engaging in strategic philanthropy can "do well by doing good" and can "get as well as give." The opening case story describes the efforts of one giant corporation, Microsoft, to increase the opportunity for poorer people to achieve more learning and knowledge.

Microsoft Helping Serbians and Roma in Hungary Reach Their Unlimited Potential

Today, for the more than 1 billion people who have access to computer technology, life has changed profoundly. Information is certainly more readily available, connections are more easily made, and commercial trade around the globe is more efficient and accessible. For the more than 5 billion people who still do not have access to the technology, however, much still needs to be accomplished. To this end, in April 2007, Microsoft made a public commitment to expand its Unlimited Potential corporate initiative. The company's long-term global business and citizenship commitment to enable new and sustained avenues of social and economic opportunity for people who have yet to realize the benefits of technology was renewed and accelerated. This initiative aligns Microsoft's technologies, partnerships, business, and corporate citizenship to impact three key areas: transforming education, fostering local innovation, and enabling jobs and opportunities.[3]

The following story describes the impact that Microsoft's educational efforts are having on the vulnerable poor in Central Eastern Europe, viewing education as the cornerstone of economic opportunity. Technology is, of course, vital in helping them achieve their education goals, and Microsoft is in a unique position to help through information and communication technology (ICT).

Serbia

The Republic of Serbia is located in the southeastern part of Europe in the central part of the Balkan Peninsula. It is home to more than 10 million people, with more than a million living in Belgrade, the country's capital. The country has faced more than a decade of social and political upheaval, leaving many of its people severely impoverished and developmentally behind many of their international peers. According to an article in the International Monetary Fund in May 2004, the highest rates of poverty are found among certain vulnerable and socially excluded groups, including refugees, victims of torture, the long-term unemployed, and the Roma population. Literacy rates are low, especially among women, with 38% of women over the age of 15 illiterate, semi-literate, or having finished only elementary school (eight years), versus 52% of men.[4] In 2007, unemployment rates were around 18%.[5]

Free IT Education for Vulnerable Groups

In October 2005, a project supported by Microsoft called *Free IT Education for Vulnerable Groups* was launched. Its aim was to increase computer literacy and the practical use of information technology (IT) among refugees, internationally displaced persons, Roma people, self-supporting parents, torture victims, and other underprivileged people in Serbia. Microsoft worked in partnership with the International Aid Network (IAN), a local nongovernment humanitarian organization, to offer 800 free information and communication technology courses to the most destitute and socially excluded groups in Serbia.

The classroom has 13 computers and is equipped with a library that includes Microsoft Press books, manuals, and multimedia CDs for self-paced independent learning. Participants are taught basic ICT skills needed for working in a modern business office, including word processing, working with spreadsheets, and information and communication using the Internet (see Figure 12.1). A typical course includes 20 classes lasting 45 minutes each and is based on a detailed curriculum with practical exercises for teachers and a short course plan for the participants, a manual, and a standardized exam. At the end of each course, successful participants are awarded a certificate of completion, one they can then show to potential and existing employers. And with these increased skills, they are then more likely to become integrated in the local community and become economically independent, either by getting employment, starting their own business, or potentially increasing their income.

By 2008, more than 1200 people had participated in the project. IAN project manager Ivan Stojilovic believes the project is "a perfect example of how society can benefit from cooperation between the private and public sector. As an international corporation, Microsoft supports ICT education of the most vulnerable groups at a local level... Together, we have helped hundreds of people get their life back on track and improved the local economy... This project increases each participant's chances of employment. It encourages social contact and interaction between different vulnerable groups and local authorities, and in this way, it facilitates social inclusion. Using their IT knowledge and skills, participants can improve their position on the job market and rebuild their confidence."[6]

FIGURE 12.1 **Learning basic information and communication technology skills prepares students for the modern business office.**

Hungary

Hungary, also in central Europe, has been a member state of the European Union (EU) since 2004 and has a population of more than 10 million, 700,000 (7%) of which are members of the Roma community. This disadvantaged group has been one of the nation's most serious sociocultural problems since the transition of the regime in 1990. Estimates are that for each employed person within the Roma community, six dependents rely on some form of government subsidy.[7] Economists point to the low education level of the Roma community as the principal reason for its poor position in the labor market. Only one third of Roma children attend secondary education programs, and less than 1% of the population holds a third-level educational certificate. This low status in the job market and higher unemployment rates cause poverty and widespread social problems. The situation is most dire among the Roma gypsy population, most of whom live in the northeastern and southern regions of Hungary. Within this group, 85% of the potentially employed are unemployed. In this catch-22 situation, the low education level of parents is the main reason for their unemployment, and their poverty is the main reason for the next generation's poor education prospects.[8]

In 2002, the Equal Chances of the Roma Association was established to improve opportunities available to these gypsy people. The Knowledge Center program was launched in 2004 to provide vocational training. And Microsoft is assisting them in their efforts.

The Knowledge Center

Under the Microsoft Unlimited Potential program and with the support of the European Union's EQUAL Community Initiative, the Knowledge Center program received grants in software and funding. This gives disadvantaged people more equal opportunities for full participation in the information-based economy. And specialists from Microsoft provide lecturers from the Microsoft Hungary team on an ad hoc basis to the training centers.

After the first year, the Knowledge Center established a formal distance-education program. This increased the number of students in classes, because students needed to migrate or relocate to undertake these studies. During the second semester of their training, these students receive their course work and study package to prepare for their exams via the Internet. Internet skills are also seen as essential for other sectors of life,

such as communicating with potential employers when searching for a job. In addition to a high-school education, each student receives computer-operation training and European
Computer Driving License qualifications (see Figure 12.2).
And to help them understand their ethnicity, students receive
Romanology training, composed of language, culture, history,
and literature.

FIGURE 12.2   Receiving computer-operation training in Hungary

Gabor Axtom-Varga, project leader of the Knowledge Center,
says: "The support of Microsoft and Equal has helped us ren-
der a solid foundation from which we can grow our services for
the future. We can expand the range of operations gradually
and thereby reach an increasingly wide audience and help
them obtain competitive knowledge and skills."[9] And strengthening the knowledge-based economy in Hungary is a task not
only for the government, but also for multinational companies
as responsible corporate citizens.

The Unique Role That the Private Sector Plays in Poverty Reduction

In our book *Corporate Social Responsibility* (Wiley, 2005), we identified six areas that represent most strategies that the private sector uses to contribute to local and global communities. Examples of poverty-related corporate initiatives are presented in the next section. We've added a seventh strategy to this list—developing and delivering affordable products for the large market at "the bottom of the pyramid."

1. *Corporate philanthropy.* Perhaps the most traditional role that corporations play is that of making direct contributions to charities and causes in one or more ways: providing *cash donations* (for victims of a natural disaster), offering *grants* (for small farmers to purchase new, higher-yield seeds), awarding *scholarships* (for women to attend job-training workshops), donating *products* (food, clothing, and hygiene items), donating *services* (for dental care), providing *technical expertise* (for purifying water), allowing the use of *facilities and distribution channels* (grocery stores providing space for collecting canned goods for food banks), and offering the use of *equipment* (vans for transporting mosquito nets to remote villages).

2. *Community volunteering.* Corporations often support and encourage employees, retail partners, and/or franchise members to volunteer their time to support local community organizations and causes. For example, Levi Strauss & Co., headquartered in San Francisco, gives employees time off to volunteer at local HIV/AIDS service organizations. It also supports their participation in annual walks to raise funds for AIDS victims, and delivering food to patients.

3. *Socially responsible business practices.* With this strategy, a corporation adopts and conducts discretionary business practices

and investments that support social causes to improve community well-being and protect the environment. A good example of this type of initiative is Starbucks' efforts to encourage production of coffee using cultivation methods that protect biodiversity and provide improved economic opportunities for coffee farmers.

4. *Cause promotions.* This initiative is distinguished by a corporation providing funds, in-kind contributions, or other corporate resources to increase awareness of and concern about a social cause or to support fund-raising, participation, or volunteer recruitment for a cause. For several years, *Parade* magazine, in partnership with Share Our Strength, a leading nonprofit anti-hunger organization, has sponsored "The Great American Bake Sale" to raise awareness of childhood hunger in the United States and to also raise funds for hunger relief. In 2003, they raised $1.1 million for food banks across the country.[10]

5. *Cause-related marketing.* In this scenario, a corporation commits to making a contribution or donating a percentage of revenues to a specific cause based on product sales. Most commonly this offer is for an announced period of time, for a specific product, and for a specified charity. The Project Red Campaign mentioned in Chapter 2, "Examining a Barrel of Current Solutions," is a great example. Organizations such as American Express and Apple make contributions to the Global Fund to fight poverty based on volumes of sales.

6. *Corporate social marketing.* As the phrase implies, this corporate initiative supports the development and/or implementation of a behavior change campaign intended to improve public health, safety, the environment, or community well-being. The distinguishing feature is the behavior change focus, which differentiates this effort from cause promotions that focus on supporting awareness, fund-raising, and volunteer recruitment for

a cause. Crest's Healthy Smiles 2010 program, for example, works to influence and support underserved minorities to seek frequent dental checkups and to brush and floss regularly.

7. *Developing and delivering affordable products and services.* This strategy has been described several times in this book in reference to those 2 billion, or even 4 billion, people at "the bottom of the pyramid." These people represent significant opportunities for corporations to tap immense entrepreneurial capabilities as well as buying power. In India, for example, the largest soap manufacturer, Hindustan Lever Limited, increased sales significantly when its communications began focusing on the importance of using soap when washing hands to help prevent diarrheal disease in the country.

Business Behavior in the Past

Corporate social responsibility is a relatively recent development in any corporation's life. Throughout the past century, corporations have asked for and demanded more rights rather than rendering the commensurate responsibilities attached to those rights. Many critics of corporations say that corporations' sales come at the expense of serious damage to the environment, and that collectively they are a leading cause of life-threatening air, water, and land pollution.

Serious commitment to corporate social responsibility started when government and citizens' groups demanded reforms and asked erring corporations to make amends for each publicized corporate abuse of power. Ralph Nader, the activist lawyer, is considered the father of consumer advocacy in opposing the power of large corporations.[11] In 1965, he published his book *Unsafe at Any Speed.* This well-researched book showed careful evidence of how structurally defective many American cars were, especially those made by General Motors.

Reacting quickly, General Motors tried to discredit Nader. It hired private investigators to look into his past and tried to trap him in compromising situations. All these attempts failed. Then it was Nader's turn to respond to the harassment. He sued GM for invasion of privacy. In the end, Nader won. The court made GM publicly apologize, and Nader netted $284,000 as a case settlement. Nader used much of the settlement money to expand his consumer-rights advocacy.

Soon after, he organized his "Nader's Raiders" when hundreds of young inspired activists joined him in Washington, D.C. Nader led his energetic converts to investigate government corruption. Dozens of books documented the results of these investigations.

In 1971, Nader established the NGO Public Citizen as an umbrella organization for his widening efforts and projects investigating Congress, health, environment, corporations, and economic issues. Public Citizen has over 150,000 members and a battalion of legal researchers. Its works have been credited with enabling the passage of the Safe Drinking Water Act and the Freedom of Information Act. The creation of the Occupational Safety and Health Administration (OSHA), the Environmental Protection Agency (EPA), and the Consumer Product Safety Commission (CPSC) is said to have come from the tireless efforts of Public Citizen.

In the years following the development of Nader's Public Citizen, a succession of corporate abuses and misconduct raised public, government, and civil society demand for a more responsible corporate citizenship. The abuses were varied and wide-ranging. They involved issues relating to the following:[12]

- Executive greed, taking the form of excessive salaries and share options
- Corruption and fraud, represented by the series of corporate meltdowns among large, high-profile companies like Enron, Worldcom, Arthur Andersen, Tyco Laboratories, and Adelphia

- Environmental degradation caused by industrial practices in toxic waste disposal, and other air, water, and land pollution
- Human-rights abuses, such as knowingly using child or prison labor to make clothes, shoes, and sporting goods
- Fair trade and the increasing injustices in current global trade practices
- Flawed corporate governance practices among corporate board members and shareholders

Another civil society advocate and writer, David Korten, believes that all these abuses come from corporations' single-minded focus "centered on the love of money."[13] However, the intensifying and almost unrelenting scrutiny that corporations are getting from the government, the media, other civil societies, and the general public has been leading to a change in this narrow centeredness. It is now clear that corporations are going in the direction of a more socially responsible commitment.

Business Needs to Reform

That reforms are needed in the business sector is no longer the issue. The issue is what shape those reforms should take. The needed reforms can go in two basic directions.

One direction is the radical reform that angry civil societies are talking about. They want a "reinvention" of corporations. That means no less than dismantling multinational and large corporations and replacing them with localized businesses. Why? Because big government needs reinvention in the same way. Korten says, "As business is localized, it will be possible to localize government as well. ... it is big business that creates the need for big government. ... The more we cut our giant corporations down to human scale, the more we will be able to reduce the size of government."[14]

Nader's advocacy, though much less radical, still belongs to this category of called-for corporate reforms. In the case of Nader's

Public Citizen, the focus is on securing corporations' commitment to good citizenship. The targeted commitment behavior is simple compliance with the law or laws that Nader's Raiders were able to get Congress to pass.[15]

The other direction that business sector reform may take is self-reform. Corporations voluntarily practice corporate social responsibility (CSR).[16] It is commitment by "internalization."[17] In contrast to compliance, it is the highest form of commitment.

Commitment from internalization and via self-reform is more realistic. Large and global corporations are here to stay because the world has a true and distinct need for them. They have done a lot of good in spite of their share of wrongdoings. The issue is not how to get rid of them. It is how to rechannel them along more constructive and responsible routes. One group of CSR advocates predicts that "the successful companies of the future are likely to be those which discover how to make full use of their relationship (with their communities) as a normal part of running their business, and so will move along...towards *full* citizenship."[18]

Responsible corporate citizenship behavior will span the continuum of compliance to internalization. A compliance program will take care of instances where the fear of punishment will act as deterrent to corrupt behavior. There is also an ethics program through which company owners and executives acquire the right value formation to behave responsibly and ethically when it comes to important company decisions.[19]

Corporations Engage in the Poverty Problem

In its 2003 Human Development Report addressing the issue of "ending human poverty," the United Nations Development Programme (UNDP) valiantly attempted to define the business sector's role and responsibility in poverty reduction.[20] For countries following the model that poverty reduction is mainly a function of economic growth, corporations and enterprises must play the critical role of generating and raising income as well as creating employment. In addition, because sustained economic growth is seriously hampered by a culture of corruption, corporations and business enterprises must stop their practice of corrupting the government and each other.

In terms of direct support for poverty reduction, many corporations are known to be philanthropic. Some establish their own foundation that takes on poverty-alleviation projects, such as the Coca-Cola Foundation. Others regularly contribute to an NGO dedicated to helping the poor, such as the 118 large companies in the Philippines that formed and supported the Philippine Business for Social Progress (PBSP).

Coca-Cola Joins with Others to Fight HIV/AIDS

In Africa, Coca-Cola is the largest private-sector employer. In April 2002, the company set up the Coca-Cola Africa Foundation. Its primary avowed purpose was to "improve the quality of life in the communities" where the Coca-Cola Company is doing business.[21]

The foundation got directly involved, for example, in flood relief in Mozambique and in providing Angola with electrical supplies. However, its more important initiative that relates to poverty alleviation is its work in the Global Business Coalition on HIV/AIDS (GBC).

The *Global Business Coalition* is an alliance of some 170 international corporations that have committed themselves to helping combat the AIDS epidemic. This alliance has extended this help through assistance from member businesses' expertise in anti-AIDS drugs and products, in service delivery and distribution, in mass communication and advertising, and in program management planning and implementation. The UN has commended pharmaceutical companies that agreed to substantially discount the prices of essential AIDS medicines in affected African countries. A database is available of many other company case studies of corporate initiatives in this critical area of poverty alleviation for the vulnerable poor segment of men, women, and children who are AIDS victims. The database can be accessed at http://www.businessfightsaids.org.

The Philippine Business for Social Progress (PBSP)

In 1970, member companies of three business associations—the Philippine Council for Economic Development, the Philippine Business Council, and the Philippine Association for Social Action—decided to establish PBSP as an umbrella NGO.[22] The concept was to coordinate through PBSP the funds that member companies in the three business associations were contributing to social and economic projects in different parts of the country. PBSP member companies committed themselves to annually contributing 0.6% of each company's before-tax net income to PBSP's antipoverty programs.

The specific role that PBSP defined for itself in poverty alleviation was as a "direct lender" and "broker" to the poverty market's microentrepreneurs in need of microfinancing. As a lender, PBSP used member companies' annual contributions to provide funds that local community-based organizations such as cooperatives and village-level NGOs can loan to their own microentrepreneur members. For its brokering role, PBSP has linked with domestic and foreign agencies in the formal economy whose resources were "denied the poor for one reason or another." It has offered its services as a conduit of those funds to support its "credit-based income-generating program" (CIGP). In both roles, PBSP stated that it was guided by its vision of becoming the foundation that will establish throughout the country "community-based credit structures that will enable the poor who do not have access to formal credit sources to improve their livelihood prospects."

Businessmen offered managers some other ways in which businesses can engage in poverty reduction.[23] For example, businessmen who were in the processed food industry were challenged to do a "Monde Nissin." This is a recommendation to produce processed food products specifically tailored to the needs of the urban poor family but priced at no more than 10 cents (or 5 pesos in local currency) a pack. Monde Nissin Corporation is the local manufacturer of the leading brand of instant noodles. It has specifically targeted the poor segment of the market (Class D and Class E consumers) and priced a pouch pack of its instant noodles for about 9 cents. Urban poor consumers can afford to spend only 20 cents (or 10 pesos) for one family meal.[24] To create a meal for a family of four, an urban poor mother prepares the instant-noodles pouch as a meal by boiling it with as many vegetables as she could buy for another 9 or 10 cents. For three square meals each day, the Class DE mother has a budget of 30 cents. That amount is the average daily earnings of an urban poor family in Metro Manila and two other urban centers.

Then companies that wanted to follow the example of Monde Nissin were further challenged to sustain and "Kaizen" this effort. These companies were to invest in two types of research. One type was in product research and development aimed at developing and continuing to develop products specifically tailored to the needs of the poor. The recommended research budget for this was 5 to 10% of total company annual product development research investment. The other type was researching the needs of the poor for better-quality food and beverage products. The research investment was also suggested to come to about 5 to 10% of the company's total market research budget.

Businesses that are not producing food products were asked to think about contributing in another way. Each corporation may want to adopt one poverty-alleviation program. Then this adopting corporation can lend sustained monetary and/or consulting assistance to the adopted poverty-alleviation program for making, say, its service delivery more efficient.

An interested corporation was urged to do something similar with the study's eight poverty segments and the eight poverty-assistance services offered by poverty-alleviation programs. A corporation could choose one pair consisting of a segment and an assistance service, and then it could lend to the adopted antipoverty program for this pair its management and social marketing assistance.

Those who are in management training services were asked, "What about helping improve the effective and efficient management of poverty-alleviation programs by giving sustained consulting assistance for three critical program-management items?" These three concerns are a management audit of a poverty-alleviation program, a management development training program after the audit, and program implementation and control consulting assistance after the training program.

Company Efforts to Bring Down the Cost of Goods and Services

Companies have traditionally neglected developing products and services for the poor precisely because poor individuals have little money. More recently, some companies have changed their thinking to see the poor as an opportunity market rather than a loss market. C. K. Prahalad describes many examples in his book *The Fortune at the Bottom of the Pyramid: Eradicating Poverty Through Profits*.[25]

The formation of "Dollar Stores" is one retail example striving to bring down the cost of ordinary products. These stores carry many items priced less than a dollar. Some items are specifically packaged in smaller sizes so that they are more affordable. Although the profit margins are smaller, this is made up by the large number of poor buyers who buy small amounts.

In a sense, stores like Wal-Mart and IKEA have worked hard to bring down the cost of many products. There is a double benefit in their sourcing an increasing number of products from poorer countries, because they also increase employment of the poor.

Ultimately, manufacturers have to innovate new ways to bring down the cost of products. Tata Motors in India has introduced the Tata Nano as the world's cheapest car (selling at $2,500) to enable more people to afford a car. The MIT Media Lab has been working on creating a $100 laptop to be distributed to third-world children. Jaipur Foot in India has created a way to customize a prosthetic foot that costs under $25. Annapurna Salt has developed an affordable microencapsulated iodized salt to fight iodine deficiency disorder (IDD). (Most salt in India lacks iodine.)

Services are being developed that would sell at a lower cost. Doctors at Aravind Eye Care (AEC) in India can now repair cataract-diseased eyes at a low cost by implementing mass-production medical procedures. Banks have used microfinance to make small loans to poor people with an excellent chance of payback.

Social Marketing in the Private Sector

How Does the Social Marketing Approach Differ from Current Traditional Approaches?

As noted earlier in this chapter, corporations have a variety of ways to contribute to reducing poverty. These methods include initiatives related to cause promotions, cause-related marketing, philanthropy, altering business practices, employee volunteering, and social marketing efforts. Table 12.1 contrasts the more traditional corporate solutions and social marketing-oriented ones. As you saw in the descriptions of the other sectors, the social marketing solution focuses on initiatives that influence specific behaviors that will help prevent poverty and/or help the poor improve their physical, emotional, and financial well being.

TABLE 12.1   Adding the Social Marketing Solution to the Mix for Corporations

Poverty-Related Issue	Traditional Solution	Social Marketing Solution
Agricultural productivity	Provide direct financing to suppliers to support technological improvements.	Provide an infusion of capital into the local microfinance community. This money then provides financing to farmers and their suppliers for technological improvements at more reasonable interest rates than they could get in their local market.
HIV/AIDS	Provide employee health-care coverage that includes access to antiretroviral drugs.	Develop workplace programs that include distribution of free condoms and confidential free testing and counseling.
Flooding	Provide employee volunteers to help homeowners in the community clean up their homes and properties after extreme flooding from hurricanes.	Host flood prevention and preparedness workshops at local facilities, including tips on how to be prepared for next year's hurricane season.
Retirement savings	Offer an option for employees to enroll in retirement savings programs, with automatic deductions from their paychecks.	Provide a "nudge" for retirement savings by offering a system in which the employee must indicate he wants to "opt out" of the program versus one in which he needs to sign up.

How Will Social Marketing Solutions Benefit Corporations?

Not only do social marketing initiatives provide an important and often missing solution for corporations that want to contribute to poverty reduction, but they also provide numerous additional benefits to the corporation. We think this is one of the best options for "doing well by doing good," because corporations often report one or more of the following outcomes:

- *Enhanced reputation.* Social marketing efforts tend to be more visible, to both current and potential customers of the company, as well as the campaign's target audience. When an organization such as Microsoft provides instructors, computers, and software for job training in developing countries, recipients as well as observers are more likely to realize the company's contribution than if they had just "written a check" to assist the poor in the community.

- *Enhanced ability to support real behavior change.* By their very nature, social marketing initiatives are designed to change behaviors that improve quality of life for the target audience. Corporations that support these efforts are likely to see positive, concrete results that they have helped produce. This benefit is often lacking with other types of support.

- *Enhanced brand loyalty.* Consider Crest's Healthy Smiles 2010 program, mentioned earlier. It seeks to influence important oral health practices for underserved minorities. Product managers know that early positive brand experiences can greatly influence lifelong brand loyalty. Certainly Crest's efforts will create positive associations for both these children and their families.

- *Enhanced product sales.* This is often possible when natural connections exist between the desired behaviors and the company's products and services. Increasing the visibility and use of mosquito nets among the poor, for example, is also likely to make their installation and use more of a norm in the community. In turn, this will increase sales for manufacturers and retailers among those who can pay.

- *Enhanced employee satisfaction.* When employees also see the positive social change that the company's efforts helped make possible, it is not uncommon for the company to experience increased employee retention, as well as productivity. Imagine your pride in your employer if you learned that its efforts to increase tuberculosis testing and treatment had saved thousands of lives in South America.

Summary

Companies can play a growing role in abating poverty. After many years of focusing only on profit making, they are beginning to assume social responsibilities, partly as a result of citizen activists' pressure (such as Nader's Raiders) and new laws and compliance, and partly out of conscience. Companies have acted individually as well as collectively to address problems of HIV, malaria, and other diseases as well as to bring down the costs of food and other products and services to make them more affordable to the poor.

Endnotes

[1] Bill Shore, *Revolution of the Heart* (New York: Riverhead Books, 1995), p. 118.

[2] From David Korten, *When Corporations Rule the World* (2nd edition) (Bloomfield, CT: Kumarian Press and Barrett-Koehler Publishers, 2001).

[3] About Microsoft Unlimited Potential. Retrieved June 25, 2008 from http://www.microsoft.com/About/CorporateCitizenship/US/AboutUnlimited Potential.mspx.

[4] European Association for Education of Adults. "Adult Education and Gender Issues in Serbia," May 5, 2007. Retrieved June 26, 2008 from http://www.eaea.org/news.php?aid=13515&k=2088&%20d=2007-05.

[5] CIA. The World Factbook—Serbia. Retrieved June 26, 2008 from https://www.cia.gov/library/publications/the-world-factbook/geos/rb.html#Econ.

[6] Microsoft Unlimited Potential Report, November 2007, "Vulnerable Groups in Serbia Receive IT Training and Realize Their Unlimited Potential."

[7] Microsoft Unlimited Potential Report, November 2007. "Roma Gain Equal Opportunities Through Unlimited Potential," p. 27. Retrieved June 26, 2008 from http://download.microsoft.com/download/7/5/f/75faafde-c447-4638-ae7b-ec99cc0f2f9c/MS_CEE_UP_Nov_2007_lowres.pdf.

[8] Retrieved June 26, 2008 from https://www.cia.gov/library/publications/the-world-factbook/geos/hu.html.

[9] Microsoft Unlimited Potential Report, November 2007. "Roma Gain Equal Opportunities through Unlimited Potential," p. 28.

[10] Philip Kotler and Nancy Lee, *Corporate Social Responsibility: Doing the Most Good for Your Company and Your Cause* (Wiley, 2005), p. 63.

[11] Sourced from http://en.wikipedia.org/wiki/Ralph_Nader. Viewed December 14, 2004.

12. M. McIntosh, D. Leipziger, K. Jones, and G. Coleman, *Corporate Citizenship: Successful Strategies for Responsible Companies* (London: Financial Times Professional Ltd., 1998), p. 44.

13. Korten, op. cit. Korten speaks with disdain about this centeredness and rejects it in favor of "one centered on the love of life."

14. Korten, op. cit., p. 275.

15. This discussion of engaging for commitment draws on the framework of Herbert Kelman (1958), "Compliance, Identification, and Internalization: Three Processes of Attitude Change," *Journal of Conflict Resolution*, 2: 51–60.

16. See, for example, Kotler and Lee, *Corporate Social Responsibility: Doing the Most Good for Your Company and Your Cause*; and McIntosh, Leipziger, Jones, and Coleman, *Corporate Citizenship: Successful Strategies for Responsible Companies*.

17. Kelman, op. cit.

18. McIntosh, et al., op. cit., p. xxi.

19. Ned Roberto in his *Survey of CEO Perceptions of Corporate Corruption and Misconduct at the Rank and File and Senior Management Levels* (Makati City: AIM Center for Corporate Responsibility, 2004) found that for petty wrongdoings and for rank-and-file employees (as seen by CEOs), it is the compliance program that works in controlling corrupt practices. On the other hand, for grand corrupt practices, the ethics program is more effective.

20. United Nations Development Programme. Human Development Report 2003. Millennium Development Goals: A compact among nations to end human poverty. pp. 23-24.

21. Sourced from http://www2.coca-cola.com/citizenship/foundation_africa/html. Viewed December 22, 2004.

22. Sourced from http://www.gdrc.org/icon/pbsp.html. Viewed December 22, 2004.

23. Ned Roberto, A Survey of Program Managers' Perceptions of the Poverty Problem and the Effectiveness of Their Poverty Alleviation Programs (Makati City: AIM Center for Corporate Responsibility, 2004).

24. Ned Roberto, Consumer Coping Behavior Survey of Metro Manila, Metro Cebu and Davao City (Makati City: Roberto & Associates, Inc., 2001).

25. C. K. Prahalad, *The Fortune at the Bottom of the Pyramid: Eradicating Poverty Through Profits* (Upper Saddle River, NJ: Wharton School Publishing-Pearson, 2005).

13

Getting the Three Sectors
to Work Together

*"The rashes first appeared when I was six... At school I could-
n't concentrate because of the incessant itching. The children
in class used to laugh at me, so I stopped going to school when
I was nine. I married in 1989. My father arranged the marriage... When we met and he saw my skin, he was very angry.
I lived with him for a few months and became pregnant...
Despite the pregnancy, he sent me home to my parents. ...I
had no support from my husband, no money for me or my
baby."*

—Agnes, a Nigerian mother, 1995[1]

Following treatment with the drug Mectizan®, Agnes's symptoms
disappeared, and she reconciled with her husband. Their story of the
devastating effects of river blindness is common, although it does not
always have the same happy ending—one that depended on a global
partnership with the public, private, and nonprofit sectors working
together in Africa. This is what we believe it will take to address, as
Bill Gates calls it, "the roughly a billion people in the world who don't
get enough food, who don't have clean drinking water, and who don't
have electricity—the things that we take for granted."[2]

If there is one fundamental lesson that the United Nations has
learned from its more than five decades of experience in poverty alleviation, it is this: *No program for alleviating poverty can attain lasting*

*success if the three sectors—government agencies, nonprofit organi-
zations, and private enterprise—do not learn to work together
effectively.*

This chapter begins with a case story describing the African Programme for Riverblindness, launched in the mid-1990s. Then we
elaborate on the nature of developing a three-way strategy and the
keys to its success.

Conquering River Blindness: It Takes a Global Partnership

The Disease

Onchocerciasis is most commonly called river blindness
because this parasitic disease causes blindness and is prevalent
around fast-flowing rivers. The disease is transmitted by the
bites of small blackflies that breed in rapidly flowing streams
and rivers. Among the 120 million people worldwide who are at
risk of contracting river blindness, more than 95% live in Africa,
with the remainder concentrated in Central and South America
and the Arabian Peninsula. Among those infected, over 6.5 million suffer from severe itching, and 270,000 are blind.[3]

The Link to Poverty

To contract river blindness, a person typically must be bitten
hundreds of times by infected blackflies, since only a small percentage carry the infection. As a result, the disease is not common among travelers or visitors to endemic countries.[4] It is, in
fact, the poorest of the poor living in rural areas who lack protection from the blackflies who are at the greatest risk, with
huge socioeconomic consequences. Infected people face physical disability and social stigma. The unbearable itching and

blindness are debilitating. When blindness in a village reaches epidemic proportions, it leaves too few able-bodied people to tend the fields. Food shortages and economic collapse then force residents to abandon their homelands in fertile river valleys. Moving to higher elevations and forested areas offers some protection from further infection, but then farmers end up struggling with poor soil and water shortages on overcrowded lands. Eventually, river blindness pushes prosperous communities into poverty.[5]

The Strategy: A Global Partnership

River blindness control began in 1974 in West Africa as a large regional project called the Onchocerciasis Control Programme using the only available approach at the time—vector control, the treating of breeding sites of disease-transmitting flies with insecticides. However, the second program, APOC, introduced in the mid-1990s, is of particular interest for this case story. The core of this program is the distribution of Mectizan, the drug developed by Merck & Co. in the 1980s and then donated for river blindness. It involves influencing community and individual behaviors through what the World Bank calls *community-directed treatment systems*.[6]

As described in the World Bank case study "West Africa: Defeating Riverblindness—Success in Scaling Up and Lessons Learned," in community-directed treatment systems, the community receives training and support from cross-sector partners, including international agencies, participating country governments, NGOs, and donor countries.[7] In coordination with these partners, the communities themselves decide how to organize treatment for their citizens. They select the drug distributor, determine the timing and method of drug collection and distribution, and report to local health providers. Authors of the case study tout that "the role of the community changes from being solely the recipient of services within the guidelines and limits set by outside providers to a position of prominence as the lead stakeholder and decision maker in community-level health services."[8] Organizers, they cite, are motivated by numerous advantages:

- Less work for local health providers
- Better treatment and geographic coverage
- Stronger ability to adapt the drug distribution and treatment program as the communities' needs and requirements change
- A greater sense of commitment to and ownership of the program, which in turn promotes sustainability and the possibility of eventual integration into the local health system

Results

The World Bank reports that in West Africa alone, 600,000 cases of blindness have been prevented, 18 million children born in the now-protected areas have been spared the risk of disease, productive labor has increased, and 25 million hectares of formerly evacuated arable lands have been made safe for settlement and agriculture. Impressively, these lands have the potential to feed an additional 17 million people per year using indigenous technologies and methods. The increased agricultural production from these lands has "transformed the region from aid-dependent to food-exporting." And in terms of return on investment, the West Africa program has achieved a 20%

economic rate of return. Elsewhere in Africa, operations that began in 1996 have achieved a 17% economic rate of return.[9]

Partners are also hopeful that the success of this community-directed distribution network and collaborative partnership approach will inspire the application of this strategy to deliver other basic health interventions in the river blindness areas, especially those that are almost exclusively remote, rural, and poor and not reached by other programs or national governments (see Figure 13.1).

FIGURE 13.1   Defeating onchocerciasis (river blindness) in Africa
Source: Merck & Co. Inc.

Developing a Three-Way Strategy

We can start by reminding ourselves of what each of the sectors is counted on to contribute to poverty reduction and what they bring to the partnership, as summarized in Table 13.1.

TABLE 13.1   The Distinct Roles of Each Sector for Poverty Reduction

Public Sector (Government Agencies)	Private Sector (Businesses)	Nonprofit Sector (Sometimes Called NGOs, NPOs, or Civil Organizations)
Build a robust economy	Corporate philanthropy	Funding
Protect and enhance public health and safety	Community volunteering	Resources and supplies
Provide basic infrastructures	Socially responsible business practices	Direct services
Educate children and youth	Cause promotions	Expertise
Provide public assistance	Cause-related marketing	Volunteering
Protect the environment	Corporate social marketing	Advocacy
Provide grants and subsidies	Develop and deliver affordable products and services	Public awareness

As we imagine the sectors partnering for poverty-reduction programs, it is apparent how important the following *seven partnership principles* will be to maximize and leverage every needed contribution. Each principle is illustrated by revisiting case examples from prior chapters that exemplify "practicing the principle."

1. *Agree on common goals.* Remember Uganda's dramatic success story in reducing AIDS from 15% to 6.5%, described in Chapter 4, "Segmenting the Poverty Marketplace"? Many who studied the program agreed that this would not have been achieved without a high level of political commitment to the goal that led to providing support for sex education programs in schools and subsidies for condoms. And the commitment of private-sector and NGO partners to the goal resulted in the ability to offer same-day results for HIV tests, which decreased the need to travel back, and increased the availability of condoms in remote locations.

2. *Develop clear roles and responsibilities.* At the core of Net-Mark's effort described in Chapter 8, "Developing a Desired Positioning and Strategic Marketing Mix," to get 15 million more people covered by malaria nets was a public-private partnership founded on the premise that each sector had a unique role to play, as well as a desired benefit. For-profit businesses wanted to promote and sell nets to those who could afford them. The government wanted to be able to provide subsidies to those who could not afford the nets. The NGO, the Academy for Educational Development, worked to coordinate the approach to ensure that nets would be available and affordable even after funding disappeared.

3. *Work toward mutual respect and appreciation.* Certainly the "Condom King," mentioned in several chapters, was eventually successful in gaining the respect of other Thai politicians and the sex-trade industry by demonstrating that publicizing the AIDS crisis would help, not hinder, its business and would decrease, not increase, the spread of HIV/AIDS. His clear recognition of their real concerns and needs increased their trust in his projections that without this social marketing effort, millions were at risk of infection, and hundreds of thousands would die.

4. *Be willing to negotiate and compromise.* It seems that the government of Malawi and the World Bank understood this principle. As described in Chapter 7, "Understanding Barriers, Benefits, and the Competition for Change," in response to the World Bank and others' serious concerns about universal subsidies, the Government of Malawi and the World Bank sponsored a fertilizer workshop, bringing together all stakeholders to discuss best practices for fertilizer and to address the mistrust between the government and private-sector fertilizer suppliers. In the end, the government agreed to involve the private sector in developing workable strategies for subsidies.

5. *Maintain open communications.* Consider the complexity of communications that must have been involved in World Vision's disaster mitigation efforts in Honduras alone, described in Chapter 11, "The Nonprofit Sector's Role in Poverty Reduction." Multiple audiences were critical to success. Local governments needed to be persuaded to take major actions, including installing early-warning systems and training citizens in basic first aid. Key individuals in communities needed to be trained in each of the essential areas of disaster management. Funders such as USAID needed progress reports and evidence for the program's ultimate efficacy.

6. *Establish systems for accountability.* The Sound Families Initiative, supported by the Bill & Melinda Gates Foundation and described in Chapter 5, "Evaluating and Choosing Target Market Priorities," helped ensure success for the homeless by establishing stringent criteria for funding. Grantees would need to demonstrate that in addition to providing housing for the poor, they would partner with social services agencies that would help the homeless families move on, decreasing their chances of returning to homelessness. In the end, this system helped many families maintain permanent housing after exiting the temporary housing program.

7. *Measure and report outcomes.* PSI's family planning program in Romania, described in Chapter 6, "Determining Desired Behavior Changes," established significant credibility with the government by taking the time to measure the impact that the workshops were having on increasing the use of contraceptives among women working in factories. A rigorous study design conducted in two factories and a control group at a third factory reported with confidence that use of contraceptives increased by more than 10%, and modern methods (such as birth control pills) increased by more than 25%.

More About How the Three-Way Relationship Works

Perhaps the importance of these seven principles will be even more apparent if you understand the nature of this three-way relationship. As shown in Figure 13.2, this relationship is made up of three two-way relationship components: the government-civil society relationship, the government-business relationship, and the civil society-business relationship.

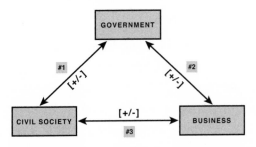

FIGURE 13.2   The three-way relationship among government, civil society, and business, with its three two-way relationships

Figure 13.2 shows that each relationship can take either of two directions, as suggested by the [+/–]. The relationship can be one of partnership (the + sign) or opposition (the – sign). We'll examine the relationship of partnership first, and then we'll discuss the negative relationship.

The Government-Civil Society Partnership

Ideally, the government and civil society organizations should find it easy to join forces to run programs to alleviate poverty. Many governments have funds to give to a cause but lack the manpower and know-how to disperse the funds efficiently and effectively. They rely on a multitude of NGOs to deliver the services to the right persons.

Yet different hurdles and misunderstandings can occur. For example, government is used to working by following to the letter the legal requirements of the partnership contract. On the other hand, most NGOs are impatient with bureaucratic procedures and like to take the most expedient path to go from point A to point B. This clash of working styles has often caused the government agency, which is attentive to the details of the partnership project, to raise questions about the NGO's sense of accountability and professionalism.

Consider the following three examples of government and civil society alliance and the lessons to be learned:

Example 1: To solve the country's unemployment problem, the Japanese government asked leading nonprofit organizations to accept a considerable amount of government money to expand NGO operations and hire more people.[10] Yet some people considered this a bad idea. The government's gesture was thought to be insulting to the NGOs on two counts. First, it treated the NGOs as if they were government "subsidiaries" that can be ordered to do what the government wants. Second, the government was telling the NGOs what it wanted them to do, not what the NGOs wanted to do. This approach to a relationship runs counter to the social marketing concept of the right way to start a partnership. You should *start from where the stakeholder (here, the NGO) is, not from where the change agent (here, the government) is.*

Example 2: A national government agency director of an antipoverty program was explaining how a partnership with one NGO went nowhere. This director said that her office had wondered from the beginning why this NGO was included among the three chosen by the government's selection committee, when another NGO was better known and had more experience. The government agency director suspected that the selected NGO had paid a bribe or benefited from favoritism. *Clearly, a partnership that starts with suspicion has nowhere to go.*

Example 3: An NGO director talked about how her government agency partner was late in disbursing the funds needed to start their project. The government also was late in choosing the members of its team in the partnership. The NGO director wanted two government staff members with whom she had worked previously to be included on the team, but their names were not on the government team membership list. The NGO director decided that instead of accusing the government of incompetence, she would meet with the government partner to find out the reasons for the delayed disbursement and the two missing members of the government partnership team. The NGO director realized that she should have known from past experience that the government is normally late in filling its obligations and that she should have factored this into the project time table. She realized that she could have obtained interim funding from another source in the meantime. And she should have checked on the availability of the two government team members she wanted. She would have learned that they were committed to another government project for the next six months. *The lesson: First get the facts about the other partner's past behavior regarding timing and resource questions.*

All these examples show that relationships between any two organizations involve delicate decisions about the right course of action, the selection of appropriate personnel, and perceptions about the other party's ability to deliver effectively and on time.

The Government-Business Sector Partnership

In most developing countries, because government and business have a longer history of partnership than either one has had with NPOs, the partnership is not as difficult to start and manage over its life cycle. Both institutions have experienced what the requirements of the partnership are like. Both understand the different types and nature of the interactions of the people involved in the partnership implementation.

When government initiates the partnership, it should choose a business partner that has a good record and experience in success-fully running poverty-alleviation projects. Thus, a government that wants to build housing for the poor should know which for-profit-bidding construction firms they can trust to deliver quality housing. The problem is not so much starting the relationship as sustaining it. The government may delay the housing disbursements because of more pressing financial commitments, or the construction firm may devote more time to other projects that deliver higher profits.

In a seminar on this subject, here is how one seminar participant from business explained the difficulty:

> "It's different in business and government. Everyone in each partnership team has his other regular job to do. The partnership project is an extra—a second job. That's unlike in an NGO, where the partnership project is the only job for the head and his people.

> "When everyone has some other things they need to do first, everyone gives to the partnership project the extra time that every now and then comes to them. And that's not the same for everyone. The free time for one team member may happen now but not for another. That's why it's so hard to have even near 100% presence of members of the two teams for follow-up and feedback partnership meetings.

> "When someone is absent from one meeting but present at the next, too much time is wasted on updating those who were absent. This is true even if everyone is required to have read the minutes of the most recent meeting and to do their homework, among those asked to do something for the next meeting. That's the other problem. Suppose I've been assigned homework. Even if I want to do it in between the two meetings, it often happens that there's a rush item to attend to. So the next partnership meeting is sometimes post-poned until the homework assignments are completed and can be presented and discussed. Even three or four post-ponements get the partnership project considerably off its timetable.

"And there's nobody to blame. The partnership project is everyone's second job. It's not your primary job."

So it turns out that government and business alliances can be started easily, but sustaining the partners' enthusiasm is sabotaged by conflicting job loyalties.

The Business-Civil Society Partnership

NPOs often initiate projects with businesses because they see businesses as having the money and other resources they need. But many NPO staffers have a cynical attitude toward business. When it was suggested to an NGO director to approach a business for help, he quickly said no. Asked why, he answered, "Businessmen don't have the right values."

Religious NPOs often hold this cynical attitude toward business. One church wanted to expand its food program for poor children. Often these children come to school hungry. So this church wanted to have a "feeding program for hunger." Someone suggested that the church should partner with a large food company like Nestlé or McDonald's. The church in need of help responded this way: "We're certain Nestlé or McDonald's would not come and help out of the pure kindness of their hearts. They'll only come and help if they can make money out of the project."

Too many NGO people are suspicious of business's motives for doing good. It would be better if they would acknowledge that business is in the business of making money for its investors but it also wants to give some support to good causes.

The next sections describe two civil society organizations and their models for working with business-oriented people to help reduce poverty.

Acumen Fund

Jacqueline Novogratz is the founder and CEO of the Acumen Fund, a venture capital firm with a philanthropic heart. Her experience told her that neither microfinance nor foreign aid are enough to make a sufficient dent in the problem of poverty. With seed money from the Rockefeller Foundation and Cisco Foundation, in 2001 she formed a "nonprofit global venture fund" dedicated to lending money to companies that aim to fight poverty by providing affordable goods and services—water, health, and housing—to the world's poorest people.

For example, Acumen made a $600,000 equity investment in an Indian water company called Water Health International to help it build small-scale water filtration plants in Indian villages. This company now operates water filtration plants in 50 villages in India. As another example, Acumen invested $1 million worth of equity in an East African company called A to Z Textile Mills that produces durable, antimalarial bed nets made out of plastic fibers that are impregnated with an organic insecticide. The company now has 5,000 employees who manufacture about 7 million nets a year. A to Z's biggest customer is the UN, which gives away the nets. Other examples include Acumen's funding of an Indian company that sells low-cost eyeglasses, an Indian Internet kiosk company, and a Pakistan company that provides home financing to squatters in Pakistan.

Clearly, there is promise in setting up a venture fund to make investments in companies that have plans to reduce some aspect of the poverty problem.[11]

Ashoka: Innovators for the Public

Another prominent "do-gooder" organization, Ashoka, makes loans to social entrepreneurs—business "change makers" who want to contribute to such issues as poverty reduction, environmental protection, human rights, health improvement, and school improvement.

Ashoka uses a rigorous five-step process to identify the most important social-change ideas and the entrepreneurs behind them. Ashoka wants social entrepreneurs who have a big, pattern-setting new idea, creativity in goal-setting and problem-solving, entrepreneurial quality, a high expected social impact for the new idea, and ethical fiber.

Today Ashoka works with more than 2,000 leading social entrepreneurs called Ashoka Fellows in over 70 countries. Ashoka provides them with a launch stipend for an average of three years, with full freedom to pursue their civic-oriented projects. Ashoka found that five years after being selected, 90% of the fellows had seen independent institutions copy their idea, and over half had changed public policy in their nation.

One Ashoka Fellow, Seham Ibrahim, works in Egypt on the problem of street children and seeks to heal them through inclusion in the larger community. Her organization arranges medical care, psychiatric support, and training that encourages the children to gain confidence and trust themselves and the world around them. Her organization's services have benefited 11,000 children so far.

Another Ashoka Fellow, Andres Randazzo, works in Mexico's poorest rural areas to implement eco-technologies to create clean water and adequate housing. His organization has created houses, cisterns, and ovens that are 70% less expensive than their regular counterparts. The pilot projects in six regions have resulted in the installation of nearly 3,000 cisterns, ovens, houses, and fish farms, impacting nearly 100,000 people. Randazzo is helping Mexican government agencies replicate and spread his models to a much larger number of rural areas in Mexico.[12]

Back to the Three-Way Partnership

Many of the problems of starting and sustaining any of the three two-way partnership components shown in Figure 13.2 are an issue of effective and efficient management. Managers in each sector encounter problems with which they have little experience. It would help if the managers of the partnership on both sides were given the official designation of "partnership officer." A partnership officer needs more than ordinary preparation for the job. Partnership officers must inspire respect and trust at the very start of the partnership. Over the life of the partnership project, partnership officers must manage their own interactions and those of their staff members with their counterparts in the partner agencies with objectivity and empathy.

Managing Adversarial and Opposing Institutions

We have examined the importance of partnerships and some of the issues in making them work. We now turn to the problem of handling adversarial groups who oppose the partnership. We will illustrate this with the 2001 three-way partnership project in Kerala called the "Health in Your Hands: Handwash with Soap" campaign that aimed to get citizens to wash their hands. While initially considered a success, it was later plagued with adversaries. The partners in the project did not do as good a job of anticipating sources of opposition. If they had segmented likely sources of opposition, they could have taken preventive measures.

Figure 13.3 shows one way of segmenting the opposition marketplace.[13] Five potential sources of opposition are identified:

- *Interest segments*. These are people or organizations affected positively or negatively by the partnership project. If harmed, they are probable opposition sources. If helped, they are potential opposition sources should the project turn out to be disappointing.
- *Knowledge segments*. These are people or organizations that possess critical information that can help or harm the partnership project. Universities, scientists, think tanks, and even indigenous people can constitute knowledge segments.

- *Implementer segments.* These are people who either control or provide the resources necessary to carry out the partnership project, or directly carry it out. They can become project opponents should they become unhappy with how the project is turning out.
- *Support segments.* These are individuals or organizations who share and believe in the project's vision, mission, and objectives. They can become opponents when they see that the project is unjustifiably deviating from its vision, mission, or objectives.
- *Communicator segments.* These include media people and organizations, elected officials, and legislators. They become project opponents when they see that the project is not delivering on its promised benefits or is in fact doing harm to the target poverty segment.

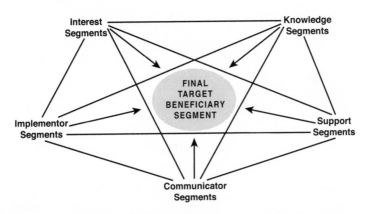

FIGURE 13.3 **Potential opposition segments and their interactions**

Figure 13.3 makes it clear that all potential opponent segments are interested in the good of the final target beneficiary segment. It is this common interest in the final target beneficiary segment that defines the interactions among these five potential opponent segments.

In the Kerala campaign, several opposition segments ultimately came to attack the partnership project. The attack was started in the spring of 2002 by a knowledge segment individual, Dr. Vandana Shiva. He was a known environmental and antiglobalization activist who served as director of Kerala's Research Foundation for Science, Technology, and Natural Resource Policy. In his published attack, Dr. Shiva argued that:

> "Kerala has the highest access to safe water, highest knowledge of prevention of diarrhea because of high female literacy and local health practices such as use of *jeera* water and high use of fluids during diarrhea. The World Bank project is an insult to Kerala's knowledge regarding health and hygiene. It is in fact Kerala from where cleanliness and hygiene should be exported to the rest of the world. People of Kerala do not need a World Bank loan for being taught cleanliness."[14]

A politician and leader of the political opposition in Kerala's State Assembly (a communicator segment individual), V. S. Achuthanandran, read Dr. Shiva's *AgBioIndia* journal article. He found in it a provocative "cause" to champion as the opposition leader. He proceeded to speak out strongly against the project. The media (a communication organization) followed with adverse news and press releases.

As the attack gained momentum, World Bank officials in India asked the Kerala state government to officially respond to the growing criticism of the project. The state government decided to turn down the request. Then, the state cabinet (a support segment member) withheld approval of the project's proposal for expansion. As a consequence, the project was brought to a standstill. This forced the partnership project team to downsize the project budget from its intended $10 million over the next three years to $2 million for one year.

The lesson is clear. In a typically high-profile three-way partnership project where government is a leading partner, it is risky not to integrate into the project plan the management of opposition segments. A carefully crafted segmentation analysis of the opposition marketplace is a most helpful starting point in this integration.

Summary

This chapter was intended to strengthen the case that poverty reduction relies on a strong partnership relationship between the three sectors. Seven principles for successful partnerships were discussed: agreement on common goals, clear roles and responsibilities, mutual respect and appreciation, negotiation and compromise, open communications, systems for accountability, and measurement and reporting of outcomes. Without these practices, we imagine not only waste of scarce resources, but personal disappointments and frustrations among program managers and others involved in developing and implementing well-intended poverty-reduction programs.

Endnotes

[1] World Bank. "West Africa: Defeating Riverblindness—Success in Scaling Up and Lessons Learned." 2004. J. Bump, B. Benton, A. Seketeli, B. Liese, and C. Novinskey, p .8.

[2] Bill Gates speech at the annual meeting of the World Economic Forum in Davos, Switzerland, January 24, 2008.

[3] World Bank. "Global Partnership to Eliminate Riverblindness." Retrieved on August 28, 2008 from http://www.worldbank.org/afr/gper/defeating.htm.

[4] The Carter Center. "The Carter Center River Blindness (Onchocerciasis) Program." Retrieved on April 14, 2008 from http://cartercenter.org/health/river_blindness/index.html.

[5] World Bank. "West Africa: Defeating Riverblindness—Success in Scaling Up and Lessons Learned." op. cit.

[6] World Bank. "West Africa: Defeating Riverblindness—Success in Scaling Up and Lessons Learned." op. cit.

[7] World Bank. "West Africa: Defeating Riverblindness—Success in Scaling Up and Lessons Learned." op. cit.

[8] World Bank. "West Africa: Defeating Riverblindness—Success in Scaling Up and Lessons Learned." op. cit.

[9] World Bank. "Global Partnership to Eliminate Riverblindness." op. cit.

[10] Tadashi Yamamoto, "Corporate-NGO Partnership: Learning from Case Studies," in Tadashi Yamamoto and Kim Gould Ashizawa (eds.), *Corporate-NGO Partnership in Asia Pacific* (Tokyo: Japan Center for International Exchange, 1999), pp. 13–38.

[11] This post originally appeared on MarcGunther.com.

[12] See Ashoka's booklet titled *Leading Social Entrepreneurs*, published by Ashoka in 2008.

[13] Constructed from the discussion of the five opposition segments in handout material at the Seminar-Workshop Program on Strategic Communications for Local Governance conducted by the World Bank's Development Communications Office in Delhi, India, December 2004.

[14] C. K. Prahalad, *The Fortune at the Bottom of the Pyramid: Eradicating Poverty Through Profits* (Upper Saddle River, NJ: Wharton School Publishing-Pearson, 2005).

INDEX

UL Wharton School Publishing

In the face of accelerating turbulence and change, business leaders and policy makers need new ways of thinking to sustain performance and growth.

Wharton School Publishing offers a trusted source for stimulating ideas from thought leaders who provide new mental models to address changes in strategy, management, and finance. We seek out authors from diverse disciplines with a profound understanding of change and its implications. We offer books and tools that help executives respond to the challenge of change.

Every book and management tool we publish meets quality standards set by The Wharton School of the University of Pennsylvania. Each title is reviewed by the Wharton School Publishing Editorial Board before being given Wharton's seal of approval. This ensures that Wharton publications are timely, relevant, important, conceptually sound or empirically based, and implementable.

To fit our readers' learning preferences, Wharton publications are available in multiple formats, including books, audio, and electronic.

To find out more about our books and management tools, visit us at whartonsp.com and Wharton's executive education site, exceed.wharton.upenn.edu.